Dark clouds are gathering.
Just ask any of the local trout.

HOUSE OF HARDY

THE WORLD'S FINEST FISHING TACKLE

For further details about House of Hardy products, contact John Dickson & Son Ltd, 21 Frederick Street, Edinburgh EH2 2NE. Telephone: 0131 225 4218. Fax: 0131 225 3658

CONTENTS

Published by Pastime Publications Ltd,
42 Raeburn Place, Edinburgh EH4 1HL.
Tel/fax: 0131-332 9099.
First published by The Scottish Tourist Board 1970.
UK & Worldwide Distribution.

INTRODUCTION

Now in its 29th year, *Scotland for Fishing* continues to offer its readers the most comprehensive guide to fishing in Scotland with the gazetteer updated yet again to ensure that information on permits, fishing rights, season/dates and other useful details is as current as it can be.

An important event happened late last year when the ownership of Pastime Publications (publisher of *Scotland for Fishing*) changed and a new management team brought in to improve what is already regarded as 'the definitive guide to fishing in Scotland'. Some of the changes can be seen in the new presentation with a redesigned front cover and a change of style for the text pages.

In addition to the usual informative editorial, we have been lucky enough to engage the help of David Wilson, celebrated owner/chef of The Peat Inn in Fife, to give us three recipes on "How to Cook your Catch". As ever, Bill Currie continues with his invaluable contribution as do a number of others.

Another innovation introduced for the first time this year is the establishment of our own Web Site, which can be found at www.scotland-for-fishing.com and is being hosted by The Gamefishing Partnership at www.gamefishing.co.uk, run by our old friend Bill Currie and his partner Dr. Colin Bradshaw. The aim of the site is obviously to promote the Guide on a worldwide basis as well as to offer our readers more accessibility and our advertisers more exposure. So visit the site!

I hope you enjoy 'the new' *Scotland for Fishing* as much as you obviously have in the past and thank you for buying our Guide.

The Publisher

4

HOW TO COOK YOUR CATCH

SCOTTISH SALMON ON A BED OF VEGETABLES WITH BASIL BUTTER SAUCE

Serves 4 (as a starter portion)
4 times 30oz (100g) Fillets Scottish Salmon (with skin on but de-scaled)
1 level teaspoons sea salt

Vegetables
1 Fennel bulb
1 Courgette
1 Leek (white part only)
½ Yellow Pepper (skin off)
NOTE: Vegetables can be changed to suit season or personal choice.

Sauce
1 ½ ozs (40g) Shallots
2 tblsp White wine vinegar
3 ozs (100g) Unsalted butter
Salt/Pepper
1 tblsp Fresh Basil leaves

Method
1   Chop shallots finely, put in pan with a knob of the butter. Sweat over a low heat without browning.
2   Add vinegar. Reduce over high heat until almost evaporated.
3   Remove from heat and whisk in remainder of butter in small pieces.
4   Place sauce in liquidiser, add Basil leaves and process until Basil is incorporated into sauce. Check seasoning, adjust with salt/pepper as necessary.

SAUCE CAN BE MADE IN ADVANCE, KEPT WARM BUT DO NOT BOIL.

Vegetables
Cut all vegetables into battons and cook separately in boiling water until tender. Keep warm.

To Cook Salmon
1   Put sea salt on skin of salmon.
2   Put a film of oil in a sauté pan on a high heat and when oil begins to smoke place salmon fillets skin side down in pan. Cook for about 5 minutes on the one side only (this time can vary depending on thickness of salmon), then turn over for a few seconds to seal underside. The salmon should be very crisp on the skin side with good brown colour but still moist and undercooked on the underside.

To Serve
1   Put vegetables on centre of plate, coat vegetables with sauce then spoon sauce around the plate.
2   Place cooked salmon skin side uppermost on top of vegetables.

Serve immediately

Recipes courtesy of David Wilson - celebrated proprietor and chef of the acclaimed Peat Inn in Fife

5

The following are the statutory open seasons for fishing for Salmon and Trout in Scotland:

SALMON

River	Rod Season	River	Rod Season
Add	Feb 16 - Oct 31	Fyne	Feb 16 - Oct 31
Aline	Feb 11 - Oct 31	Girvan	Feb 25 - Oct 31
Allan	Mar15 - Oct 31	Gruinard	
Alness	Feb 11 - Oct 15	& Little Gruinard	Feb 11 - Oct 31
Annan	Feb 26 - Nov 15	Halladale	Jan 12 - Sep 30
Applecross	Feb 25 - Nov 15	Helmsdale	Jan 11 - Sep 30
Awe	Feb 12 - Oct 15	Hope	Jan 12 - Sep 30
Ayr	Feb 11 - Oct 31	Inver	Feb 11 - Oct 31
Beauly	Feb 11 - Oct 15	Irvine	Feb 25 - Nov 15
Berriedale	Feb 11 - Oct 31	Kannaird	Feb 11 - Oct 31
Bervie	Feb 25 - Oct 31	Kirkaig	Feb 11 - Oct 31
Bladnoch	Feb 11 - Oct 31	Kishorn	Feb 11 - Oct 31
Borgie	Jan 12 - Sep 30	Laxford	Feb 11 - Oct 31
Broom	Feb 11 - Oct 31	Lochy	Feb 11 - Oct 31
Brora	Feb 1 - Oct 15	Lomond (Clyde)	Feb 12 - Oct 31
Carron (E. Ross)	Jan 11 - Sep 30	Moidart	Feb 11 - Oct 31
Carron (W. Ross)	Feb 11 - Oct 31	Morar	Feb 11 - Oct 31
Conon	Jan 26 - Sep 30	Nairn	Feb 12 - Oct 30
Cree	Mar 1 - Oct 14	Naver	Jan 12 - Sep 30
Creed	Feb 11 - Oct 16	Ness	Jan 15 - Oct 15
Croe	Feb 11 - Oct 31	Nith	Feb 26 - Nov 30
Dee (Aberdeenshire)	Mar 1 - Sep 30	Orchy	Feb 12 - Oct 15
Dee (Kirkcudbrightshire)	Feb 11 - Oct 31	Oykel	Jan 11 - Sep 30
Deveron	Feb 12 - Oct 31	Shiel	Feb 11 - Oct 31
Dionard	Feb 11 - Oct 31	Shin	Jan 11 - Sep 30
Don	Feb 12 - Oct 31	Spey	Feb 12 - Sep 30
Doon	Feb 11 - Oct 31	Stinchar	Feb 24 - Oct 31
Dunbeath	Feb 11 - Oct 15	Strathy	Jan 12 - Sep 30
Eachaig	Feb 16 - Oct 31	Tay	Jan 15 - Oct 15
Earn	Feb 1 - Oct 31	Teith	Feb 1 - Oct 31
Esk (North & South)	Feb 16 - Oct 31	Thurso	Jan 11 - Oct 5
Ewe	Feb 11 - Oct 31	Torridon	Feb11 - Oct 31
Findhorn	Feb 12 - Sep 30	Tweed	Feb 1 - Nov 30
Fleet (Kirkcudbrightshire)	Feb 25 - Oct 31	Ugie	Feb 16 - Oct 31
Fleet (Sutherland)	Feb 25 - Oct 31	Ullapool	Feb 11 - Oct 31
Forss	Feb 11 - Oct 31	Wick	Feb 11 - Oct 31
Forth	Feb 1 - Oct 31	Ythan	Feb 12 - Oct 15

TROUT: The season for trout is from **March 15 to October 6**.
For conservation reasons, some clubs or associations have slightly shorter seasons.
Shortening of seasons for conservation also applies to certain salmon rivers.

THE SALMON RIVERS OF SCOTLAND

Pentland Firth

North Minch

MAP I

Dornoch Firth

Moray Firth

Inverness

MAP III

MAP II

Aberdeen

Oban

Firth of Tay

Firth of Forth

Edinburgh

Glasgow

Firth of Clyde

MAP IV

The GLENMORANGIE

FISHERMAN'S CODE

1.

He who'd be a fisher true,
Should know the proper thing to do.
Since brother anglers everywhere,
Are known for courtesy and care.
For love of fishing always mellows,
To love of nature and your fellows.

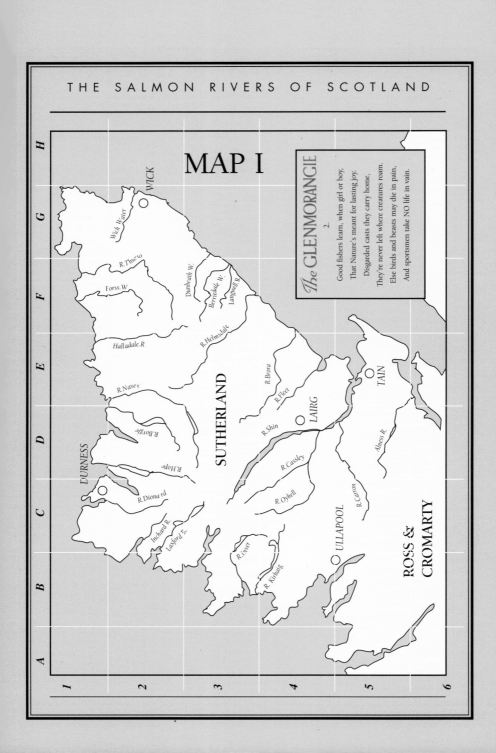

THE SALMON RIVERS OF SCOTLAND

MAP I

The GLENMORANGIE

2.

Good fishers learn, when girl or boy,
That Nature's meant for lasting joy.
Disgarded casts they carry home,
They're never left where creatures roam.
Else birds and beasts may die in pain,
And sportsmen take NO life in vain.

H
G
F
E
D
C
B
A

1 2 3 4 5 6

WICK

Wick Water

R.Thurso

Forss.W.

Halladale.R

R.Naver

DURNESS

R.Borgie

R.Hope

R.Diona rd

Inchard R.

Laxford R.

Dunbeath W.

Berriedale W.

Langwell.R.

R.Helmsdale

SUTHERLAND

R.Brora

R.Fleet

R.Shin

LAIRG

R.Cassley

R.Oykell

R.river

R.Kirkaig

ULLAPOOL

TAIN

Alness R.

R.Carron

ROSS &
CROMARTY

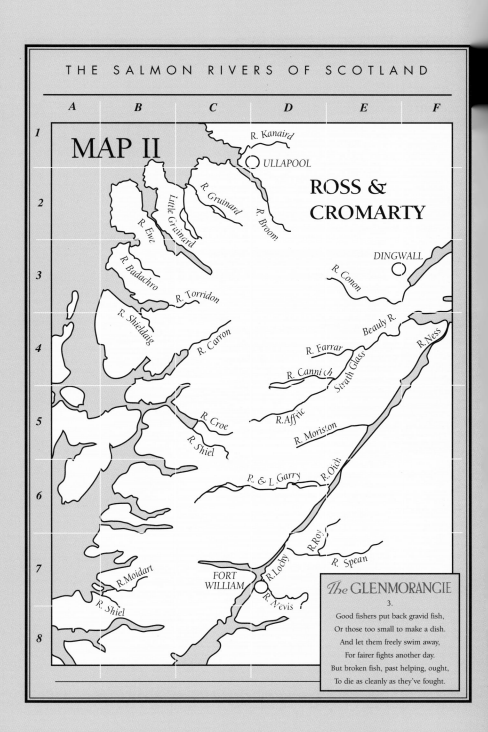

THE SALMON RIVERS OF SCOTLAND

	A	B	C	D	E	F
1						

MAP II

R. Kanaird

○ ULLAPOOL

ROSS & CROMARTY

R. Ewe

Little Gruinard

R. Gruinard

R. Broom

DINGWALL ○

R. Badachro

R. Conon

R. Shieldaig

R. Torridon

Beauly R.

R. Carron

R. Farrar

R. Ness

R. Cannich

Strath Glass

R. Croe

R. Affric

R. Moriston

R. Shiel

R. Oich

R. & L. Garry

R. Roy

R. Spean

R. Moidart

R. Lochy

R. Shiel

FORT WILLIAM ○

R. Nevis

The GLENMORANGIE

3.

Good fishers put back gravid fish,
Or those too small to make a dish.
And let them freely swim away,
For fairer fights another day.
But broken fish, past helping, ought,
To die as cleanly as they've fought.

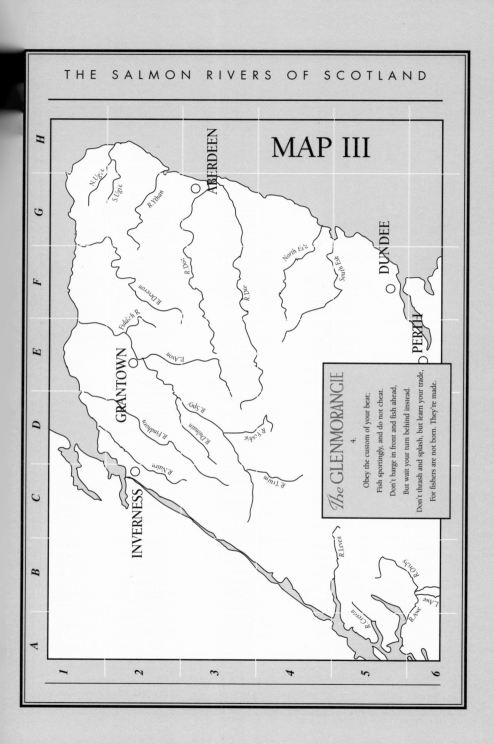

THE SALMON RIVERS OF SCOTLAND

MAP III

H

G

F

E

D

C

B

A

1

2

3

4

5

6

ABERDEEN

DUNDEE

PERTH

GRANTOWN

INVERNESS

N. Ugie

S. Ugie

R. Ythan

R. Don

R. Deveron

Fiddich R.

R. Avon

R. Findhorn

R. Nairn

R. Spey

R. Dulnain

R. Feshie

R. Truim

North Esk

South Esk

R. Dee

R. Leven

R. Teven

R. Awe

L. Awe

R. Orchy

The GLENMORANGIE

4.

Obey the custom of your beat;
Fish sportingly, and do not cheat.
Don't barge in front and fish ahead,
But wait your turn behind instead.
Don't thrash and splash, but learn your trade,
For fishers are not born. They're made.

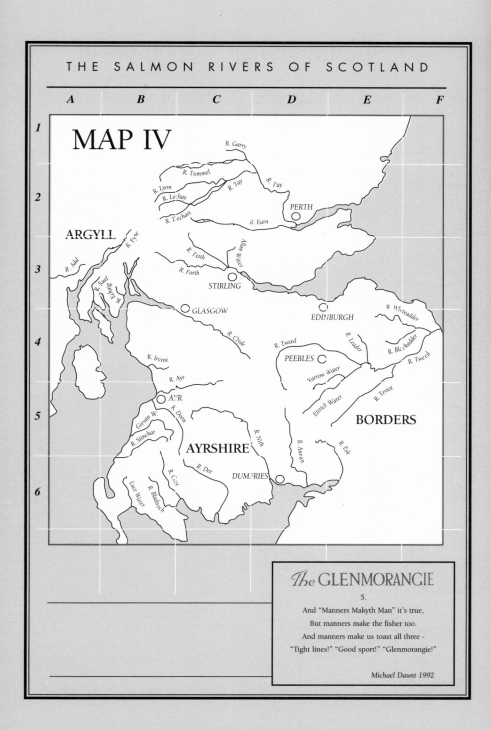

THE SALMON RIVERS OF SCOTLAND

	A	B	C	D	E	F
1						

MAP IV

R. Garry

R. Tummel

R. Lyon

R. Tay

R. Tay

R. Lochay

R. Lochart

PERTH

R. Earn

ARGYLL

R. Fyne

R. Add

R. Teith

Allan Water

R. Kinel

R. Echaig

R. Forth

STIRLING

GLASGOW

EDINBURGH

R. Whiteadder

R. Clyde

R. Tweed

R. Leader

R. Blackadder

PEEBLES

R. Tweed

R. Irvine

Yarrow Water

R. Ayr

R. Teviot

AYR

Etrick Water

Girvan W.

R. Doon

BORDERS

R. Stinchar

R. Nith

R. Esk

AYRSHIRE

R. Annan

R. Dee

R. Cree

DUMFRIES

Luce Water

R. Bladnoch

The GLENMORANGIE

5.

And "Manners Makyth Man" it's true,
But manners make the fisher too.
And manners make us toast all three -
"Tight lines!" "Good sport!" "Glenmorangie!"

Michael Daunt 1992

Glenmorangie – Sponsors of the Salmon & Trout Association

During 1996, Glenmorangie launched a three year sponsorship initiative with the Salmon & Trout Association to support their new member recruitment activities at over 50 game-fishing shows and related events across the country The company also provides a miniature of Glenmorangie 10 Years Old for every new member, helping to make the joining experience even more enjoyable!

Many of the S&TA branch meetings held regularly during the year also benefit from the Association with Glenmorangie, through the provision of raffle prizes and the organisation of whisky tastings.

Glenmorangie is Scotland's best selling malt whisky. For over 150 years it has been produced by a small group of dedicated craftsmen at the historic distillery near Tain on the shores of the Dornoch Firth in Ross-shire. The craftsmen - known as 'the Sixteen Men of Tain' - use the best natural products from the surrounding environment for producing Glenmorangie. Water from the nearby Tarlogie Springs and malted barley from the Black Isle help create Glenmorangie's distinctive taste and aroma.

Glenmorangie is proud to support the S&TA and encourages all gamefishing anglers to join the Association in order to safeguard fish stocks and the sport of game-fishing for future generations.

Glenmorangie House – The Perfect Retreat

Glenmorangie House is situated in Cadboll in historic Easter Ross near the Glenmorangie Distillery in Tain and stands "in the shadow" of the picturesque ruins of Cadboll Castle. The earliest part of the house dates from the 1500's and most of the rest from the 1800's.

It was bought by Glenmorangie in 1989 and restored and refurbished to the highest standards of taste and comfort. Its ambience is that of a peaceful country house firmly rooted in pastoral tranquillity and its approach to guests is very much "tell us what you want and we'll do our very best to provide it".

It has six attractive bedrooms, each with twin beds, en-suite bathrooms and splendid views. Public rooms include the light-fitted and luxurious Morning room and the snug Buffalo Room. Log fires burn in each, with vases of cut flowers, magazines and books to hand and the house-party atmosphere encourages guests to get to know one another. The extensive grounds and walled gardens are only two hundred

Glenmorangie House

yards from the sea where rocky and sandy beach provides great walks. There are an astonishing number of interesting things to see within easy reach - not least The Glenmorangie Distillery itself.

Your hosts, Andrew and Jacquie Taylor, are both skilled managers and Andrew is a Master Chef and a member of the exclusive Craft Guild of Chefs. At his disposal is the finest produce you could wish for: salmon is landed on the beach below the house; shellfish a mile away; beef and lamb raised on Ross-shire's coastal grazings; game is bought in from neighbouring estates; vegetables, herbs and soft fruits, in season, coming from the house's own kitchen garden and glass-houses.

Fishing is available as part of any visit to Glenmorangie House. Sea fishing, with sea-going boats and equipment which cater for groups up to a maximum of 20 people are available of hire. For Trout fishing, many lochs are within an hour's drive of the House, and for Salmon fishing Glenmorangie House has access to River Shin, Carron, Cassley, Alness, Brora, Fleet and many more.

We can arrange experienced Ghillies for both Trout and Salmon fishing, and can supply all equipment, transport and, of course, lunches.

Bespoke packages are available, as is exclusive use of the House for parties of more than six people. There are, of course, alternative activities for non-fishers which include golfing, horse-riding etc.

Glenmorangie House is the perfect retreat!

Dinner, Bed and Breakfast from £110 per person, per night (includes all wine, soft drinks and Glenmorangie 10 year old).

Glenmorangie House has just become the first hotel in the Highlands to be awarded the Scottish Tourist Board's (STB) prestigious Five Star Grade for Quality Assurance.

Glenmorangie House can be reached on: 01862 871671.

FISHING HILL LOCHS

1998 SEASON ON THE ROAD TO THE ISLES

John Brown is the Secretary of the Rannoch and District Angling club. Each year he collects the returns and presents invaluable reports on the fishing in the Rannoch district, an area well known for its diversity of hill lochs. There are various lochs in this district that have limited access, are hidden or simply secret. In this article John details some of the better known lochs of the area. With well over fifty years fishing experience, John's information continues to be of benefit to many a fisherman, world over.

Loch Bhac which lies in Allean forest and managed by Pitlochry Angling has fished very well with most anglers this season. They have had no problems getting the 3-bag limit of either, Brown, Rainbow or Brook Trout. A party of four anglers from Dunalastair Hotel, Kinloch Rannoch caught fifty plus in one day and returned them all. The heaviest a Brown trout of 2.5 lbs taken on a blue and black fly. This catch was in the latter days of June. Loch Kinnardochy which is in the Schiehallion road area has so far been a bit disappointing, although there have been one or two trout over 1 lb taken. The flies which are favourite is black pennel. This loch is also managed by Pitlochry Angling club and has a 6-bag limit. Permits for both the above lochs are available from mitchells tackle Shop in Pitlochry or from J. Brown, The Square, Kinloch Rannoch. Fly fishing only allowed on both lochs. Electric outboards are allowed and fish under 10 inches must be returned.

Loch Rannoch

Loch Eigheach near Rannoch Station has also been fishing very well . Although there are numerous small brown trout caught, the average weight of the fish returned has been about 6 ounces. Again black flies are favourite although the heaviest fish taken so far this season of 1.5 lbs, was caught on a Peter Ross fly. This loch is managed by Rannoch and District Angling Club. Permits are available from J. Brown, The Square, Kinloch Rannoch also from Colin Robertson, Dunan Lodge Near Rannoch Station and at the Tearoom at Rannoch Railway Station.

An unusual venue is Loch Stronsmere which is on Dunan Estate and has been stocked this year with half pound brown trout. Permits for this loch are available from Colin Robertson at Dunan Lodge. The charge is £10 per day with a 4-bag limit. Standard loch flies are best with black pennel and grouse patterns favourites. This loch is well worth a visit, and contact with Colin is advisable as he can provide a welcome lift to the loch.

Loch Errochty in the Trinafour area near Blair Atholl is quite a favourite for those who like wild brownies. Some large Brown trout have been caught this season. Fishing is by any legal method and permits are available from the Highland shop in Blair Atholl.

Dunalastair reservoir has been fishing better in the evenings and some large trout have been taken mostly on sedges. One trout of 4.5 lbs has been taken so far, but it is encouraging to see quite a lot of fish of about 2 lbs. Again being taken as was the case 5 or 6 years ago. Permits are available for fishing from Dunalastair Estate and Dunalastair Hotel. Boat fishing only is allowed.

On a recent visit to Loch Garry at Dalnaspiddal with my local club on a very poor fishing day I was very pleased to have caught eight Char which I returned. It was nice to catch them during the day as in previous visits years ago they seemed to feed just as it was getting dark. Permits to fish Loch Garry can be had from Mr and Mrs Kennedy at Dalmaspiddal Lodge.

And finally to Loch Rannoch. The fishing at the loch from both boat and bank has been its best for 10-12 years. The average weight of trout is about 3/4 - 1lb. One trout of 10lbs has been caught. The standard loch flies are best with various patterns all catching trout. The loch is managed by Loch Rannoch Conservation Association and permits are available from shops and Hotels in Kinloch Rannoch. Boats are available for hire on the loch from the Dunalastair Hotel.

It is encouraging to see a big increase in the number of smaller trout which in recent years have not been seen. We have also seen an increase in enthusiasts who are keen to catch wild brown trout, one man in particular had gone three years without catching a salmon and had instead turned to catching wild brownies, and was delighted to catch a 3 lbs trout on Dunalastair water.

John Brown

15

Delnashaugh Inn

THE BALLINDALLOCH BEAT

The fishing belongs to Ballindalloch Estate, which is situated in Speyside 14 miles north-east of Grantown-on-Spey. The Estate is owned by the Macpherson-Grant family and is centred around Ballindalloch Castle, the family home since 1546, which is now open to the public.

This beautiful river flows out of Loch Avon in the heart of the Cairngorm mountains and joins the famous River Spey beside Ballindalloch Castle. The Estate owns the first six miles of the River Avon (pronounced A'an) from its junction with the River Spey to the march with the Crown Estate at the Alt na Criche burn on the left bank. The Avon is the largest tributary of the Spey and attracts good runs of Salmon, Grilse and Seatrout. These migratory fish normally start appearing in the river in late April and the fishing season ends on the 30th September annually.

The Avon is an intriguing river to fish. The fast flowing clear water does not yield up its secrets easily. The rocky pools have numerous individual lies and the streamy water is particularly attractive for fly fishing. Flies such as Silver Stoat, Garry Dog, Munro Killer, Stoat's Tail and Ally's Shrimp sizes 8 to 12 fished with an 11-14 foot rod are recommended. Spinning is only permitted if the conditions are unsuitable for the fly.

Over four miles of the best water with fishing on both banks from Livet Mouth downstream to Fire Pump Pool below the Bridge of Avon have been divided up into six beats known as the Lower Beats. Each beat is fished by two rods on a daily rota system. There are over 30 named pools on these beats all of which may be fished twice during a weeks stay at Ballindalloch. Good access to the river has been provided for vehicles and most beats have small fishing huts. Guests are provided with maps and rotas and are shown where to fish. There is a fishing Ghillie on hand to help newcomers to the river. From the march with the Crown Estate downstream to the Livet Mouth the fishing is from the left bank only. This stretch of water is known as Beat A and is let separately. Worming is permitted on Beat A up to 31st August.

The fishing is let by the week, but day permits may be issued if there are any rods available. Day permits are normally let on Beat A. Each month of the season has its attractions. In May when the wild cherry blossom is out Strathavon looks at its best and there is the exciting prospect of catching a large fresh run spring salmon. June and July see the main runs of grilse and seatrout and the long hours of daylight in these northern latitudes make it possible to fish all night. In August and September the river holds its full complement of summer fish and large catches can be made if the water conditions are right. For further details contact:

The Estates Office,
Ballindalloch,
Banffshire AB37 9AX
Tel: (01807) 500205
Fax: (01807) 500210

The Delnashaugh Inn

The Delnashaugh Inn also belongs to the Estate. Conveniently situated near the river at the Bridge of Avon, the Inn has established a good reputation with visiting fishermen and their families and has a well-equipped rod room with deep freeze.

Self Catering Cottages are also available on the Estate.

Enquiries about accommodation should be addressed to the Inn on Tel. no: **(01807) 500255** or the Estate office on Tel. no: **(01807) 500205.**

CINDERELLA NO MORE!

SCOTTISH COARSE FISHING

Many people think that freshwater angling in Scotland was until very recently confined to trout and salmon, but our sport has always been more diverse than that. The largest pike, chub and grayling ever caught in Britain were all Scottish fish. Nor were fish like these just isolated specimens or accidental captures. Tommy Morgan, for instance, whose 47lb 11oz Loch Lomond pike still beats even the best of its easily-living cousins from today's generation of stocked trout reservoirs, was a skilled and experienced pike angler who knew both the loch and his quarry intimately. It's true that few Scottish anglers in the past fished exclusively for coarse species, but some of the best of our game fishers were actually all-rounders who honed their watercraft on the demands of finicky grayling in the ice-fringed upper reaches of the Clyde, or perhaps by teasing spoons through the reeds and weeds of our larger lochs for the voracious, acrobatic pike which abounded – and still do – in them.

Pike and perch have been in Scotland for hundreds – perhaps thousands – of years. Both species probably spread more widely because of their value as a cheap food source. Nevertheless, around the mid-nineteenth century pike were being stocked in a number of highland lochs specifically for sporting purposes and grayling were similarly introduced in several Scottish rivers to provide year-round angling. Advertisements for local hotels as early as the twenties were highlighting Loch Lomond's pike fishing as a particular attraction. Carp and tench may also have found their way here as a food source – there is mention of both on

A fine 2lb Perch from Danskine Loch - 1990

SCOTTISH COARSE FISHING

the menu of a banquet at Dunkeld Cathedral several hundred years ago – and were certainly stocked during the last century as ornamental additions to various estate ponds. Some of those landowners – or their estate workers – were no doubt tempted to do more than just watch when the shadowy bronze shapes materialised in the muddy shallows on warm summer evenings.

In the sixties Scottish sea angling was blossoming rapidly, fuelled by spectacular catches of cod in the Clyde and the development of the virgin resources of the Hebrides and the Northern Isles. At the same time Scottish coarse fishing was also attracting increasing publicity and generating a small stream of visitors. They came particularly for the challenging and almost untapped reserves of pike fishing in the larger lochs, and to a lesser extend

for the prolific roach shoals which were to be found in the lower reaches of the Clyde, Forth Tay and Tweed. This coincided, however, with a substantial expansion of carp and barbel fishing in England and the opening up of the prolific Irish bream, tench and rudd waters. Scottish coarse fishing at the time offered exceptional quality, but less variety than the touring angler could find elsewhere. For that reason the development of coarse fishing as a tourist activity in Scotland was steady rather than dramatic.

The most significant step forward in the growth of coarse fishing by Scottish-based anglers came around 1967, when a small group of afficionados formed the Glasgow & West of Scotland Coarse Fishing Association. Although its name suggested a local bias, the club was a focal point for enthusiasts throughout

21½lb Pike from a Borders Loch

Scotland and did a great deal to promote fishing. Club members, particularly the tireless secretary Bryan Hewitt, located and in many cases opened up (sometimes literally) new waters. Young members, including myself, learnt their craft from more experienced hands. The club played a major part in creating the first generation of home-grown Scottish coarse anglers: people who grew up with the spring spawners as their main area of interest. As well as development of the sport itself, the Glasgow & West club was active on the match fishing front. By 1970 it was able to mount annual open events which attracted hundreds of anglers from as far away as Yorkshire and the Midlands.

Over the next ten years or so there was an expansion of the number of coarse fishing clubs, some concentrating on particular species and others focussed on the competitive side. By the early eighties the Scottish Federation for Coarse Angling had been established to act as an umbrella body for the sport. A national team was competing at World Championship level – collectively with only modest success but gaining great credit from an individual runner-up medal won by the late Rab Stephens. There was also some expansion in the range of species available. Carp had been stocked in Lanark Loch in the mid seventies, for instance, and fish of nearly twenty lbs were starting to be caught by the end of the decade. Tench had similarly spread throughout the Forth & Clyde canal after small scale introductions in the late sixties, and big bags could be taken in various locations. The twin themes from the mid eighties to

the present day are of continued steady growth in participation, and increasing diversity in the species and opportunities available. The Federation runs a small but enthusiastically-supported match league, which provides the breeding ground for our international team. Without the resources available to our English counterparts we face an unequal task at the highest levels of the competitive fishing world; but our best home-grown anglers are nevertheless a match for anyone in the right conditions. Some of our specialist anglers – particularly among the pike enthusiasts – are nationally respected experts. Several have even been among the pioneers of fishing for unfamiliar species in exotic locations across the world.

Thanks to sympathetic and forward-looking policies by a number of local authorities, carp and to a lesser degree tench and bream have become well established in various public waters across the central belt. Stocks in some private waters, largely in Dumfries & Galloway, have also been nutrured as hotel and guest house owners realise the tourism potential. Individual clubs, notably the Scottish Carp Group, have stocked their own waters as have one or two private syndicates. Less honourable, but very much a fact of life, has been the spread of species such as dace, chub and – unfortunately – ruffe, from discarded livebaits brought here by visiting pike anglers.

The Federation has also established its status as the authoritative voice of the sport in legislative and administrative circles. It has ensured that coarse fishing interests are taken into consideration by,

.....even the smaller loch Awe Pike are acrobatic fighters!

for instance, having representatives sitting on the Secretary of State's Advisory Committee on statutory Protection Orders and contributing to the debate on the Wild Rivers report which forms a blueprint for public policy on the future of fisheries management in Scotland.

So where does Scottish coarse fishing go from here? I am confident the answer is onwards and upwards. Most of the current generation of Scottish Anglers have outgrown the prejudies which saw coarse fish treated as vermin in all too many game fisheries. The more scientific approach to managing natural resources which is emerging from, for instance, the Wild Rivers project recognises a legitimate place for coarse species in the ecosystem and as a sporting resource. The catch-and-return philosophy which is central to coarse fishing is very much in tune with the current state of public opinion on "green" issues, making it attractive both to younger participants and to the owners, many of them local councils, of waters which could be developed. Participation therefore looks set to continue to grow over the next decade, and with that it will become increasingly viable to manage waters as commercial coarse fisheries. In addition to creating a better range of facilities for visitors, these will provide the breeding ground for home-based coarse anglers which can only serve to accelerate the growth of the sport even further.

If you are interested in coarse fishing you can call the Scottish Federation for Coarse Angling (Steve Clerkin, tel 01592-642242) for details of general coarse fishing clubs. Specialist anglers may like to contact the Scottish Carp Group (Ron Woods, tel 0141-637 4645) or the Regional Association of the Pike Anglers' Club of GB (Alistair McPhee, tel 01259-210877).

DISCOVERING THE Wilderness

Good gamefishing nearly always has a strong element of the wilderness in it. I do not mean, of course, that you must always travel to the margins of the map to find it. I can imagine a conversation in a comfortable bar which might hold that true wilderness – whatever that is – has vanished from our modern world. As a Scottish fisher, if I said anything to follow this, it

On the banks of the Tweed at Scrogbank.

might be 'I hear you'. The facts are that finding the wildplace, understanding them and cherishing them is right at the heart of our fishing. Of course, if it were not for the trout, sea trout and salmon, we might never discover these places where wilderness and paradise are blended. When we say that good fishing has something of the wilderness within it, at least we mean that we find in Scotland a host of natural water, set in landscape which has not been 'improved' by the bulldozer or intensive modern agriculture. Wild fishing waters are places where the environment is pure and where the fish themselves are wild or have adopted wildness. Fishers also mean something more detailed. The fishing place with echoes of the wilderness in it is often found in a mini-landscape, – a bay on a loch, a pool on a river. As a fisher, let me tell you that Scotland is very rich in landscapes and waterscapes of this order. It would, of course, be absurd to say that Scotland was unexplored or its fishing waters virgin, but it would be very true to say that Scotland has a great and exciting range of fishing with memorable elements of the wilderness in it.

I may be repeating myself, but I say and say again that, for fishers, the real Scotland begins half a mile (or less) off any of the roads through it. This is a way of reminding us that we have some excellent wild territory in our country, often open to easy walking access, sometimes over a ridge in the hills. Once there, just a short walk away, you could be in a timeless zone, indeed, almost on another planet. Fishing is undoubtedly an excellent way to discover, reach and enjoy wild Scotland, because the fish themselves draw you into unspoiled landscapes and, in a detailed way, help you to discover a Scotland which the road-bound tourist never gets near.

Let me begin with a trout loch story. I have often found wilderness Scotland by just fishing the side of a loch away from the road which brought you down the glen.

I was spending a few days in the Great Glen – that remarkable Scottish 'rift valley' running west through Loch Ness, Loch Oich and Loch Lochy and providing

An attractive Bay on Loch Affric.

a route for the Caledonian canal from Inverness to Fort William. The main road running beside Loch Lochy looks over one of the deepest lochs in Scotland. It is a dramatic place. You look across to the far shore to the impressive sight of steep slopes rising abruptly to three thousand feet. The glen walls rise high and loch waters run deep. It's a lovely prospect. I first fished Loch Lochy on the south side close to the main road and didn't move much to my flies. I looked again at the far bank and thought I saw a different world. I drove across the bridge at Gairlochy, – crossing the River Lochy at the Caledonian Canal – and turned east, following the road on the far side past the Arkaig river and on through the trees of Clunie forest to where the road becomes a forestry track, and there I found a different Loch Lochy. Trees hung over the loch edge, often trailing branches in the water. Most lochs have good shallow water and wadable bays where

the best trout lie. Loch Lochy, a deep narrow loch, is different. I was faced with a boulder-strewn, quite narrow shelf running down its long bank, under the branches of the trees. Thirty yards out, the shelf abruptly plunges out of sight into the loch depths. Yes, that place had more than a whiff of the wilderness within it. The question was, how could I fish it? I had a pair of salmon waders in the car and with these, wading quite deeply, I picked my way down the stony shelf among the trailing branches, and rolling my line out (there was no room to cast overhead) I found trout splashing at my flies all the way. I had nine in an hour of which I kept the four best. These were lovely trout up to three quarters of a pound, taken from a wild and exciting place, within sight of the unproductive main-road side of the loch. Wilderness and all the delights of fishing were alive and well in that curious place.

On the New Pool of the Laggan Beat of the Ness.

This really is more of an example than a recommend-ation. Not every visiting loch fisher has belly waders and not everyone wants to pick their way through bankside branches to get their trout. But transfer the principle to another water. Have a day on Loch Arkaig, lying in the hills north west of Loch Lochy you will find a whole south bank untracked and promising wilderness fishing. If you fish Arkaig from the boat, use it to explore the narrow band of

Returning a summer fish on the Doon in Ayrshire. Smithston Fishings.

shallows and small bays. On this, and on a great array of other Inverness-shire hill lochs, wilderness and wild fish are waiting to be discovered.

Migratory fish like sea trout, grilse and salmon might be said to carry their own wilderness with them. They come up from the sea and in the case of grilse and salmon, they may come from great

distances and hazardous return journeys to their home river. We have had problems with sea trout in certain areas in Scotland. The West Highlands has been suffering a serious decline. Interestingly, the Solway fish, right down in the West of Scotland have shown some recovery recently. The Border Esk has begun to revive; the Annan has had some good signs of recovery also.

On the other side of the country in the east and north east – Dee and Spey particularly – sea trout were present in 1998 in better numbers than in recent years. Anyone who has hooked a fresh sea trout knows that it is a wilderness fish. I had a three pounder in the dusk a few nights before writing this introduction and, just before netting it, my friend said, 'There are not many salmon which would run like that.'

The attractive wilderness

A small sea Trout from a Hebridean loch.

elements of Scottish fishing, then, are partly in our exciting and varied landscape and partly in the character of our wild fish, trout, sea trout and salmon. For me, all three fish are strongly associated with the landscape. Although I have fished for more than half a century on the mainland and in the Hebrides, I am still finding whole tracts of land with waters, – particularly trout waters – which I have not yet really got to know. For example, the mountainous and most beautiful land lying north west of the Great Glen, has deep valleys with long lochs, nearly all showing a west or north west trend. They include Cluanie, the lochs of Glen Affric, Mullardoch and Monar. Several of these lochs are not on through routes. The roads lead to the lochs, then peter out. Make your arrangements locally and take a day or so to explore these fisheries. Remember, in a long glen, say like Strath Glass and Glen Affric, you will find fishing not only in the main waters, but in smaller fisheries in the hills beside them for example, the Glen Affic Hill lochs. Glen Moriston has main valley salmon and trout fishing , but also has a wealth of loch fishing (21 lochs and one estate alone) in marvellous hill country. Take a good look at the 'Great Glen and Skye' section of Scotland for Fishing to get details.

Taking a let of salmon or sea trout fishing is sometimes as easy as asking in the Highland hotel of your choice. Sometimes it might involve getting in touch with the estates concerned. Local fisheries sometimes offer short term lets or even day tickets. Most major salmon and sea trout beats are let by the week and prior arrangements ought to be made. In the last few seasons, however, partly because of reduced runs on some rivers and lochs, more short-span vacancies are becoming available. This is particularly true in June and September, when the tenants or owners of the lodges go home. Your local hotel or fishing agents know the game plan and may be able to let fishers have unexpected, interesting and potentially good water to fish. Salmon fishing particularly is a question of luck with the weather. To a slightly lesser extent, this is also true of sea trout. In Scotland for Fishing you will find Agencies and estate offices listed for each area. You will also find club and hotel fishing details. Local fishing tackle shops are not only fascinating places to call on during a fishing trip, but can offer good fishings on a day or short term basis. Local angling clubs sometimes have very interesting water available for visitors, and sometimes, as on Spey at Grantown, the water open to

Choosing a fly on the Helmsdale.

visiting fishers is extensive. Just because a river has a famous name does not mean that the local club will not have access to some part of it. For example, Highland rivers like the Brora and Helmsdale have a certain number of visitor tickets available for Club water – properly restricted to visitors staying in a hotel or boarding house etc. in the area during the fishing dates.

With these 'doors' into Scottish fishing – many of

A good wild trout, well fed and hard fighting.

which will open willingly to your knock – the quality of what Scotland offers will become clear. That quality, as we said earlier, is not always up-front, – in the shop window, as it were, it lies in the places you fish, and, in particular, in the detail of each. The wilderness is there, wiith that wild quality of sport which we are famous for. It is sometimes a shy wilderness, having to be discovered in certain bays or on certain pools of a river. But it is there and, for me, this element is the vital one in enjoying a fishing holiday in Scotland. Our fishing is seldom without a feeling of wildness and of being unspoiled. We are not, of course, offering a rural utopia; we are welcoming fishers to a real landscape with more that a little magnificence, to real waters, many of which are unspoiled and above all to fish which are wild. Fishing Scottish waters is often the best way to discover the true, wild nature of Scotland and its memorable wild fish.

Bill Currie

On the Ness, looking up from the Laggan to Dochfour.

BORDERS - RIVERS & LOCHS

Area Tourist Board
Scottish Borders Tourist Board
Chief Executive,
Shepherds Mill,
Whinfield Road,
Selkirk TD7 5DT.
Tel: (01750) 20555.

Scottish Environment Protection Agency
Galashiels Office
Burnbrae,
Mossilee Road,
Galashiels TD1 1NF.
Tel: (01896) 752797 or 752425.
Fax: (01896) 754412 (24 hour emergency number).

RIVERS

Water	Location	Species	Season	Permit available from	Other information
Blackadder (Map IV F4)	Greenlaw	Brown Trout	1 Apr. to 6 Oct.	Greenlaw Angling Club T. Waldie, 26 East High St., Greenlaw TD10 6UF. All hotels.	No bait fishing until 1st May. Sunday fishing. No spinning.
	Kimmerghame	Brown Trout	1 Apr. to 6 Oct.	Mrs McCosh, Kimmerghame Mill, Duns Kimmerghame House, Tel:01361 883277. R. Welsh & Son, 28 Castle Street, Duns. Tel: 01361 883466.	
Bowmont Water	Morebattle	Trout Grayling	15 Mar. to 6 Oct.	Keith Rothwell, Eildon View, Mainsfield Ave., Morebattle TD5 8QP. Tel: (01573) 44247.	No ground baiting. No Sunday fishing from Primeside Mill up.
Eden Water	Kelso	Brown Trout	1 Apr. to 30 Sep.	Forrest & Sons, 40 The Square, Kelso. Tel: (01573) 224687. Intersport, 43 The Square, Kelso. Tel: (01573) 223381. Border Hotel, Woodmarket, Kelso TD5 7AX. Tel: (01573) 224791.	Fly only. No spinning. Restricted to 3 rods.
	Gordon	Brown Trout	15 Mar. to 6 Oct.	J.H. Fairgrieve, Burnbrae, Gordon. Tel: (01573) 410357.	No spinning. No Sunday fishing.
Ettrick & Yarrow (Map IV E4)	Bowhill	Salmon Trout	1 Feb. to 30 Nov. 15 Mar. to 30 Sep.	Buccleuch Estates Ltd., Estate Office, Bowhill, Selkirk. Tel: (01750) 20753.	Tweed Rules. No Sunday Fishing.
	Selkirk	Brown Trout	1 Apr. to 30 Sep.	P. & E. Scott (Newsagent), 6 High Street, Selkirk. Tel: (01750) 20749.	Night fishing (15 May to 14 Sep.). Week ticket only. No minnows or spinning. No Sunday fishing.
Ettrick (Map IV D5)	Ettrick Bridge	Brown Trout Salmon	1 Apr. to 30 Sep. 1 Feb. to 30 Nov.	Ettrickshaws Hotel. Tel: (01750) 52229.	Packed lunches and flasks for residents. Permits also available for other waters.
Kale Water	Eckford	Trout Grayling	1 Apr. to 30 Sep.	Mr. Graham, Eckford Cottage, Eckford, Kelso. Tel: (01835) 850255.	No Sunday fishing.

Water	Location	Species	Season	Permit available from	Other information
	Morebattle	Trout Grayling	15 Mar. to 6 Oct.	Keith Rothwell, Eildon View, Mainsfield Ave., Morebattle TD5 8QP. Tel: (01573) 44247. Templehall Hotel, Morebattle. Tel: (01573) 440249.	No ground baiting. No Sunday fishing.
Leader Water (Map IV E4)	Lauderdale	Trout	15 Mar. to 6 Oct.	M. & I. Rattray (Newsagent), Lauder. J.S. Main, Saddler, 87 High Street, Haddington. Tel: (01620) 822148. Lauder Post Office. Tower Hotel, Oxton, by Lauder. Tel: (01578) 750235. Anglers Choice, 23 Market Square, Melrose TD6 9PL. Tel: (01896) 823070.	No spinning. Sunday fishing. No grayling fishing.
Leader Water/ Tweed	Earlston	Trout	15 Mar. to 30 Sep.	Earlston Angling Assoc., C.T. Austin, 23 Summerfield, Earlston. Tel: (01896) 849548. D. & B. Welsh Newsagents, The Square, Earlston. E. & R. Anderson Newsagent, The Square, Earlston. Tel: (01896) 849330. Anglers Choice, 23 Market Square, Melrose. Tel: (01896) 823070. Hotels and pubs.	No Sunday fishing. Other restrictions as per permit.
Liddle Water	Newcastleton	Sea Trout	1 May to 30 Sep.	J.D. Ewart, Fishing Tackle Shop, Newcastleton. Tel: (01387) 375257.	Day and weekly tickets available.
	South Roxburgh- shire	Salmon Sea Trout Brown Trout	1 Feb. to 31 Oct. 15 Apr. to 30 Sep. 1 May to 30 Sep.	Esk & Liddle Fisheries, R.J.B. Hill, Bank of Scotland Buildings, Langholm. Tel: (013873) 80428. George Graham, Hagg-on-Esk, Old School, Canonbie. Tel: (013873) 71416.	Spinning allowed until 14 April and otherwise only when water is above markers at Newcastleton, Kershopefoot and Penton Bridges. No Sunday fishing.
Lyne Water	Tweed Junction to Flemington Bridge	Trout Grayling	1 Apr. to 30 Sep.	Peeblesshire Trout Fishing Assoc., D.G. Fyfe, 39 High Street, Peebles. Tel: (01721) 720131. Tweeddale Tackle Centre, 1 Bridgegate, Peebles. Tel: (01721) 720979. Sonny's Sports Shop, Innerleithen. Tel: (01896) 830806. Tweed Valley Hotel, Walkerburn EH43 6AA. Tel: (01896) 870636. J. Dickson & Son, 21 Frederick Street, Edinburgh. Tel: 0131-225 4218. Crook Inn, Tweedsmuir. Tel: (01899) 880272.	No Sunday fishing. No spinning. No bait fishing April & September. Tickets also cover Tweed. Catch and release policy for native trout. Bag limit for stocked trout.
Oxnam Water	Morebattle	Trout Grayling	15 Mar. to 6 Oct.	Keith Rothwell, Eildon View, Mainsfield Ave., Morebattle TD5 8QP. Tel: (01573) 44247.	No ground baiting. No Sunday fishing from Bloodylaws up.

Water	Location	Species	Season	Permit available from	Other information
Teviot (Map IV E5)	Above Chesters	Salmon Sea Trout	1 Feb. to 30 Nov.	The Pet Store, Union Street, Hawick. Tel: (01450) 373543.	All rules and regulations on ticket. Limited to 9 rods on 3 beats per day. (9 day tickets Mon–Fri. 6 visitor season tickets only on application to:) Mr. R. Kohler, Hawick Angling Club, 8 Twirlees Terrace, Hawick. Tel: (01450) 373903.
	Eckford	Salmon Sea Trout Brown Trout	1 Feb. to 30 Nov. 15 Mar. to 30 Sep.	Mr. Graham, Eckford Cottage, Eckford, Kelso. Tel: (01835) 850255.	No Sunday fishing. Limited to 4 day permits. Bait and spinning 15 Feb. to 15 Sep. only. Spinning for trout and grayling prohibited.
Teviot Cont.	Jedforest	Salmon	1 Feb. to 30 Nov.	Jedforest Angling Assoc., J. Tait, 9 Boundaries, Jedburgh TD8 6EX. Tel: (01835) 863871.	No Sunday fishing. Salmon: 6 rods per day. Spinning 15 Feb. to 14 Sep. Fly only 15 Sep. to 30 Nov. No Sunday fishing. No spinning. Fly only until 1 May.
		Trout	1 Apr. to 30 Sep.	Shaws (Newsagent), 10 Canongate, Jedburgh. Tel: (01835) 863245.	
	Kelso	Brown Trout Grayling	1 Apr. to 30 Sep.	Forrest & Sons, 40 The Square, Kelso. Tel: (01573) 224687. Intersport, 43 The Square, Kelso. Tel: (01573) 223381. Border Hotel, Woodmarket, Kelso TD5 7AX. Tel: (01573) 224791.	No Sunday fishing. Restrictions on spinning. No maggots or ground bait. Size limit 10".
Teviot (and Ale Slitrig Borthwick Rule)	Hawick	Brown Trout Salmon	15 Mar. to 30 Sep. 1 Feb. to 30 Nov.	The Pet Store, 1 Union Street, Hawick. Tel: (01450) 373543.	All rules and regulations on ticket.
Tweed (and Teviot) (Map IV F4)	Kelso	Brown Trout Coarse Fish	1 Apr. to 30 Sep.	Forrest & Sons, 40 The Square, Kelso. Tel: (01573) 224687.	
Tweed (Map IV F4)	Peeblesshire (substantial stretch of river)	Trout Grayling	1 Apr. to 30 Sep.	Peeblesshire Trout Fishing Assoc., Blackwood & Smith w.s., 39 High Street, Peebles EH45. Tel: (01721) 720131. Tweed Valley Hotel, Walkerburn EH43 6AA. Tel: (01896) 870636. F. & D. Simpson, 28/30 West Preston Street, Edinburgh EH8 9PZ. Tel: 0131-667 3058. J. Dickson & Son, 21 Frederick Street, Edinburgh. Tel: 0131-225 4218.	No spinning. No bait fishing April & September. No Sunday fishing. Tickets also cover Lyne Water. Waders desirable. Fly only on Tweed from Lynefoot upstream. New catch and release policy for native trout. Bag limit for stocked trout.
	Clovenfords (Peel Water)	Salmon Sea Trout	1 Feb. to 30 Nov.	J.H. Leeming ARICS, Salmon Fishing Agent, Stichill House, Kelso TD5 7TB. Office: (01573) 470280. Fax: (01573) 470259. Web site: http://www.scotborders.co.uk	Half mile single bank. 2 rods. Spinning or fly 15 Feb. to 14 Sep. Fly only 15 Sep. to 30 Nov. Average 5 fish caught.
	Coldstream (West Learmouth Beat)	Salmon Grilse Sea Trout	1 Feb. to 30 Nov.	J.H. Leeming ARICS, Salmon Fishing Agent, Stichill House, Kelso TD5 7TB. Office: (01573) 470280. Fax: (01573) 470259. Web site: http://www.scotborders.co.uk	2/3 of a mile of south bank. Average catch 263 fish. No spinning before 15 Feb. or after 15 Sep.

Water	Location	Species	Season	Permit available from	Other information
Tweed cont.	Galashiels (Fairnilee Beat)	Salmon Sea Trout	(salmon) 1 Feb. to 30 Nov.	J.H. Leeming ARICS, Salmon Fishing Agent, Stichill House, Kelso TD5 7TB. Office: (01573) 470280. Web site: http://www.scotborders.co.uk	3.5 miles single bank. Ghillies, rod room, hut, boat and full facilities. Average 98 fish caught. No spinning before 15 Feb. or after 15 Sep.
		Trout	1 Apr. to 30 Sep.	Messrs. J. & A. Turnbull, 30 Bank Street, Galashiels. Tel: (01896) 753191. Anglers Choice, 23 Market Square, Melrose TD6 9PL. Tel: (01896) 823070.	No Sunday fishing. Day tickets available on Saturdays. No spinning.
	Galashiels (Boleside Beat)	Salmon Sea Trout	Feb. to Nov.	J.H. Leeming ARICS, Salmon Fishing Agent, Stichill House, Kelso TD5 7TB. Office: (01573) 470280. Fax: (01573) 470259. Web site: http://www.scotborders.co.uk	1.5 miles of double bank with 9 named pools. Boleside is regarded as one of the top Tweed beats. Average catch: 419. 2 boats available.
	Galashiels (Netherbarns Beat)	Sea Trout Salmon	Feb. to Nov.	J.H. Leeming ARICS, Salmon Fishing Agent, Stichill House, Kelso TD5 7TB. Office: (01573) 470280. Fax: (01573) 470259. Web site: http://www.scotborders.co.uk	The beat forms the bottom part of Boleside Fishings and is about half a mile of double bank fishing. Average catch 33. No boats.
	Horncliffe (Tweedhill Beat)	Salmon Sea Trout	1 Feb. to 30 Nov.	J.H. Leeming ARICS, Salmon Fishing Agent, Stichill House, Kelso TD5 7TB. Office: (01573) 470280. Fax: (01573) 470259. Web site: http://www.scotborders.co.uk	3 miles of single bank. Some tidal water. Average catch 157 fish.
	Innerleithen (Traquair Beat)	Salmon Sea Trout	1 Feb. to 30 Nov.	J.H. Leeming ARICS, Salmon Fishing Agent, Stichill House, Kelso TD5 7TB. Office: (01573) 470280. Fax: (01573) 470259. Web site: http://www.scotborders.co.uk Mrs A Lerette, 23/25 High Street, Innerleithen. Tel: (01896) 830314.	2 miles above and 1 mile below Innerleithen Bridge. Ghillie, fishing hut and good access to both banks. Average catch Oct/Nov 65 salmon and sea trout. No spinning before 15 Feb. or after 15 Sep.
	Nr. Kelso (Hendersyde Beat)	Salmon Sea Trout	1 Feb. to 30 Nov.	J.H. Leeming ARICS, Salmon Fishing Agent, Stichill House, Kelso TD5 7TB. Office: (01573) 470280. Fax: (01573) 470259. Web site: http://www.scotborders.co.uk	The water is split into two beats which are fished 3 days in rotation with the opposite bank. Thus 2 rods are able to fish 1 mile of double bank fishing. Average catch 274 fish.
	Kelso	Brown Trout	1 Apr. to 30 Sep.	Border Hotel, Woodmarket, Kelso TD5 7AX. Tel: (01573) 224791.	Fly only. No spinning. Restricted to 3 rods.
	Ladykirk	Brown Trout	19 Mar. to 8 Oct.	Victoria Hotel, Norham. Tel: (01289) 382237.	No spinning. No ground baiting. Fly only above Norham Bridge to West Ford. No Sundays.
	Melrose	Trout Grayling	1 Apr. to 6 Oct.	Melrose & District Angling Assoc., Anglers Choice, 23 Market Square, Melrose. Tel: (01896) 823070.	No spinning. No ground baiting. No Sunday fishing. Minnow fishing not permitted. Spinning reels of all types prohibited.

Water	Location	Species	Season	Permit available from	Other information
Tweed cont.	Melrose (Ravenswood Tweedswood)	Brown Trout	1 Apr. to 30 Sep.	Anglers Choice, 23 Market Square, Melrose. Tel: (01896) 823070.	Fly fishing only.
	Melrose (Ravenswood Beat)	Salmon Sea Trout	Feb. to Nov.	J.H. Leeming ARICS, Salmon Fishing Agent, Stichill House, Kelso TD5 7TB. Office: (01573) 470280. Fax: (01573) 470259. Web site: http://www.scotborders.co.uk	1.5 miles of right bank with 7 named pools. The beat lies in a wooded gorge, having no road beside it. Average catch 100 fish. 1 boat available.
	Melrose (Pavilion)	Salmon Sea Trout	1 Feb. to 30 Nov.	Anglers Choice, 23 Market Square, Melrose. Tel: (01896) 823070.	Fly only: 1 to 15 Feb., and 15 Sep. to 30 Nov. 16 Feb. to 14 Sep fly and spinning.
	Nest	Salmon Sea Trout Trout	1 Feb. to 30 Nov. 1 Apr. to 30 Sep.	Tweed Valley Hotel, Walkerburn EH43 6AA. Tel: (01896) 870636.	Private salmon/sea trout beat approx. 1.75 miles, 4 rods. Fly only 15 Sep. to 30 Nov. Trout and grayling permits available to all. Week or day lets Spring/ Summer. Week lets only Oct. & Nov.
	Northam (Ladykirk Beat)	Salmon Grilse Sea Trout	1 Feb. to 30 Nov.	J.H. Leeming ARICS, Salmon Fishing Agent, Stichill House, Kelso TD5 7TB. Office: (01573) 470280. Fax: (01573) 470259. Web site: http://www.scotborders.co.uk	3 miles of the north bank. Boats and ghillies provided. Average catch 196 fish. No spinning before 15 Feb. or after 15 Sep.
	Northam (Pedwell Beat)	Salmon Grilse Sea Trout	1 Feb. to 30 Nov.	J.H. Leeming ARICS, Salmon Fishing Agent, Stichill House, Kelso TD5 7TB. Office: (01573) 470280. Fax: (01573) 470259. Web site: http://www.scotborders.co.uk	1.5 miles single bank. Average catch of 313 fish. No spinning before 15 Feb. or after 15 Sep.
	Peel	Salmon Sea Trout	1 Feb. to 30 Nov.	Tweed Valley Hotel, Walkerburn EH43 6AA. Tel: (01896) 870636.	Private 2-rod salmon beat on south bank. Week or day lets Spring/Summer. Week lets only October and November. Angling course, September.
	Peebles (Wire Bridge Pool to Nutwood Pool – excluding Kailzie)	Salmon Grilse Sea Trout	21 Feb. to 30 Nov.	Peeblesshire Salmon Fishing Assoc. Seasons:Blackwood & Smith w.s., 39 High Street, Peebles. Tel: (01721) 720131 Day Permits: Tweeddale Tackle Centre, 1 Bridgegate, Peebles EH45 8RZ. Tel: (01721) 720979.	Strictly fly fishing only. No Sunday fishing. Other regulations on tickets.
	St. Boswells (Bemersyde Beat)	Salmon Grilse Sea Trout	1 Feb. to 30 Nov.	J.H. Leeming ARICS, Salmon Fishing Agent, Stichill House, Kelso TD5 7TB. Office: (01573) 470280. Fax: (01573) 470259. Web site: http://www.scotborders.co.uk	1 mile of excellent water. Average catch 151 fish. Must be a good walker and wader as parts are difficult and access to the river bank not available to cars.

Water	Location	Species	Season	Permit available from	Other information
Tweed cont.		Brown Trout	1 Apr. to 30 Sep.	Dryburgh Abbey Hotel, St. Boswells. Tel: (01835) 822261. Anglers Choice, 23 Market Square, Melrose. Tel: (01896) 823070. Crook Inn, Tweedsmuir. Tel: (01899) 880272.	Fly only 1 Apr. to 1 May. No bait fishing until 1 May. No Sunday fishing. No spinning tackle. No coarse fishing allowed outside season. Access to restricted beats by special permits only.
	Tweedsmuir Walkerburn	Brown Trout Grayling Salmon Sea Trout Trout	1 Apr. to 30 Sep. 1 Feb. to 30 Nov. 1 Apr. to 30 Sep.	Tweed Valley Hotel, Walkerburn EH43 6AA. Tel: (01896) 870636.	All rules and regulations on permits. Salmon tickets for hotel guests only after 14 Sep. Special salmon and trout weeks tuition. Trout and grayling permits available to all.
	Haystoun (Beat 1.5 miles)	Salmon Sea Trout	15 Feb. to 30 Nov.	Fraser's Salmon Fishing & Hire Ltd., 16 Kingsmuir Crescent, Peebles. Tel: (01721) 722362.	No spinning in autumn – fly only. No Sunday fishing. Rods limited to 6 per day. Part-time ghillie included in permit price. 8 named salmon pools.
	Kingsmeadow (Beat [3/4] mile)	Salmon Sea Trout	15 Feb. to 30 Nov.	Fraser's Salmon Fishing & Hire Ltd., 16 Kingsmuir Crescent, Peebles. Tel: (01721) 722362.	Spinning allowed 15 Feb. to 14 Sep. Rods limited to 2 per day. Easy car access to beat. Part-time ghillie included in permit price. 5 named salmon pools.
Whiteadder & Dye & Tributaries	30 miles	Brown/ Rainbow Trout	15 Mar. to 30 Sep.	J.S. Main, Saddlers, 87 High Street, Haddington. Tel: (01620) 822148. R. Welsh & Son, 28 Castle Street, Duns, Berwickshire TD11 3DP. Tel: 01361 883466.	No Sundays. Fly only before 15 Apr. Worm from 15 Apr. only. Minnow from 1 May only. Size limit 8 inches.
Whiteadder (Map IV F4)	Allanton	Trout	15 Mar. to 30 Sep.	Berwick & District Angling Association, Mr. D. Cowan, 129 Etal Road, Tweedmouth, Berwick-upon-Tweed. Tel: (01289) 306985. R. Welsh & Son, 28 Castle Street, Duns, Berwickshire TD11 3DP. Tel: 01361 883466.	Fly only before May. No spinning. No threadline. No maggot fishing. No ground baiting. 9 inch min.

LOCHS & RESERVOIRS

Water	Location	Species	Season	Permit available from	Other information
Acreknowe Reservoir	Hawick	Brown Trout	15 Mar. to end Sep.	The Pet Shop, 1 Union Street, Hawick. Tel: (01450) 373543. Mr. D Smith, "Wellogate Bank", Wellowgate Brae, Hawick. Tel: (01450) 373142.	Ticket covers all other trout waters managed by Hawick Angling Club. Boat available from Pet Shop. Fly fishing only.
Alemoor Loch	Hawick	Brown Trout Perch Pike		As Acreknowe	Bank fishing only.
Alton Loch	2 miles N. of Hawick	Brown/ Rainbow Trout	1 Mar. to 31 Oct.	At loch only. Further details from: Mr. Morand, Flat 7, 3 Quay Walls, Berwick-upon-Tweed, Northumberland. Tel: 0836 339757 (mobile).	Average weight of fish caught: 1.5 to 3 lbs. Fly fishing only. 4 boats plus 4 on bank. Sessions: Day 8am–4pm; Evening 4.30 pm–dusk.
Clearburn Loch	Nr. Hawick	Trout		Tushielaw Inn, Ettrick Valley, Selkirkshire. Tel: (01750) 62205. Clerklands Fly Fishery,	Boat supplied free.

Water	Location	Species	Season	Permit available from	Other information
Clerklands Loch	Nr. Selkirk	Rainbow/ Brown Trout	All year.	Nr. Selkirk. Tel: (01835) 870757.	Fly fishing only. Trout Master available. Open daily. 3 Boats.
Coldingham Loch	Reston	Brown/ Rainbow Trout	15 Mar. to 30 Oct.	Dr E.J. Wise, West Loch House, Coldingham. Tel: (01890) 771270.	Fly only. 6 boats (max 12 rods). 10 bank rods. Sunday fishing. Advance booking essential.
Fruid Reservoir	Tweedsmuir	Brown Trout	Apr. to Sep.	Crook Inn, Tweedsmuir. Tel: (01899) 880272.	Bank fishing only. Fly, bait, spinning.
Heatherhope Reservoir	Hownam	Trout	15 Mar. to 6 Oct.	David Gray, 17 Mainsfield Avenue, Morebattle TD5 8QW. Tel: (01573) 440528. The Garage, Morebattle. Templehall Hotel, Morebattle. Tel: (01573) 440249.	No ground baiting. No Sunday fishing.
Hellmoor Loch	Hawick	Brown Trout		As Acreknowe.	No boat. No competitions. Limit 6 trout.
Knowesdean Reservoir	Galashiels	Brown/ Rainbow Trout	15 Mar. to 31 Oct.	J. & A. Turnbull, 30 Bank Street, Galashiels. Tel: (01896) 753191.	Bag limit 3 fish. 2 sessions per day. Advance booking advisable.
Loch Lindean	Selkirk	Brown Trout	Apr.–Oct.	P. & E. Scott, Newsagent, 6 High Street, Selkirk TD7 4DA. Tel: (01750) 20749.	2 boats available.
Loch of the Lowes and St. Mary's Loch	Selkirk	Brown Trout Pike Perch Eels	1 Apr. to 30 Sep. 1 May to 30 Sep.	St. Mary's A.C. per Sec., N. MacIntyre, "Whincroft" 8 Rosetta Road, Peebles EH45 8JU. Tel: (01721) 722278. Gordon Arms Hotel, Yarrow. Hook, Line & Sinker, 20 Morningside Road, Edinburgh. Tel: 0131-447 9172. Tibbie Shiels Inn, St. Mary's Loch, Yarrow, Selkirk. Tel: (01750) 42231. Anglers Choice, 23 Market Square, Melrose. Tel: (01896) 823070. Glen Cafe (lochside). Tweeddale Tackle Centre, 1 Bridgegate, Peebles. Tel: (01721) 720979. Mikes Tackle Shop, 46 Portobello High Street, Edinburgh. Tel: 0131-657 3258.	Fly fishing only, until 30 April thereafter spinning and bait allowed. Club fishing apply Secretary or keeper. Sunday fishing. Weekly permits and rowing boats from keeper, Mr. Brown (01750) 42243. Outboard engines of up to 5 h.p. may be used, but none available for hire. No float fishing. Loch of the Lowes is bank fishing only. River Tweed Protection order applies. Club memberships available.
Megget Reservoir	Tweedsmuir	Brown Trout	Closed till mid 1999.	Tibbie Shiels Inn, St, Mary's Loch, Yarrow, Selkirk. Tel: (01750) 42231. East of Scotland Water. Tel:(01786) 458827.	No bait fishing. 6 Boats available. Max. bag limit 10 fish.
Peebles-shire Lochs	Tweed Valley	Brown/ Rainbow Trout	Apr. to Oct.	Tweed Valley Hotel, Walkerburn EH43 6AA. Tel: (01896) 870636.	Stocked private lochans. Wild brown trout loch.

Water	Location	Species	Season	Permit available from	Other information
Portmore Game Fisheries	Peebles-Eddleston	Wild Brown Trout Rainbow Trout	1 Apr. to 31 Oct.	Portmore Game Fisheries at the loch. Tel: (01968) 675684. Moblie: 0374 127467	Average weight of fish caught: 2lbs. Popular flies, Buzzers: Lures at beginning; from May, dry & wet. Boats are avail- able, contact: Steve McGeachie at number opposite. Fly fishing only.
Purdom Stone Reservoir (Map IV D6)	Hoddom & Kinmount Estates Ecclefechan	Brown Trout	1 Apr. to 15 Sep.	The Water Bailiff, Hoddem & Kinmort Estates, Esatae Office, Hoddem, Lockerbie DG11 1BE. Tel: (01576) 300417. Mobile: 0411 681507.	2 sessions: 10am–4pm, 5pm–dusk. Bag limit 4 per day, 3 per evening. From end Oct. to start Apr., 1 day session only, 10am–3.30pm.
Sunlaws Trout Pond	Heston nr Kelso	Rainbow Trout	All year.	Sunlaws House Hotel, Kelso. Tel: (01573) 450331.	Boats available from Pet Store, 1 Union Street, Hawick. Fly only.
Synton Loch	Hawick	Brown Trout		As Acreknowe Reservoir.	Fly fishing only. 2 boats.
Talla Reservoir	Tweedsmuir	Brown Trout Arctic Char	Apr. to Sep.	Crook Inn, Tweedsmuir. Tel: (01899) 880272.	Boat and Bank fishing. 2 boats available. Fly fishing only.
Upper Loch	Bowhill	Brown/ Rainbow Trout	1 Apr. to 31 Oct.	Buccleuch Estate Ltd., Estate Office, Bowhill, Selkirk. Tel: (01750) 20753.	Fly only. 2 rods per boat and limit of 8 fish per boat. No fishing Sundays.
Watch Reservoir	Longformacus	Brown Trout Rainbow Trout	1 Mar. to 30 Sep. All year.	W.F. Renton, The Watch Fly Reservoir. Tel: (01361) 890331 & 0860 868144.	Sunday fishing. Fly only. Strictly no use of bait/ maggots, etc. Restaurant, Tearoom and disabled facilities available.
West Water Reservoir	West Linton	Brown Trout	1 May to 30 Sep.	Contact: 0131-445 6300.	2 boats. Fly fishing only. Boat fishing only.
Whiteadder Reservoir	Gifford	Brown Trout	Apr. to Sep.	Goblin Ha Hotel, Gifford. Tel: (01620) 810244.	Fly fishing only. 8 boats are available. Boat and Bank fishing
Willies-truther Loch	Hawick	Brown/ Rainbow Trout		As Acreknowe Reservoir.	Any legal method.
Wooden Loch	Eckford	Rainbow Trout	1 Apr. to 31 Oct.	Mr. Graham, Eckford Cottage, Eckford, Kelso. Tel: (01835) 850255.	1 boat. No bank fishing. Only rainbow trout after 30 Sep. Only 2 rods at any time. Advance booking necessary. No Sundays.

Dumfries & Galloway Council
52-60 Queensberry street,
Dumfries DG1 1BF.
Tel: (01387) 260765.

Scottish Environment Protection Agency
River's House,
Irongray Road,
Dumfries DG2 OJE.
Tel: (01387) 720502.
Fax: (01387) 721154.
Emergency Tel: 0800 807060.

RIVERS

Water	Location	Species	Season	Permit available from	Other information
Annan (Map IV D6)	Halleaths Estate Lockerbie	Salmon Sea Trout	25 Feb. to 15 Nov.	Messrs. McJerrow & Stevenson (Solicitors), 55 High Street, Lockerbie. Tel: (01576) 202123.	Limited number of weekly tickets.
	Kirkwood & Jardine Hall Beats	Salmon Sea Trout Brown Trout	25 Feb. to 15 Nov.	Mr. Anthony Steel, Kirkwood, Lockerbie. Tel: (01576) 510212/510200.	Kirkwood is mainly fly fishing (spinning and worming only in spate conditions). Jardine Hall – spinning and worming allowed.
	Royal Four Towns Water Lockerbie	Salmon Sea Trout Brown Trout	25 Feb. to 15 Nov.	Castle Milk Estates Office, Norwood, Lockerbie. Tel: (01576) 510203.	Fly fishing only. No Sunday fishing.
	St. Mungo Parish	Salmon Sea Trout Brown Trout	25 Feb. to 15 Nov.	Warmanbie Hotel & Restaurant, Annan DG12 5LL. Tel: (01461) 204015.	Fly, spinning, worm all season. Access to many other stretches. For residents only.
	Warmanbie Estate	Salmon Sea Trout Brown Trout	25 Feb. to 15 Nov.	Newton Stewart A.A. Galloway Guns & Tackle, 36 Arthur Street, Newton Stewart. Tel: (01671) 403404.	
Bladnoch (Map IV B6)	Newton Stewart	Salmon	1 Mar. to 31 Oct.	Palakona Guest House, Queen Street, Newton Stewart DG8 6JL. Tel: (01671) 402323. (For guests only.)	
Cairn	Dumfries	Brown Trout Salmon Sea Trout	15 Mar. to 6 Oct. 1 Apr. to end Oct.	Dumfries & Galloway A.A. Secretary: D. Byers, 4 Bloomfield, Edinburgh Road, Dumfries DG1 1SG. Tel: (01387) 253850.	Limited number of permits. No Sunday fishing. Restrictions depend on water level. Visitors Mon.–Fri. only.

Water	Location	Species	Season	Permit available from	Other information
Cree (and Pencill Burn) (Map IV B6)	Drumlamford Estate	Salmon Trout	Apr. to Oct.	The Keeper, The Kennels, Drumlamford Estate, Barrhill. Tel: (01465) 821256.	No Sunday fishing.
	Newton Stewart	Salmon Sea Trout	1 Mar. to 14 Oct.	Newton Stewart A.A. Galloway Guns & Tackle, 36 Arthur Street, Newton Stewart. Tel: (01671) 403404. Palakona Guest House, Queen Street, Newton Stewart DG8 6JL. Tel: (01671) 402323. (For guests only.)	No Sunday fishing. Rules printed on permits.
Black Water of Dee (Map IV C6)	Mossdale	Trout Pike Perch Salmon	15 Mar. to 30 Sep. 11 Feb. to 31 Oct.	Local hotels and shops.	
Esk (Map IV E5)	East Dumfriesshire	Salmon Sea Trout/ Herling Brown Trout	1 Feb. to 31. Oct. 1 May to 30 Sep. 15 Apr. to 30 Sep.	Esk & Liddle Fisheries R.J.B. Hill, Bank of Scotland Buildings, Langholm. Tel: (013873) 80428. George Graham, Hagg-on-Esk, Old School, Canonbie. Tel: (013873) 71416.	Spinning allowed until 14 Apr. and otherwise only when water is above markers at Skippers Bridge, Canonbie Bridge and Willow Pool.
Ken	New Galloway	Brown/ Rainbow Trout Perch Pike Roach Salmon	15 Mar. to 30 Sep.	Mr. Swain, Kenmure Arms Hotel, High Street, New Galloway. Tel: (01644) 420240/420360.	Boats available from hotel. Free fishing at hotel on River Ken.
Kirkwood	Annan	Chub Graying	All year	Anthony Steel, Kirkwood, Lockerbie. Tel: (01576) 510200.	Big fish. Record Chub caught here.
Liddle	Newcastletor Ticket	Salmon Sea Trout Brown Trout	15 Apr. to 31. Oct. 1 May to 30 Sep. 15 Apr. to 30 Sep.	J.D. Ewart, Tackle Agent, Newcastleton. Tel: (01387) 375257. R.J.B. Hill, Bank of Scotland Buildings, Langholm. Tel: (01387) 380428.	Spinning allowed when water is above markers at Newcastleton and Kershopefoot Bridges. No Sunday fishing. Day tickets available.
Milk	Scroggs Bridge	Sea/ Brown Trout Carp Salmon	1 Apr. to 6 Nov.	Mr. Anthony Steel, Kirkwood, Lockerbie. Tel: (01576) 510200.	Mainly fly fishing. No Sunday fishing.
Minnoch	Newton Stewart	Salmon	1 Mar. to 30 Sep.	Galloway Guns & Tackle, 36 Arthur Street, Newton Stewart. Tel: (01671) 403404.	Fly, spin or worm.
Nith (Map IV D5)	Dumfries	Salmon Sea Trout Brown Trout	25 Feb. to 30 Nov. 15 Mar. to 6 Oct.	Dumfries & Galloway Council, Housing Services, 81-85 Irish St., Dumfreis. Tel: (01387) 259991. Dumfries & Galloway Angling Association, Secretary, D. Byers, 4 Bloomfield Edinburgh Road, Dumfries DG1 1SG. Tel: (01387) 253850.	No Sunday fishing. Advance booking. Limited number of permits. Weekly permits from Mon. to Fri. Advance booking possible. Spinning restrictions.

Water	Location	Species	Season	Permit available from	Other information
	Thornhill	Salmon Sea Trout Brown Trout	25 Feb. to 30 Nov. 1 Apr. to 31 Sep.	The Drumlanrig Castle Fishings, The Buccleuch Estates Ltd., Drumlanrig Mains, Thornhill DG3 4AG. Tel: (01848) 600283.	Lower, Middle & Upper beats. Average weight of fish caught: Salmon 9lbs 8oz, Grilse 6 lbs, Sea Trout 2lbs, Brown Trout 8 oz, Grayling, 8 oz. Popular flies: Stoats Tail, General Practitioner, Silver Doctor, Flying C, Silver Toby. Spinning, worming (until 31 Aug.). Weekly and daily lets up to 3 rods/beat.
		Salmon Sea Trout Brown Trout	25 Feb. to 30 Nov. 1 Apr. to 30 Sep.	The Drumlanrig Castle Fishings, The Buccleuch Estates Ltd., Drumlanrig Mains, Thornhill DG3 4AG. Tel: (01848) 600283.	Lower, Middle & Upper beats. Average weight of fish caught: Salmon 9lbs 8oz, Grilse 6 lbs, Sea Trout 2lbs, Brown Trout 8 oz, Grayling, 8 oz. Weekly and daily lets up to 3 rods/beat.
		Salmon Sea Trout Brown Trout	25 Feb. to 30 Nov.	Mid Nithsdale A.A. Secretary. Tel/Fax:(01548) 330555. Mr. I.R. Milligan, 37 Drumlanrig Street, Thornhill DG3 5LS. Tel: (01848) 330555.	No day permits on Saturdays. Spinning and worming allowed only in flood conditions. Advisable to book for autumn fishing.
Nith (and tributaries Kello Crawick Euchan Mennock)	Sanquhar	Salmon Sea Trout Brown Trout Grayling	15 Mar. to 30 Nov. Jan., Feb.	Upper Nithsdale Angling Club, Pollock & McLean, Solicitors, 61 High Street, Sanquhar. Tel: (01659) 50241.	No Sunday fishing. Visitors and residents. Day tickets (Mon.–Fri.) – limit of 30 per day during months: Sep., Oct. & Nov. Week tickets – limit of 10 per week during season.
Tarf	Kirkcowan	Sea Trout Brown Trout	Easter to 30 Sep.	A. Brown, Three Lochs Holiday Park, Kirkcowan, Newton Stewart. Tel: (01671) 830304.	
Upper Tarf	Nr. Newton Stewart	Salmon Trout	1 Mar. to 14 Oct. 15 Mar. to 6 Oct.	Palakona Guest House, Queen Street, Newton Stewart DG8 6JL. Tel: (01670) 402323. (For guests only.) Galloway Country Sports. Tel: (01988) 402346 – all day tickets.	Fly, spin or worm.
Urr	Castle Douglas	Salmon Sea Trout Brown Trout	25 Feb. to 30 Nov. 15 Mar. to 6 Oct.	Castle Douglas & District A.A. Tommy's Sport Shop, 178 King Street, Castle Douglas. Tel: (01556) 502851. Dalbeattie A.A. Ticket Secretary: M. McCowan & Son, 43 High Street, Dalbeattie. Tel: (01556) 610270.	
Urr cont.	Dalbeattie	Salmon Sea Trout Brown Trout	25 Feb. to 30 Nov. 15 Mar. to 6 Oct.	Dalbeattie A.A. Ticket Secretary: M. McCowan & Son, 43 High Street, Dalbeattie. Tel: (01556) 610270.	

Water	Location	Species	Season	Permit available from	Other information
White Esk	Eskdalemuir	Salmon Sea Trout	15 Apr. to 30 Oct. 15 Apr. to 30 Sep.	Hart Manor Hotel, Eskdalemuir, by Langholm. Tel: (01387) 373217.	Fly and spinner and worm.

LOCHS & RESERVOIRS

Water	Location	Species	Season	Permit available from	Other information
Barend Loch	Sandyhills	Carp	Open all year	Barend Properties, Reception, Sandyhills, Dalbeattie. Tel: (01387) 780663.	
Barscobe Loch	Balmaclellan	Brown Trout	15 Mar. to 6 Oct.	Lady Wontner, Barscobe, Balmaclellan, Castle Douglas. Tel: (01644) 420245/420294.	Fly fishing only. Obtain permit first.
Black Loch	Newton Stewart	Brown Trout	15 Mar. to 30 Sep.	Forest Enterprise, Creebridge, Newton Stewart. Tel: (01671) 402420. Talnotry Campsite, Queens Way, Newton Stewart. Tel: (01671) 402170. Clatteringshaws Wildlife Visitors Centre, New Galloway. Tel: (01644) 420285.	Fly only until 1 July. Sunday fishing.
Black Loch	Nr. Kirkcowan	(Stocked) Brown Trout Pike	15 Mar. to 6 Oct. No close season.	Palakona Guest House, Queen Street, Newton Stewart. Tel: (01671) 402323. (Guests only.) Galloway Country Sports. Tel: (01988) 402346 – all day tickets.	Any legal method permitted.
Bruntis Loch	Newton Stewart	Brown/ Rainbow Trout	1 May to 30 Sep.	Newton Stewart A.A., Galloway Guns & Tackle, 36 Arthur Street, Newton Stewart. Tel: (01671) 403404.	Fly fishing only (fly and worm from 1 June). Bank fishing only. Sunday fishing.
Clattering-shaws Loch	6 miles west of New Galloway	Brown Trout Pike Perch	Open all year for coarse fish	Galloway Guns & Tackle, 36 Arthur Street, Newton Stewart. Tel: (01671) 403404. Kenmure Arms Hotel, High Street, New Galloway. Tel: (01644) 420240.	Fly fishing, spinning or worm fishing permitted.
Dalbeattie Reservoir	Dalbeattie	Brown/ Rainbow Trout	1 Apr. to 30 Sep.	Dalbeattie A.A. Ticket Secretary: M. McCowan & Son, 43 High Street, Dalbeattie. Tel: (01556) 610270.	Bank fishing. Fly only. Boats for hire.
Loch Dee	Castle Douglas	Brown Trout	15 Mar. to 30 Sep.	Forest Enterprise, Creebridge, Newton Stewart. Tel: (01671) 402420. Talnotry Campsite, Queens Way, Newton Stewart. Tel: (01671) 402170. Clatteringshaws Wildlife Visitors Centre, New Galloway. Tel: (01644) 420285.	Annual fly fishing competition in August.
Dindinnie Reservoir	Stranraer	Brown Trout	1 May to 30 Sep.	Stranraer & District A.A. The Sports Shop, 90 George Street, Stranraer. Tel: (01776) 702705. Local hotels.	Fly fishing only. Sunday fishing.
Loch Dornal	Drumlamford Estate	Coarse Stocked Trout	Apr. to Oct.	Jim McGure, The Lodge Cottage, Drumlamford Estate, Barrhill, South Ayrshire. Tel: (01465) 821243. Galloway Guns & Tackle, Newton Stewart. Tel: (01671) 403404.	Spinning allowed. Boats available. Fly fishing. Average 2.5 lbs.

41

Water	Location	Species	Season	Permit available from	Other information
Loch Drumlamford	Drumlamford Estate	Stocked Trout	Apr. to Oct.	Jim McGure, The Lodge Cottage, Drumlamford Estate, Barrhill, South Ayrshire. Tel: (01465) 821243. Galloway Guns & Tackle, Newton Stewart. Tel: (01671) 403404.	Fly fishing only. Boats available. Average weight of fish 1½ to 2lbs.
Loch Dunskey (lower)	Portpatrick	Rainbow & Brown Trout	Apr. to Oct.	The Keeper, Dunsky Estate, Portpatrick. Tel: (01776) 810364/810848.	Max 4 rods. Boat available. 11 acres.
	Portpatrick	Rainbow & Brown Trout	Apr. to Oct.	The Keeper, Dunsky Estate, Portpatrick. Tel: (01776) 810364/810848.	Max 2 rods. Boat avaialbe. 5 acres.
Loch Ettrick	Closeburn	Rainbow Trout (stocked) Brown Trout	1 Apr. to 30 Nov.	John Crofts, Blawbare, Ettrick, Closeburn, Thornhill DG3 5HL. Tel: (01848) 330154. Closeburn Post Office. Tel: (01848) 331230.	Average weight of fish: 1½ to 3lbs. Popular flies: Nymphs. Fly fishing only. 4 boats availble.
Loch Fern	Dalbeattie	(stocked) Brown Trout	1 Apr to 31 Oct.	John Crofts, Blawbare, Ettrick, Closeburn, Thornhill DG3 5HL. Tel: (01848) 330154.	
Loch Fern Fishery	nr Dalbeattie	Rainbow (stocked) Brown Trout	1 Apr to 30 Nov.	Tel: (01848) 330154	Bait fishing only.
Fynntalloch Loch	Newton Stewart	Brown/Rainbow Trout	1 May to 6 Oct.	Newton Stewart A.A., Galloway Guns & Tackle, 36 Arthur Street, Newton Stewart. Tel: (01671) 403404.	Fly fishing only. Bank fishing only.
Glenkiln Reservoir	Dumfries	Brown Trout (stocked) Rainbow Trout	1 Apr. to 30 Sep.	District Manager, West of Scotland Water, Dumfries and Galloway District, Marchmount House, Dumfries DG1 1PW. Tel: (01387) 250000.	Enquiries to Mr. Ling at number opposite.
Jericho Loch	Dumfries	Brown/Rainbow Trout Brook Trout	1 Apr. to 31 Oct.	McMillan's Tackle Shop, Friars Vennel, Dumfries. Pattie's Tackle Shop, Queensberry Street, Dumfries. Club bookings – contact Jimmy Younger. Tel: (01387) 750247. Day-tickets from Grove Service Station, Heath Hall Dumfries.	Bank fishing only. Fly fishing only. Popular flies: lures, nymphs, traditionals. Sunday fishing.
Loch Ken	New Galloway	Brown Trout Salmon Pike Perch Roach	15 Mar. to 30 Sep. All year round	Kenmure Arms Hotel, High Street, New Galloway. Tel: (01644) 420240. Local shops.	Sunday fishing allowed except for salmon. Worm and spinning permitted. Boats available.
Kettleton Reservoir	Thornhill	Brown/Rainbow Trout	1 Apr. to 30 Sep.	I.R. Milligan, 37 Drumlanrig Street, Thornhill. Tel/Fax: (01848) 330555.	Fly fishing only. Popular flies: Muddler, Black Pennel.
Kirriereoch Loch	Newton Stewart	Brown Trout (stocked)	1 May to 6 Oct.	Newton Stewart A.A. Galloway Guns & Tackle, 36 Arthur Street, Newton Stewart. Tel: (01671) 403404. Glentrool Holiday Park, Glentrool. Tel: (01671) 840280.	Fly fishing only (fly & worm after 1 June). Bank fishing only. Sunday fishing.

Water	Location	Species	Season	Permit available from	Other information
Knock-quassan Reservoir	Stranraer	Brown Trout	1 May to 30 Sep.	Stranraer & District A.A. The Sports Shop, 90 George Street, Stranraer. Tel: (01776) 702705. Local hotels.	Bank fishing only. Fly and spinning. Sunday fishing.
Laird-mannoch Loch	Twynholm	Wild Brown Trout	1 Apr. to 30 Sep.	G.M. Thomson & Co. Ltd., 27 King Street, Castle Douglas. Tel: (01556) 504030.	Fly fishing only. Boats available. Limited days. Self-catering accommodation available.
Lillies Loch	Castle Douglas	Brown Trout	15 Mar. to 30 Sep.	Forest Enterprise, Creebridge, Newton Stewart. Tel: (01671) 402420.	Bank fishing only. Any legal method. Sunday fishing.
Lochenbreck Loch	Lauriston	Brown/ Rainbow Trout	1 Apr. to 30 Sep.	Watson McKinnel, 15 St. Cuthbert Street, Kirkcudbright. Tel: (01557) 330693.	8.30am–10pm. Bank and fly fishing. Five boats. Sunday fishing.
Loch of the Lowes	Newton Stewart	Brown Trout (stocked)	15 Mar. to 30 Sep.	Forest Enterprise, Creebridge, Newton Stewart. Tel: (01671) 402420. Talnotry Campsite, Queens Way, Newton Stewart. Tel: (01671) 402170. Clatteringshaws Wildlife Visitors Centre, New Galloway. Tel: (01644) 420285.	Fly only. Sunday fishing.
Morton Castle Loch	Thornhill	Stocked Brown/ Rainbow Trout	1 Apr. to 30 Sep. Including Sundays.	The Buccleuch Estates Ltd., Drumlanrig Mains, Thornhill DG3 4AG. Tel: (01848) 600283. Particulars available.	Average weight of fish: 2¼ lbs. Popular flies: Montana, Damsel, P/T Nymph, Ace of Spades, Coachman (dry). Fly fishing only. Bank and boat fishing. Let on a daily basis for up to 3 rods. Full day or evenings only.
Mossdale Loch	Mossdale Nr. New Galloway	Stocked Rainbow Trout Wild Brown Trout	15 Mar. to 30 Sep.	The Mossdale Post Office, Mossdale, Castle Douglas DG7 2NF. Tel: (01644) 450281.	Fly fishing only from boat. Boats available from Post Office. Sunday fishing.
Loch Nahinie	Drumlamford Estate	Stocked Trout	Apr. to Oct.	Jim McGure, The Lodge Cottage, Drumlamford Estate, Barrhill, South Ayreshire. Tel: (01465) 821243.	Fly fishing only. Boats available.
Ochiltree Loch	Newton Stewart	Brown/ Rainbow Trout	1 May to 6 Oct.	Newton Stewart A.A. Galloway Guns & Tackle, 36 Arthur Street, Newton Stewart. Tel: (01671) 403404	Fly fishing only. Bank fishing only. Sunday fishing.
Penwhirn Reservoir	Stranraer	Brown Trout	15 Mar. to 30 Sep.	Stranraer & District A.A. The Sports Shop, 90 George Street, Stranraer. Tel: (01776) 702705. Local hotels.	Fly fishing and spinning. Bank fishing. Sunday fishing.
Piltanton Burn	Dunragit	Brown/ Rainbow Trout Salmon	1 May to 31 Oct.	Mr J. Duffy, 2 Orchard Road, Dunragit, Stranraer. The Sports Shop, 90 George Street, Stranraer. Tel: (01671) 403403.	Spinning and worming allowed. Fly fishing.
Loch Roan	Castle Douglas	Brown/ Rainbow Trout	1 Apr. to 6 Oct.	Tommy's Sports Shop, 178 King Street, Castle Douglas. Tel: (01556) 502851.	Fly fishing only. Four boats.

Water	Location	Species	Season	Permit available from	Other information
Slatehouse Loch	Thronhill	Rainbow Trout	1 Apr. to 30 Sep. Including Sundays.	Buccleuch Estates Ltd., Drumlanrig Mains, Thronhill, DG3 4AG. Tel: (01848) 600283. Particulars available.	Average weight 2½lb. Popular flies include Montana, Damsel, Nymph. Ace of Spades. Fly fishing only. Bank fishing only, let on a daily basis for up to 3 rods. Tuition is available at an additional cost. Full day or evenings only.
Soulseat Loch	Stranraer	Brown/ Rainbow Trout	15 Mar. to 30 Sep.	Stranraer & District A.A. The Sports Shop, 90 George Street, Stranraer. Tel: (01776) 702705. Local hotels.	Fly, spinning and bait. Bank fishing and two boats. Sunday fishing.
Spa-wood Loch	Nr. Newton Stewart	Wild Brown Trout	15 Mar. to 30 Sep.	Palakona Guest House, Queen Street, Newton Stewart DG8 6JL. Tel: (0671) 402323.	Guests only.
Starburn Loch	Thornhill	Wild Brown Trout Rainbow Trout	1 Apr. to 31 Aug. Including Sundays.	The Buccleuch Estates Ltd., Drumlanrig Mains, Thornhill DG3 4AG. Tel: (01848) 600283. Particulars available.	Average weight of fish: 2.2 lbs. Popular flies: Montana, Damsel, P/T Nymph, Ace of Spades, Coachman (dry). Fly fishing only. Bank and boat fishing available. Let on a daily basis for up to 3 rods. Full day or evenings only.
Stroan Loch	Mossdale	Brown Trout Pike Perch	1 Apr. to 30 Sep.	Forest Enterprise, 21 King Street, Castle Douglas. Tel: (01556) 503626. Kenmure Arms Hotel, High Street, New Galloway. Tel: (01644) 420240.	On Raiders Road Forest Drive.
Loch Whinyeon	Gatehouse of Fleet	Brown Trout	1 Apr. to 30 Sep.	Watson McKinnel, 15 St. Cuthbert Street, Kirkcudbright. Tel: (01557) 330693.	8am to 10pm. Bank and boat fishing. 2 boats available. Fly fishing only.

STRATHCLYDE (SOUTH) - RIVERS & LOCHS

STRATHCLYDE (SOUTH) - RIVERS & LOCHS

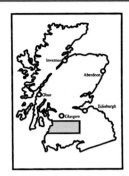

Constituent Area Tourist Boards
Ayrshire Tourist Board
Director of Tourism, Tourist Information
Centre, Burns House, Park House Street, Ayr.
Tel: (01292) 284196.

Greater Glasgow and Clyde Valley
Tourist Board
11 George Square,
Glasgow G2 1DY
Tel: 0141- 204 4400.

Tourist Information Centre
Tourism Officer,
Promenade, Largs,
Ayrshire KA30 8BG.
Tel: (01475) 673765.

Isle of Arran Tourist Board
Area Tourist Officer,
Information Centre, The Pier,
Brodick, Isle of Arran KA27 8AU
Tel: (01770) 302140.
Greater Glasgow Tourist Board,
Chief Executive, Greater Glasgow
Tourist Board,
35 St. Vincent Place,
Glasgow G1 2ER.
Tel: 0141-204 4400.

Scottish Environment
Protection Agency
Ayr Office,
2 Adoway Place,
Ayr KA7 2AA.
Tel: (01292) 264047.

RIVERS

Water	Location	Species	Season	Permit available from	Other information
Annick	Irvine	Salmon Sea Trout Brown Trout	15 Mar.to 31 Oct. 15 Mar. to 6 Oct.	Mr N. Galloway, 13 Marble Avenue, Dreghorn. Tel: (01294) 214944.	
Annick (and Glazert)	Kilmaurs	Salmon Sea Trout Brown Trout	15 Mar. to 31Oct. 15 Mar. to 6 Oct.	Kilmaurs A.C., T.C McCabe, 8 East Park Crescent, Kilmaurs. Mr. D. Dunn, 22 Habbieauld Road, Kilmaurs. Tel: (01563) 523846. Kasasim., Main Street, Kilmaurs. Tel: (01563) 538570.	
Avon	Strathaven	Brown Trout Grayling	15 Mar. to 6 Oct. No close season	Country Lines, 29 Main Street, The Village, East Kilbride. Tel: (01355) 228952. Sports Emporium, Hamilton. Tel: (01698) 283903.	Any legal method.
Ayr	Failford	Salmon Sea Trout Trout	10 Feb. to 31 Oct.	Gamesport of Ayr, 60 Sandgate, Ayr. Tel: (01292) 263822.	No Saturday or Sunday visitor permits.
	Mauchline	Salmon Sea Trout Brown Trout	15 Mar. to 31 Oct. 15 Mar.to 15 Sep.	Linwood & Johnstone, Newsagent, The Cross, Mauchline. Tel: (01290) 550219.	

45

Water	Location	Species	Season	Permit available from	Other information
Ayr (Cessnock Lugar)	Mauchline	Salmon Sea Trout Brown Trout	11 Feb. to 31 Oct. 15 May to 6 Oct.	Linwood & Johnstone, Newsagents, The Cross, Mauchline. Tel: (01290) 550219.	
Ayr (Lugar)	Mauchline	Salmon Sea Trout Brown Trout	15 Mar. to 30 Oct. 15 Mar. to 15 Sep.	Linwood & Johnstone, Newsagents, The Cross, Mauchline. Tel: (01290) 550219.	
Cart	Busby	Brown Trout	15 Mar. to 6 Oct.	Tackle & Guns, 920 Pollokshaws Road, Glasgow G41 2ET. Tel: 0141-632 2005.	Average weight of fish caught: 8–10 oz. Popular flies: small spider flies. Bait fishing allowed, no spinning.
Cessnock	Mauchline	Brown Trout	15 Mar. to 15 Sep.	Linwood & Johnstone, Newsagents, The Cross, Mauchline. Tel: (01290) 550219.	
Clyde (Map IV C4)	Thankerton and Roberton	Brown Trout Grayling	15 Mar. to 5 Oct. 7 Oct. to 14 Mar.	B.F. Dexter, Secretary, 18 Boghall Park, Biggar. H. Bryden, Newsagent, 153 High Street, Biggar. J & A O'Hara, Grocers, Mill Rd., Thankerton. Anglers Attic, 44 Kirk Rd., Wishaw. Wyndales Hotel, Symington. Tinto Hotel, Symington. Esso Garage, Coulter Road, Biggar. D. M'Mahon, 23 Cormiston Road, Biggar. P&R Torbet, 15 Strand Street, Kilmarnock. Tel: (01563) 541734. Tackle & Guns, 920 Pollockshaws Road, Glasgow G41 2ET. Tel: (0141) 632 2005	Protection order in force. **Permits to be obtained before going to river.** Spinning with legal lures allowed from 1 May. Fly fishing at all times. Flies in normal use size 14. Ground baiting and keep nets are not allowed. No Sunday fishing.
Douglas (and Clyde)	Douglas Water	Brown Trout Grayling	15 Mar. to 30 Sep. All year.		Permits widely available in tackle shops in Glasgow and Lanarkshire.
Garnock	Kilbirnie	Brown Trout Salmon Sea Trout	15 Mar. to 6 Oct. 15 Mar. to 31 Oct.	R.T. Cycles, Glengarnock. Tel: (01505) 682191.	No Sunday fishing after 1 July.
Garnock (and Lugton)	Kilwinning	Salmon Sea Trout Brown Trout	15 Mar. to 31 Oct. 15 Mar. to 6 Oct.		Day permits.
Gryfe	Bridge of Weir	Brown Trout	15 Mar. to 6 Oct. 15 Mar. to 31 Oct.	M. Duncan, Newsagent, Main Street, Bridge of Weir. Tel: (01505) 612477.	No Saturday or Sunday fishing.
Iorsa	Isle of Arran	Salmon Sea Trout	Jun. to Oct.	The Estate Office, Dougarie, Isle of Arran. Tel: (01770) 840259.	
Irvine (Map IV B4)	Hurlford and Crookedholm	Salmon Sea Trout	15 Mar. to 31 Oct. 15 Mar. to 6 Oct.	P. & R. Torbet, 15 Strand Street, Kilmarnock. Tel: (01563) 541734.	

Water	Location	Species	Season	Permit available from	Other information
	Kilmarnock	Salmon Sea Trout Brown Trout	15 Mar. to 31 Oct. 15 Mar. to 6 Oct.	P. & R. Torbet, 15 Strand Street, Kilmarnock. Tel: (01563) 541734.	No Sunday fishing after 31 July.
Irvine (and Annick)	Dreghorn	Salmon Sea Trout Brown Trout	31 Oct. 15 Mar. to 6 Oct.	Mr N. Galloway, 13 Marble Avenue, Dreghorn. Tel: (01292) 214944.	River Irvine only, extension of season for salmon and sea trout – 1 to 15 November. Fly only.
Kelvin	Glasgow– Strathkelvin	Salmon Sea Trout	11 Feb. to 31 Oct.	Tackle & Guns Ltd., 920 Pollokshaws Road, Glasgow G41 2ET. Tel: 0141-632 2005.	Any legal bait permitted.
Machrie	Arran	Salmon Sea Trout	Jun. to Oct.	Margo M. Wilson, Boltachan House, Aberfeldy PH15 2LA. Tel: (01887) 820496.	No Sunday fishing. Booking: Nov.–Oct.
Rotten Calder	East Kilbride	Brown Trout	15 Mar. to 6 Oct.	Country Lines, 29 Main Street, The Village, East Kilbride. Tel: (013552) 28952.	Any legal method.
Stinchar (Map IV B5)	Bardrochart Beat	Salmon Sea Trout	25 Oct. to 31 Oct.	Bardrochart Estate, Oaknowe, Colmonell, Ayrshire KA26 0SG. Tel: (01465) 88202.	Fly only. Fishing restricted to left bank.
	Dalreoch Estate	Salmon Sea Trout	25 Feb. to 31 Oct.	D. Overend, Dalreoch Lodge, Colmonell, Ayrshire KA26 0SQ. Tel: (01465) 881214.	Fly only, except in high water when spinning is allowed. Double bank fishing.

LOCHS & RESERVOIRS

Water	Location	Species	Season	Permit available from	Other information
Ardgowan Loch	Greenock	Brown/ Rainbow Trout	All year	At Ardgowan Loch. Tel: (01475) 522492.	Average weight of fish caught: from 1 lb 4 oz. Popular flies: Buzzers, Muddlers, traditional wet and drys. Lures in winter. Fly fishing only on 37 acres. 55 acres of bait Fishery available. 6 boats available. Bank fishing. Stocked weekly.
Loch Arklet	Stirling & Trossachs	Brown Trout	30 Mar. to 28 Sep.	West of Scotland Water, 419 Balmore Road, Glasgow. Tel: 0141-355 5333. Or on location.	Fly fishing by rowing boat only. No live bait/ spinning. Rowing boats supplied. 7 days fishing.
Loch Belston	Sinclairston	Brown Trout Rainbow Trout Rainbow Trout	15 Mar. to 15 Sep. No close season	Bailiffs at loch. Gamesport of Ayr, 60 Sandgate, Ayr. Tel: (01292) 263822.	Boats available.
Loch Bradan	Straiton	Brown Trout (stocked)	15 Mar. to 30 Sep.	Forest Enterprise, Straiton. Tel: (01655) 770637. Mr. R. Heaney, Tallaminnoch, Straiton. Tel: (01655) 770617.	Five boats. Sunday fishing.
Loch Brecbowie	Straiton	Brown Trout	15 Mar. to 30 Sep.	Forest Enterprise, Straiton. Tel: (01655) 770637. Straiton Stores.	Fly fishing advised. Sunday fishing.

47

Water	Location	Species	Season	Permit available from	Other information
Burnfoot Reservoir	Nr. Fenwick	Brown/ Rainbow Trout	15 Mar. to 6 Oct.	Kilmaurs A.C., Mr. T.C. McCabe, 8 East Park Crescent, Kilmaurs. Mr. D. Dunn, 22 Habbieauld Road, Kilmaurs. Tel: (01563) 523846. J. L. McGarrity, 18, Main Street, Kilmaurs. Tel: (01563) 538287.	Average weight of fish caught: 1 lb–5 lbs. Popular flies: Butcher, Montana, Nymph, Viva, Soldier Palmer. Any legal method – no swim feeders or floats.
Busbie Muir Reservoir	Ardrossan	Brown Trout	1 Apr. to 6 Oct.		Obtain permits before fishing. Average weight of fish caught: 8–12 oz. Two boats, keys available from Alpine Store.
Camphill Reservoir	Kilbirnie	Brown Trout	1 Apr. to 6 Oct.	Kilbirnie A.C., V. Donati, 12 Newhouse Drive. Tel: (01505) 683923. R.T. Cycles, Glengarnock. Tel: (01505) 682191.	Fly only. Boat only.
Glen Finglas	Stirling & Trossachs	Brown Trout	30 Mar. to 28 Sep.	Mr N Meikle, 41 Buchany, Doune. Tel: (0850) 558869. (The Trossachs Fishings). Or on location.	Fly fishing by rowing boat only. No live bait/ spinning. Rowing boats supplied. 7 days fishing.
Loch Goin (between orange markers)	Nr. Eaglesham	Brown Trout	15 Mar. to 6 Oct.	Kilmaurs A.C., Mr T.C. McCabe, 8 East Park Crescent, Kilmaurs. Mr. D. Dunn, 22 Habbieauld Road, Kilmaurs. Tel: (01563) 523846.	Average weight of fish caught: 8 oz to 3 lbs. No other baits – fly only.
Craigen-dun-ton Reservoir	Nr. Kilmarnock	Rainbow/ Brown Trout	15 Mar. to 6 Oct.		Average weight of fish caught: Rainbow 1 lb 8 oz, Brown Trout 12 oz. Fly and spinning only; no live bait.
Harelaw Dam	Neilston	Brown Trout	15 Mar. to 6 Oct.	Tackle & Guns, 920 Pollokshaws Road, Glasgow. Tel: 0141-632 2005.	Average weight of fish caught: 1 lb 2 oz. For boats day or evening contact: Dougie Brown, 10 Garrioch Drive, Glasgow. Tel: 0141-946 6060.
Headshaw Loch	Nr. Ashkirk Village	Brown/ Rainbow Trout	Apr. to Nov.	Manager at Headshaw Loch. Tel: (0374) 287762, or Headshaw Farm. Tel: (01750) 32233.	Average weight of fish caught: 2–4 lbs. Fly only. 7 boats, bank fishing. Bag limit 3 fish.
Hillend Reservoir	Nr. Caldercruix	Brown Trout Pike Perch	15 Mar. to 6 Oct.	Bailiff at Reservoir. Tel: (01236) 843611. Cafaro Bros., 140 Renfield Street, Glasgow. Tel: 0141-332 6224. Outside In, 120 Stirling Street, Airdrie. Tel: (01236) 755532.	Average weight of fish caught: 1 lb 4 oz – 3½lbs. No ground baiting or swim feeders or illegal sub-stances. 10 boats available. Bank fishing. For further details: Mt. Potter, Secretary, 12 Sharp Avenue, Kirkwood, Coatbridge ML5 5RT. Hut number: (01236) 843611.
Howwood Fishery (Bowfield Dam)	Nr. Howwood	Brown/ Rainbow/ Brook/ Golden Trout	All year	Armadale Sports, Armadale. Bailiff. Tel: (01505) 702688. Howwood Trout Fishery. Tel: (01505) 702688.	Average weight of fish caught: 1½lbs +. Fly only. 3 boats available. Bank fishing. Refreshments sold. Resident qualified instructor.

Water	Location	Species	Season	Permit available from	Other information
Loch Katrine	Stirling & Trossachs	Brown Trout	30 Mar. to 28 Sep.	Mr N Meikle, 41 Buchany, Doune. Tel: (0850) 558869. (The Trossachs Fishings). Or on location.	Fly fishing by rowing boat only. No live bait/ spinning. Rowing boats supplied. 7 days fishing.
Kilbirnie Loch	Kilbirnie	Brown/ Rainbow Trout	15 Mar. to 6 Oct.	Kilbirnie A.C., 12 Newhouse Drive, Kilbirnie. Tel: (01505) 683923. R.T. Cycles, Glengarnock. Tel: (01505) 682191.	All legal methods. Boats available.
Maich Water	Lochwinnoch	Brown/ Rainbow Trout	All year	From Maich Water Fishery. Tel: (01505) 842341. Average weight of fish caught: 1.5 lbs.	Popular flies: Damsels, Buzzers, Nymphs & Sedges. Fly and bait. 1 boat and bank fishing. Stocked 3 times weekly. Amenities for disabled. Clubhouse serving refreshments.
Newmills (6 lochs)	Cleghorn	Rainbow Trout	All year	At Newmills. Tel: (01555) 870730.	Average weight of fish caught: 1 lb 2 oz. Popular flies: Lures, Cats Whiskers, Ace of Spades, Vivas. 2 boats (1 for disabled). Bank fishing. Tackle for sale/hire.
North Craig Reservoir	Kilmaurs	Rainbow Trout	Open all year	Kilmaurs A.C., T.C. McCabe, 8 East Park Crescent, Kilmaurs. Mr. D. Dunn, 22 Habbieauld Road, Kilmaurs. Tel: (01563) 523846. Pages etc., Main Street, Kilmaurs. Tel: (01563) 538570.	Average weight of fish caught: 1–5 lbs. Popular flies: Butcher, Soldier Palmer, Blue Zulu, Baby Doll, Viva. Any legal method.
Pen-whapple Reservoir	Nr. Girvan	Stocked Brown Trout	1 Apr. to 15 Sep.	Mrs. Stewart, Lanes Farm, nr. Girvan (1/4 mile from reservoir).	Fly fishing only (Mon –Sat). No Sunday fishing. Average weight of fish caught: 1 lb. Popular flies: Kate McLaren, Zulu, Invicta; traditional patterns. 4 boats available.
Port-na-Lochan	Black-waterfoot	Rainbow Trout	All year	Kinloch Hotel, Blackwaterfoot, Isle of Arran. Tel: (01770) 860444.	Average weight of fish caught: 1¼lbs to 1¾lbs. Fly fishing only. Popular flies: Viva, Alexandria, Montana Nymph, Peter Ross. Bait fishing at specific times only. Bank fishing only.
Raith & Prestwick Reservoir	Monkton	Rainbow Trout	15 Mar. to 15 Nov.	Gamesport of Ayr, 60 Sandgate, Ayr. Tel: (01292) 263822. Newhall's Newsagent, Monkton. Wheatsheaf Inn, Monkton.	Average weight of fish caught: 1–4 lbs. Popular flies: Butcher, Greenwell Glory. Worm fishing. No Sunday fishing. Weekdays 8am - 6pm.
Springwater Loch	Nr. Dalrymple	Rainbow/ Brown/ Brook Trout	All year	At Springwater Fishery's. Tel: (01292) 560343. Out of hours - Tel: (01292) 560300.	Average weight of fish caught: 3–4 lbs. Popular flies: Buzzers, Hoppers, Damsels, Nymphs, Cats Whiskers and Vivas. Fly only (bait loch 2 acres) available. Stocked every day. Tackle for hire.

Water	Location	Species	Season	Permit available from	Other information
Strathclyde Country Park Loch	Motherwell	Bream Tench Roach Carp Perch	All year	Booking Office, Strathclyde Country Park, 366 Hamilton Road, Motherwell. Tel: (01698) 266155.	

Constituent Area Tourist Boards

Bute and Cowal Tourist Board
Area Tourist Officer,
Information Centre,
7 Alexandra Parade,
Dunoon, Argyll PA23 8AB.
Tel: (01369) 703785.

Area Tourist Officer,
Tourist Information Centre,
15 Victoria Street,
Rothesay,
Isle of Bute PA20 0A
Tel: (01700) 502151

West Highlands & Islands of Argyll Tourist Board
Area Tourist Officer,
Tourist Information Centre,
Argyll Square, Oban,
Argyll PA34 4AR.
Tel: (01631) 563122.

Scottish Environment Protection Agency
Lochgilphead Office,
2 Smithy Lane,
Lochgilphead PA31 8TA.
Tel: (01546) 602876.

RIVERS

Water	Location	Species	Season	Permit available from	Other information
Aros	Mull	Salmon Sea Trout	End Jun. to mid-Oct.	Tackle & Books, Main Street, Tobermory, Isle of Mull. Tel: (01688) 302336.	No Sunday fishing.
Awe (Map III B6)	Inverawe Taynuilt	Salmon Sea Trout	May to Oct.	Inverawe Fisheries, Taynuilt, Argyll. Tel: (01866) 822446.	Fly fishing only.
Bellart	Mull	Sea Trout Salmon	Jun. to end Oct.	Tackle & Books, Main Street, Tobermory, Isle of Mull. Tel: (01688) 302336.	No Sunday fishing.
Cur	13 miles from Dunoon	Salmon Sea Trout Brown Trout	1 Apr. to 15 Oct.	Dunoon & District A.C. Purdies of Argyll, 112 Argyll Street, Dunoon. Tel: (01369) 703232.	Fishing all legal methods. Bookings: Hon. Sec. A.H. Young, 'Ashgrove', 28 Royal Crescent, Dunoon PA23 7AH. Tel: (01369) 705732.
Euchar	Kilninver	Salmon Sea Trout Brown Trout	1 Jun. to 15 Oct.	Mrs. Mary McCorkindale, Glenann, Kilninver, by Oban, Argyll. Tel: (01852) 316282.	No Sunday fishing.
		Salmon Sea Trout	Mid-Jul. to mid-Oct.	J.T.P. Mellor, Barncromin Farm, Knipoch, by Oban, Argyll. Tel: (01852) 316273.	(Tues., Wed. & Thurs.)
Finnart	12 miles from Dunoon	Occ. Salmon Sea Trout Brown Trout	1 Apr. to 15 Oct.	Dunoon & District A.C. Purdie's of Argyll, 112 Argyll Street, Dunoon. Tel: (01369) 703232.	Fishing all legal methods. Advanced bookings: Hon. Sec. A.H. Young, 'Ashgrove', 28 Royal Crescent, Dunoon PA23 7AH. Tel: (01369) 705732.
Goil	Lochgoilhead	Salmon Sea Trout	May to end Oct.	River Goil A.C. J. Lamont, Shore House Inn, Lochgoilhead. Tel: (01301) 703340.	Fly and worm. No spinning. No sea baits. No Sundays.
Grey	Islay	Salmon Sea Trout	Jul. to Oct.	Head Gamekeeper's House, Islay House Square, Bridgend. Tel: (01496) 810293.	Fly only. No night fishing.

Water	Location	Species	Season	Permit available from	Other information
Laggan	Islay	Salmon Sea Trout	Jul. to Oct.	Head Gamekeeper's House, Islay House Square, Bridgend. Tel: (01496) 810293.	Fly fishing only. No night fishing.
Massan	6 miles from Dunoon	Salmon Sea Trout Brown Trout	1 Apr. to 15 Oct.	Dunoon & District A.C. Purdie's of Argyll, 112 Argyll Street, Dunoon. Tel: (01369) 703232.	All legal methods. Advanced bookings: Hon. Sec. A.H. Young, 'Ashgrove', 28 Royal Crescent, Dunoon PA23 7AH. Tel: (01369) 705732.
Orchy (Map III B6)	Dalmally	Salmon	11 Feb. to 15 Oct.	W.A. Church, Croggan Crafts, Dalmally, Argyll. Tel: (01838) 200201.	
Ruel (Map IV B3)	Glendaruel	Salmon Sea Trout	16 Feb. to 31 Oct.	Glendaruel Hotel, Clachan of Glendaruel, Argyll PA22 3AA. Tel: (01369) 820274. Dunoon & District A.C. Purdie's of Argyll, 112 Argyll Street, Dunoon. Tel: (01369) 703232.	No Sunday fishing. All legal methods. Advanced booking: Hon. Sec. A.H. Young, 'Ashgrove', 28 Royal Crescent, Dunoon PA23 7AH. Tel: (01369) 705732.
Sorn	Islay	Salmon Sea Trout	October	Brian Wiles, Head Gamekeeper's House, Islay House Square, Bridgend. Tel: (01496) 810293.	Fly fishing only. No night fishing.

LOCHS & RESERVOIRS

Water	Location	Species	Season	Permit available from	Other information
Loch a'Bharrain	Nr. Oban	Brown Trout	15 Mar. to 6 Oct.	D. Graham, Combie Street, Oban. Anglers' Corner, 2 John Street, Oban. Tel: (01631) 566374. Post Office, Kilmelford. Mr. Morrison, Ledaig Leisure, Benderloch.	Standard trout flies wet or dry (12 & 14). Peaty loch with small fish.
Loch a'Chaorainn	Nr. Kilmelford	Brown Trout	15 Mar. to 6 Oct.	D. Graham, 11-15 Combie Street, Oban. Tel: (01631) 562069. Anglers' Corner, 2 John Street, Oban. Tel: (01631) 566374. Post Office, Kilmelford. Mr. Morrison, Ledaig Leisure, Benderloch.	Popular flies: imitations of natural flies. The loch contains trout up to 2 lbs.
Loch a'Cheigin	Nr. Kilmelford	Brown Trout	15 Mar. to 6 Oct.	D. Graham, Combie Street, Oban. Anglers' Corner, 2 John Street, Oban. Tel: (01631) 566374. Post Office, Kilmelford. Mr. Morrison, Ledaig Leisure, Benderloch.	Popular flies: standard trout patterns, size 14.
Loch a'Chlachain	Nr. Kilmelford	Brown Trout	15 Mar. to 6 Oct.	D. Graham, Combie Street, Oban. Oban. Tel: (01631) 562069. Anglers' Corner, 2 John Street, Oban. Tel: (01631) 566374. Post Office, Kilmelford. Mr. Morrison, Ledaig Leisure, Benderloch.	Popular flies: standard trout flies, wet or dry (12 & 14).
Loch a' Chrea-chain	Nr. Kilmelford	Brown Trout	15 Mar. to 6 Oct.	D. Graham, Combie Street, Oban. Anglers' Corner, 2 John Street, Oban. Tel: (01631) 566374. Post Office, Kilmelford. Mr. Morrison, Ledaig Leisure, Benderloch.	Popular flies: standard pattern trout flies sizes 12 & 14, also big lure type flies for the bigger trout.

Water	Location	Species	Season	Permit available from	Other information
Loch a'Cruaiche	Nr. Kilmelford	Brown Trout	15 Mar. to 6 Oct.	D. Graham, Combie Street, Oban. Anglers' Corner, 2 John Street, Oban. Tel: (01631) 566374. Post Office, Kilmelford. Mr. Morrison, Ledaig Leisure, Benderloch.	Small weedy loch with small trout.
Loch a'Mhinn	Nr. Kilmelford	Brown Trout	15 Mar. to 6 Oct.	D. Graham, Combie Street, Oban. Anglers' Corner, 2 John Street, Oban. Tel: (01631) 566374. Post Office, Kilmelford. Mr. Morrison, Ledaig Leisure, Benderloch.	Popular flies: standard trout flies, wet or dry (12 & 14). The loch contains small fat trout, frequently difficult to catch.
Loch a'Phearsain	Nr. Kilmelford	Brown Trout	15 Mar. to 6 Oct.	D. Graham, Combie Street, Oban. Anglers' Corner, 2 John Street, Oban. Tel: (01631) 566374. Post Office, Kilmelford. Mr. Morrison, Ledaig Leisure, Benderloch.	Average weight of fish: 8 oz to 1 lb. Popular flies: standard patterns, sizes 12 & 14.
Loch an Daimh	Nr. Kilmelford	Brown Trout	15 Mar. to 6 Oct.	D. Graham, Combie Street, Oban. Anglers' Corner, 2 John Street, Oban. Tel: (01631) 566374. Post Office, Kilmelford. Mr. Morrison, Ledaig Leisure, Benderloch.	The loch contains trout up to 6 oz, but they are difficult to catch. Popular flies: standard trout flies, wet or dry (10 & 14).
Loch an Losgainn Beag	Nr. Kilmelford	Brown Trout	15 Mar. to 6 Oct.	D. Graham, Combie Street, Oban. Anglers' Corner, 2 John Street, Oban. Tel: (01631) 566374. Post Office, Kilmelford. Mr. Morrison, Ledaig Leisure, Benderloch.	Popular flies: standard trout flies, wet or dry (10 to 14). The loch contains very large trout that are difficult to catch. Reputed to fish best in the evening during June.
Loch an Losgainn Mor	Nr. Kilmelford	Brown Trout	15 Mar. to 6 Oct.	D. Graham, Combie Street, Oban. Anglers' Corner, 2 John Street, Oban. Tel: (01631) 566374. Post Office, Kilmelford. Mr. Morrison, Ledaig Leisure, Benderloch.	Popular flies: standard trout flies, wet or dry (10 to 14). The loch contains trout of 6 oz but they are difficult to catch.
Loch Airigh-Shamh-raidh	Musdale	Brown Trout	15 Mar. to 6 Oct.	D. Graham, Combie Street, Oban. Anglers' Corner, 2 John Street, Oban. Tel: (01631) 566374. Post Office, Kilmelford. Mr. Morrison, Ledaig Leisure, Benderloch.	Popular flies: standard trout flies wet or dry (12 & 14). Loch is full of easily caught trout.
Aros Lake	Mull	Rainbow Trout	All year	Tobermory AA., c/o Browns Shop, Tobermory. Tel: (01688) 302020.	Bank fishing only. Spinning permitted. Bag limit 5 fish.
Loch Ascog	Argyll	Brown/ Rainbow Trout	15 Mar. to 5 Oct.	Kyles of Bute A.C. A.H. Richardson, Allt Beag, Tighnabruaich PA21 2BE. Tel: (01700) 811486.	Fly only.
Loch Assopol	Mull	Salmon Sea Trout Brown Trout	Apr. to start Oct.	Argyll Arms Hotel, Bunessan, Isle of Mull. Tel: (01681) 700240.	Fly and spinner only. No Sunday fishing.

Water	Location	Species	Season	Permit available from	Other information
Glen Astil Lochs (2)	Isle of Islay	Brown Trout	15 Mar. to 30 Sep.	I.G. Laurie, Newsagent, 19 Charlotte Street, Port Ellen, Isle of Islay. Tel: (01496) 302264.	Fly only. No Sunday fishing. No catch limit. Permit covers all 5 lochs of Port Ellen Angling Club (see Loch Kinnabus). Boat available.
Glen Dubh Reservoir	Bacaldine nr. Oban	Rainbow Brown/Trout	Mar. to Oct.	Anglers' Corner, 2 John Street, Oban. Tel: (01631) 566374.	Bank fishing only.
Loch Avich	Taynuilt	Brown Trout Rainbow Trout	15 Mar. to 6 Oct.	Mr. N.D. Clark, 11 Dalavich, by Taynuilt, Argyll PA35 1HN. Tel: (01866) 844209. Loch Awe Stores, Loch Awe, Dalmally, Argyll. Tel/Fax: (01838) 200 200.	5 boats available.
	Nr. Kilmelford	Brown Trout	15 Mar. to 6 Oct.	D. Graham, Combie Street, Oban. Anglers' Corner, 2 John Street, Oban. Tel: (01631) 566374. Post Office, Kilmelford. Mr. Morrison, Ledaig Leisure, Benderloch.	Popular flies: standard patterns sizes 12 & 14.
Loch Awe	South Lochaweside by Dalmally	Salmon Sea Trout Brown Trout Rainbow Trout Perch Char Pike	11 Feb. to 15 Oct. 15 Mar. to 6 Oct. All year	Ardbrecknish House, by Dalmally, Argyll. Tel: (01866) 833223/833256.	Boats, tackle and permits available. Clubs welcome.
		Salmon Sea Trout Brown Trout Rainbow Trout Perch Char Pike	15 Mar. to 15 Oct. 15 Mar. to 6 Oct. All year	The Portsonachan Hotel, nr. Dalmally PA33 1BL. Tel: (01866) 833224.	
		Brown/ Rainbow Trout	15 Mar. to 15 Oct.	Ford Hotel, Ford. Tel: (01546) 810273.	
	Taynuilt	Salmon Sea Trout Brown Trout Rainbow Trout	12 Feb. to 15 Oct. 15 Mar. to 6 Oct.	Mr. D.N. Clark, 11 Dalavich, by Taynuilt PA35 1HN. Tel: (01866) 844209. Anglers' Corner, 2 John Street, Oban. Tel: (01631) 566374.	Boats available.
	Argyll	Brown/ Rainbow Trout	15 Mar. to 6 Oct.	Oban Tourist Office, Boswell House, Argyll Square, Oban. Tel: (01631) 563122. W.A. Church, Croggan Crafts, Dalmally, Argyll. Tel: (01838) 200201.	Permits also available for pike fishing (no close season).
Ballygrant Loch	Ballygrant	Brown Trout	15 Mar. to 6 Oct.	Port Askaig Stores, Port Askaig, Isle of Islay. Tel: (01496) 840245.	Average weight of fish caught: 8–16 oz. Boats are available.

Water	Location	Species	Season	Permit available from	Other information
Loch Bealach Ghearran	Nr. Minard village	Brown Trout	15 Mar. to 6 Oct.	Intersport, Lochnell Street, Lochgilphead, Argyll. Forest District Office, Whitegates, Lochgilphead. Fynetackle, Argyll Street, Lochgilphead.	Average weight of fish caught: 8 oz. Popular flies: most dark flies.
Big Feinn	Nr. Kilmelford	Brown Trout	15 Mar. to 6 Oct.	D. Graham, Combie Street, Oban. Anglers' Corner, 2 John Street, Oban. Tel: (01631) 566374. Post Office, Kilmelford. Mr. Morrison, Ledaig Leisure, Benderloch.	The loch contains very large trout which are very difficult to catch. It fishes best at the beginning of the season in windy conditions. Popular flies: large salmon flies – Demons or Terrors.
Blackmill Loch	Nr. Minard village	Brown Trout	15 Mar. to 6 Oct.	Intersport, Lochnell Street, Lochgilphead, Argyll. Forest District Office, Whitegates, Lochgilphead. Fynetackle, Argyll Street, Lochgilphead.	Average weight of fish caught: 8 oz. Popular flies: most dark flies.
Cam Loch	Nr. Ford	Brown Trout	15 Mar. to 6 Oct.	Ford Hotel, Ford. Tel: (01546) 810273. West Argyll Forest Districts, Whitegates, Lochgilphead. Fynetackle, Argyll Street, Lochgilphead.	Average weight of fish caught: 8 oz. Popular flies: most dark flies.
Loch Crauch Maolachy	Nr. Kilmelford	Brown Trout	15 Mar. to 6 Oct.	D. Graham, Combie Street, Oban. Anglers' Corner, 2 John Street, Oban. Tel: (01631) 566374. Post Office, Kilmelford. Mr. Morrison, Ledaig Leisure, Benderloch.	Stocked trout reach 2 lbs or more. Standard patterns, sizes 12 & 14.
Dubh Loch	Kilninver	Loch Leven Trout Brown Trout	Apr. to mid-Oct.	J.T.P. Mellor, Barndromin Farm, Knipoch, by Oban. Tel: (01852) 316273. Anglers' Corner, 2 John Street, Oban. Tel: (01631) 566374.	Boat on loch.
Loch Dubh-Bheag	Nr. Kilmelford	Brown Trout	15 Mar. to 6 Oct.	D. Graham, Combie Street, Oban. Post Office, Kilmelford. Mr. Morrison, Ledaig Leisure, Benderloch.	Popular flies: standard trout patterns, sizes 12 & 14.
Loch Dubh-Mor	Nr. Kilmelford	Brown Trout	15 Mar. to 6 Oct.	D. Graham, Combie Street, Oban. 2 John Street, Oban. Tel: (01631) 566374. Post Office, Kilmelford. Mr. Morrison, Ledaig Leisure, Benderloch.	Average weight of fish caught: 4 oz. Popular flies: standard patterns, 10 & 12.
Dunoon Reservoir	Dunoon	Rainbow & Brook Trout	1 Mar. to 30 Nov.	Dunoon & District A.C. Purdie's of Argyll, 112 Argyll Street, Dunoon. Tel: (01369) 703232.	Fly fishing only. Regularly stocked with rainbow trout up to 4 lbs.
Ederline Lochs (18 hill lochs)	Ford	Wild Brown Trout	May to 6 Oct.	The Keeper, Keepers Cottage, Ederline, Ford, Lochgilphead. Tel: (01546) 810215.	Average weight of fish caught: 8 oz. Fly only. Boats available on 5 lochs.
Loch Ederline (& 3 smaller lochs)	Ford	Pike Perch	No close season	The Keeper, Keepers Cottage, Ederline, Ford, Lochgilphead. Tel: (01546) 810215.	All baits allowed. 3 boats available.

55

Water	Location	Species	Season	Permit available from	Other information
Loch Fad	Bute	Brown/ Rainbow Trout	15 Mar. to 6 Oct.	Bailiff at Loch. Tel: (01700) 504871. Isle of Bute Trout Co. Ltd., Ardmaleish, Isle of Bute PA20 0QJ. Tel: (01700) 502451.	23 boats available. Bank fishing. Whole day and evening tickets. No night fishing.
		Rainbow Trout Brown Trout	Mar. to Oct.	Carleol Enterprises Angling Holidays, 3 Alma Terrace, Rothesay. Tel: (01700) 503716.	Accommodation specifically for anglers. Permits arranged.
Loch Fada	Isle of Colonsay	Brown Trout	15 Mar. to 30 Sep.	The Hotel, Isle of Colonsay, Argyll PA61 7YP. Tel: (01951) 200316.	Fly fishing only.
Loch Finlaggan	Islay	Brown Trout	15 Mar. to 30 Sep.	Head Gamekeeper House, Islay House Square, Bridgend, Isle of Islay, Argyll PA44 7NZ. Tel: (01496) 810293.	Two boats.
Forestry Hill Lochs	Ford	Brown Trout	15 Mar. to 6 Oct.	Ford Hotel, Ford, Argyll. Tel: (01546) 810723.	
Loch Frisa	Mull	Brown Trout Sea Trout	Apr. to Oct.	Tobermory AA., c/o Browns Tobermory. Tel: (01680) 302020. Forest Enterprise, Millpark Road, Mull. Tel: (01680) 300346. Tackle & Boots, Tobermory. Tel: (01680) 302336. Boat Permit: Mr L. McDowall, Lettermore Farm. Aros. Tel: (01680) 300436.	Bank fishing. Spinning best.
Loch Glashan	Nr. Lochgair village	Brown Trout	15 Mar. to 6 Oct.	Intersport, Lochnell Street, Lochgilphead, Argyll. Forest District Office, Whitegates, Lochgilphead.	Average weight of fish caught: 12 oz. Popular flies: most dark flies. One boat is available.
Loch Gleann A' Bhearraidh	Lerags by Oban	Brown Trout	15 Mar. to 6 Oct.	Cologin Homes Ltd., Lerags, by Oban, Argyll. Tel: (01631) 564501. The Barn Bar, Cologin, Lerags, by Oban. Tel: (01631) 564501. Forest Enterprise, Millpark Road, Oban Tel: (01631) 566155. Anglers' Corner, 2 John Street, Oban. Tel: (01631) 566374.	One boat available. Good trout. Any method fishing.
Loch Gully	Nr. Kilmelford	Brown Trout	15 Mar. to 6 Oct.	D. Graham, Combie Street, Oban. Anglers' Corner, 2 John Street, Oban. Tel: (01631) 566374. Post Office, Kilmelford. Mr. Morrison, Ledaig Leisure, Benderloch.	The loch contains some good fat trout. Popular flies: standard patterns, 12 & 14.
Iasg Loch	Nr. Kilmelford	Brown Trout	15 Mar. to 6 Oct.	D. Graham, Combie Street, Oban. Anglers' Corner, 2 John Street, Oban. Tel: (01631) 566374. Post Office, Kilmelford. Mr. Morrison, Ledaig Leisure, Benderloch. Tel: (01631) 720393.	Popular flies: standard patterns, 10 & 12.
Inverawe	Taynuilt	Rainbow Trout	Mar. to Dec.	Inverawe Fisheries, Taynuilt, Argyll. Tel: (01866) 822446.	3 lochs and beginners loch. Fly fishing only. Fishing lessons available.

Water	Location	Species	Season	Permit available from	Other information
Kinnabus Lochs (3)	Islay	Brown Trout Arctic Char	15 Mar. to 30 Sep.	I. G. Laurie, Newsagent, 19 Charlotte Street, Port Ellen, Isle of Islay. Tel: (01496) 302264.	Boat available. Fly only. No Sunday fishing. No catch limit. Ticket covers all five lochs (see Glen Astil).
Loch Loskin	1 mile from Dunoon	Brown/ Sea Trout	1 Apr. to 30 Sep.	Dunoon & District A.C. Purdie's of Argyll, 112 Argyll Street, Dunoon. Tel: (01369) 703232.	Fly only. Boat only.
Loch Lossit	Ballygrant	Brown Trout	15 Mar. to 6 Oct.	Port Askaig Stores, Port Askaig, Isle of Islay. Tel: (01496) 840245.	Average weight of fish caught: 8–16 oz. Boats available.
Loch Lussa	Campbeltown	Brown Trout	15 Mar. to 6 Oct.	A.P. MacGrory & Co., 16/20 Main Street, Campbeltown. Tel: (01586) 552132.	
Mishnish	Mull	Brown Trout	1 Apr. to 30 Sep.	Tobermory A.A., c/o Browns Shop, Tobermory. Tel: (01688) 302020.	Average weight of fish caught: 12 oz. Standard trout flies. 3 boats available. No Sunday fishing. Bag limit 5 fish.
MacKays Loch	Oban	Brown Trout Rainbow Trout	All Year	The Angler's Cornor, 2 John Street, Oban PA34 5NS. Tel: (01631) 566374.	3 boats available. Fly only. Day and half day permits.
Loch na Curraigh	Nr. Kilmelford	Brown Trout	15 Mar. to 6 Oct.	D. Graham, Combie Street, Oban. Anglers' Corner, 2 John Street, Oban. Tel: (01631) 566374. Post Office, Kilmelford. Mr. Morrison, Ledaig Leisure, Benderloch.	The loch has some fat 8 oz–1lb trout that some-times rise freely. The south end is floating bog and fishing from this bank is not advised. Popular flies: stand-ard trout flies, wet or dry (12 & 14).
Loch nam Ban	Nr. Kilmelford	Brown Trout	15 Mar. to 6 Oct.	D. Graham, Combie Street, Oban. Anglers' Corner, 2 John Street, Oban. Tel: (01631) 566374. Post Office, Kilmelford. Mr. Morrison, Ledaig Leisure, Benderloch.	Fish up to 2 lbs have been caught on occasion. Popular flies: standard trout flies, wet or dry (12 & 14).
Loch na Sailm	Nr . Kilmelford	Brown Trout	15 Mar. to 6 Oct.	D. Graham, Combie Street, Oban. Anglers' Corner, 2 John Street, Oban. Tel: (01631) 566374. Post Office, Kilmelford. Mr. Morrison, Ledaig Leisure, Benderloch.	The loch has been dammed to improve fishing. Popular flies: standard trout pattern, sizes 12 & 14.
Loch Nell	Nr. Oban	Salmon Sea Trout Brown Trout Char	15 Mar. to 6 Oct. (Brown Trout)	D. Graham, Combie Street, Oban. Anglers' Corner, 2 John Street, Oban. Tel: (01631) 566374. Post Office, Kilmelford. Mr. Morrison, Ledaig Leisure, Benderloch.	Popular flies: standard patterns, salmon and sea trout flies (8 & 10). Fly, spinning and bubble & fly are permitted. Boat available.
Oude Reservoir	14 miles from Oban	Brown Trout	15 Mar. to 6 Oct.	D. Graham, Combie Street, Oban. Anglers' Corner, 2 John Street, Oban. Tel: (01631) 566374. Post Office, Kilmelford. Mr. Morrison, Ledaig Leisure, Benderloch.	Bank fishing can be difficult because of the fluctuating water level. Popular flies: standard trout flies, wet or dry (12 & 14). A boat is often located on this loch for periods.

Water	Location	Species	Season	Permit available from	Other information
Powder-works Dam	Argyll	Brown/ Rainbow Trout	15 Mar. to 5 Oct.	Kyles of Bute A.C., c/o Kames Hotel. Tel: (01700) 811489. Several shops in Kames and Tighnabruaich.	Fly and bait only, no spinning.
Loch Scamma-dale	Kilninver	Salmon Sea Trout Brown Trout	1 Jun. to 15 Oct. 15 Mar. to 6 Oct.	Mrs. McCorkindale, 'Glenann', Kilninver, by Oban, Argyll. Tel: (01852) 316282.	No Sunday fishing.
Loch Seil	Kilninver	Sea Trout Brown Trout	Apr. to mid-Oct.	J.T.P. Mellor, Barndromin Farm, Knipoch, by Oban, Argyll. Tel: (01852) 316273.	Boat on loch.
Sior Lochs	Nr. Oban	Brown Trout	15 Mar. to 6 Oct.	D. Graham, Combie Street, Oban. Anglers' Corner, 2 John Street, Oban. Tel: (01631) 566374. Post Office, Kilmelford. Mr. Morrison, Ledaig Leisure, Benderloch.	Popular flies: standard trout flies, wet or dry (12 & 14). The lochs fish best in April and May.
Loch Squabain	Mull	Salmon Sea Trout Brown Trout		Tackle & Books, Main Street, Tobermory, Mull. Tel: (01688) 302336.	Boat fishing only. Weedy.
Loch Tarsan	8 miles from Dunoon	Brown Trout	1 Apr. to 30 Sep.	Dunoon & District A.C. Purdie's of Argyll, 112 Argyll Street, Dunoon. Tel: (01369) 703232.	Fly only. Boats available.
Tighna-bru-aich Reservoir (2 other lochs)	Tighnabru-aich	Brown/ Rainbow Trout	15 Mar. to 5 Oct.	Kyles of Bute A.C. Sec. A.H. Richardson, Allt Beag, Tighnabruaich PA21 2BE. Tel: (01700) 811486.	Fly and bait only. No spinning.
Torr Loch	North end of Mull	Wild Brown Trout Sea Trout	Apr. to Oct.	Tackle & Books, Main Street, Tobermory, Mull. Tel: (01688) 302336.	No Sunday fishing. 1 boat. Banks clear. Fly only.
Loch Tralaig	Nr. Kilmelford	Brown Trout	15 Mar. to 30 Sep.	Mrs. E. Mellor, Barndromin Farm, Knipoch, by Oban. Tel: (01852) 316273.	Fishing from bank only.
Loch Turamin	Isle of Colonsay	Brown Trout	15 Mar. to 30 Sep.	The Hotel, Isle of Colonsay, Argyll.	Fly fishing only.
Wee Feinn Loch	Nr. Kilmelford	Brown Trout	15 Mar. to 6 Oct.	D. Graham, Combie Street, Oban. Anglers' Corner, 2 John Street, Oban. Tel: (01631) 566374. Post Office, Kilmelford. Mr. Morrison, Ledaig Leisure, Benderloch.	A small loch that contains trout up to 2 lbs. Popular flies: standard trout patterns, sizes 10 & 12.

Edinburgh and Lothian Tourist Board
Waverley Market,
3 Princes Street,
Edinburgh EH2 2QP.
Tel: 0131-473 3800.

Argyll, the Isle, Loch Lomond, Stirling and Trossachs Tourist Board
Old Town Jail,
St John Street,
Stirling FK8 1EA.
Tel: (01786) 445222.

Kingdom of Fife Tourist Board
Tourism Manager,
St. Andrews and North East Fife Tourist Board,
70 Market Street, St. Andrews,
Fife KY16 9NU.
Tel: (01334) 472021.
Fax: (01334) 478422.

Kirkcaldy District Council, Tourist Information Centre
19 Whitecausway,
Kirkcaldy, Fife KY1 1XF.
Tel: (01592) 267775.
Fax: (01592) 203154.

Tourist Information Centre
Forth Bridges,
c/o Queensferry Lodge Hotel,
St Margarets Head,
North Queensferry,
Fife KY1 1HP.
Tel: (01383)417759.

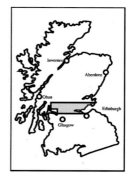

RIVERS

Water	Location	Species	Season	Permit available from	Other information
Allan (Map IV C3)	Bridge of Allan	Salmon Sea Trout Brown Trout	15 Mar. to 31 Oct. 15 Mar. to 6 Oct.	Country Pursuits, 46 Henderson Street, Bridge of Allan. Tel: (01786) 834495.	
Almond	Cramond	Salmon Sea Trout Brown Trout	1 Feb. to 31 Oct. 15 Mar. to 6 Oct.	Country Life, Balgreen Road, Edinburgh. Tel: 0131-337 6230. Davidsons Mains P.O., 49 Corbiehill Rd., Edinburgh. Tel: 0131-336 5346.	Mouth to Old Cramond Brig. East bank only.
	West Lothian	Salmon Sea Trout Brown Trout	1 Feb. to 31 Oct. 15 Mar. to 6 Oct.	City Sports, 18 Almondvale South, Livingston. Tel: (01506) 434822. Country Life, Balgreen Road, Edinburgh. Tel: 0131-337 6230.	20 miles of river.
Clatto Loch	5 miles stn of Cupar off A916	Brown Trout	1 Apr. to 29 Sept.	Waterman's Cottage, (adjacent to Loch), Mrs Watson. Tel: (01334) 652595	Boat hire. Fly only.

Water	Location	Species	Season	Permit available from	Other information
Devon	Dollar	Salmon Sea Trout Brown Trout	15 Mar. to 30 Oct. 15 Mar. to 5 Oct.	Devon Angling Assoc., R Breingan, 33 Redwell Place, Alloa. Tel: (01259) 215185. D.W. Black, The Hobby & Model Shop, 10–12 New Row, Dunfermline. Tel: (01383) 722582. Tron Sports, Tron Court, Tullibody by Alloa. Tel: (01259) 215499.	No Sunday fishing. Devonside Bridge upstream with excluded stretches. Fly fishing only from 15 Mar. to 12 Apr.
	Hillfoots	Salmon Sea Trout Brown Trout	15 Mar. to 31 Oct. 15 Mar. to 6 Oct.	Country Pursuits, 46 Henderson Street, Bridge of Allan. Tel: (01786) 834495.	No Sunday fishing.
Eden	Cupar area	Brown Trout Sea Trout Salmon	15 Mar. to 5 Oct. 15 Feb. to 31 Oct.	J. & R. Caldwell, Foodstore & Fishing Tackle, Main Street, Methilhill, Fife. Tel: (01592) 712215.	All legal methods permitted.
Endrick	Drymen Balfron Kilfarn Fintry	Salmon Sea Trout Brown Trout	11 Feb. to 31 Oct. 15 Mar. to 6 Oct.	Loch Lomond Angling Improvement Assoc., C. McCrory, P.O. Box 3559, Uddingston G71 7SJ. Tel: (01506) 655063.	Members only. No Sunday fishing. Fly only.
		Dace Chub Roach Eels	Open all year	The Bridge House, Drymen G63 0EY. Tel: (01360) 660355.	Fishes Spring to Autumn. Good dace shoals.
Esk	Musselburgh (Estuary to Buccleuch Estate both banks)	Salmon Sea Trout Brown Trout	15 Mar. to 31 Oct. 15 Mar. to 6 Oct.	Country Life, Balgreen Road, Edinburgh. Tel: 0131-337 6230.	No Sunday fishing. A max. of 6 fish per day. Spinning reels are prohibited. Further regulations on permit.
Esk (North and South)	Midlothian	Brown/ Rainbow Trout Grayling	15 Mar. to 6 Oct. 7 Oct. to 14 Mar. Special winter permit	F. & D. Simpson, 28/30 West Preston Street, Edinburgh EH8 9PZ. Tel: 0131 667 3058. Country Life, Balgreen Road, Edinburgh. Tel: 0131-337 6230. Laird & Dog Hotel, High Street, Lasswade. Bailiffs at water.	Fly rod and reel only to be used. Stocked at beginning of every month. Reductions for disabled, children and OAPs. Platform at Lasswade for disabled. Regulations on permit. Sunday fishing.
Forth (Map IV C3)	Stirling	Salmon Sea Trout Brown Trout	1 Feb. to 31 Oct. 15 Mar. to 6 Oct.	Mitchell's Tackle, 13 Bannockburn Road, Stirling. Tel: (01786) 445587. Country Pursuits, 46 Henderson Street, Bridge of Allan. Tel: (01786) 834495.	Information leaflet with maps, prices, rules. No bait fishing before 1 May or after 31 Aug.
Fruin	Helensburgh	Salmon Sea Trout Brown Trout	11 Feb. to 31 Oct. 1 Mar. to 6 Oct.	Loch Lomond Angling Improvement Assoc., P.O. Box 3559, Uddingston G71 7SJ. Tel: 0141-781 1545. Tues./Wed./Fri. - 9 a.m. till 5 p.m.	Members only. Fly fishing only.
Water of Leith	Edinburgh	Brown Trout	1 Apr. to 30 Sep.	The City of Edinburgh Council, Recreation Dept., 17 Waterloo Place, Edinburgh EH1 3BG. Tel: 0131-529 7844. Post Office, 36 Main Street, Balerno. Tel: 0131-449 3077. Post Office, Bridge Road, Colinton, Edinburgh. Tel: 0131-441 1003. Country Life, Balgreen Road, Edinburgh. Tel: 0131-337 6230.	Fly fishing above Slateford Road Bridge. No spinning. Regulations on permit.

Water	Location	Species	Season	Permit available from	Other information
Leven	Dumbarton Bulloch	Salmon Sea Trout Brown Trout	11 Feb. to 31 Oct. 15 Mar. to 6 Oct.	Loch Lomond Angling Improvement Assoc., P.O. Box 3559, Uddingston G71 7SJ. Tel: 0141-781 1545. Tue./Wed./Fri. (9-5pm). Tackle & Guns, 920 Pollokshaws Road, Glasgow. Tel: 0141-632 2005.	Members may fish all Association waters. No Sunday fishing. Day tickets available.
Leven (Fife)	Markinch to Leven	Brown Trout Salmon Sea Trout	15 Mar. to 30 Sep. 11 Feb. to 15 Oct.		All legal methods. No shrimp or prawn.
Teith (Map IV C3)	Callander	Salmon Sea Trout Brown Trout	1 Feb. to 31 Oct.	J. Bayne, Main Street, Callander. Tel: (01877) 330218. (Season permits only.) Country Pursuits, 46 Henderson Street, Bridge of Allan. Tel: (01786) 834495.	Information leaflet with maps, prices, rules. No Sunday fishing.
	Gart Farm by Callander	Salmon Sea Trout	1 Feb. to 31 Oct.	Country Pursuits, 46 Henderson Street, Bridge of Allan. Tel: (01786) 834495.	Season permits only.
Tyne	Haddington	Brown Trout Rainbow Trout Sea Trout	15 Mar. to 6 Oct.	East Lothian Angling Association, J.S. Main, Saddlers, 87 High Street, Haddington. Tel: (01620) 822148. John Dickson & Son Ltd., 21 Frederick Street, Edinburgh EH2 2NE. Tel: 0131-225 4218. Country Life, Balgreen Road, Edinburgh. Tel: 0131-337 6230.	Twenty miles of river. No Sunday fishing. No threadlines. No spinning.

LOCHS & RESERVOIRS

Water	Location	Species	Season	Permit available from	Other information
Loch Achray	By Callander	Brown Trout Perch Pike	15 Mar. to 6 Oct.	Forest Enterprise, Queen Elizabeth Forest Park Visitor Centre, Aberfoyle. Tel: (01877) 382383. Loch Achray Hotel, Trossachs. Tel: (01877) 376229/376240. Bayne's Fishing Tackle Shop, Callander.	Bank fishing no longer permitted. Boat Hire only. From An Tigm Mor. (Old Trossarms Hotel).
Allandale Tarn Fisheries	West Calder	Rainbow/ Brown Trout Landlock Salmon	All year	At Allandale Tarn Fishery. Tel: (01506) 873073.	Average weight of fish caught: 2 lbs 4 oz. Fly fishing only on lochan. Separate bait pond. Bank only. Members A.S.S.F. Trout Master Water & Premier Trout Fishery. Rods/tackle for hire. Snack bar. Smokery available.
Loch Ard	Kinlochard	Brown Trout	15 Mar. to 6 Oct.	Altskeith Hotel, Kinlochard FK8 3TL. Tel: (01877) 387266.	Average weight of fish caught:12 oz. Popular flies: Silver Butcher, Kate McLaren, Alexandra. Fly fishing only. Boats are available.
Loch Arklet	By Inversnaid	Brown Trout	15 Mar. to 27 Sep.	Morris Meikle. Tel: (01786) 841692.	Average weight of fish caught:8 to 12 oz. Popular flies: Silver Butcher, Grouse & Claret, Black Pennel, Greenwell's Glory. No live bait allowed. Rowing boats only are available.

Water	Location	Species	Season	Permit available from	Other information
Beecraigs Loch	Linlithgow	Brown Trout Rainbow Trout Brook Trout	1 Mar. to 31 Oct.	Beecraigs Country Park, The Park Centre, nr. Linlithgow. Tel: (01506) 844516.	Fly fishing only. Boat fishing only. Night fishing 11pm to 7am. May to August. Advance booking essential.
Bonaly Reservoir	Edinburgh	Brown/ Rainbow Trout	1 Apr. to 30 Sep.	None required.	
Bowden Springs	Linlithgow	Rainbow/ Brown Trout	3 Jan. to 23 Dec.	Grant Laidlaw, Bowden Springs Fishery, Carriber, Linlithgow. Tel: (01506) 847269.	Bank and boat fishing. Fly fishing only. Fish average 2lbs. Heaviest 19lbs. Float tubes for hire/sale. Corporate entertainment a speciality.
Cameron Reservoir	St. Andrews	Brown Trout	Mid-Apr. to end Sep.	St. Andrews Angling Club, Secretary, Mr. P. Malcolm, 54 St. Nicholas Street, St. Andrews. Tel: (01334) 476347. The bailiff at the fishing hut on Cameron Reservoir. During season. Tel: (01334) 840236.	Average weight of fish caught: 1 lb. Fly fishing only. 6 boats are available. Sunday fishing available.
Carron Valley Reservoir	nr. Denny	Brown Trout	Mid Apr. to Sep.	East of Scotland Water, Woodlands, St Ninians Road, Stirling FK8 2HB. Tel: (01786) 458705. (9 a.m.-4 p.m.) Tel: (01324) 823698, (0374) 832525. (Evening, weekend tel. nos).	Single session - April and September. Double session - May to August. Day - 9 a.m. to 4 p.m. Evening 4.30 p.m. to dusk. Boat fishing only, 16 boats. Fly fishing only. Bag limit 5 fish per angler.
Clubbiedean Reservoir	Edinburgh	Brown/ Rainbow Trout	1 Apr. to 30 Sep.	East of Scotland Water, Fishing Desk, 55 Buckstone Terr., Edinburgh EH10 6XH. Tel: 0131-445 6462.	Boat fishing only. 3 Boats. Double sessions: May to August. Single session Apr. and Sept. Fly fishing only.
Cocksburn Loch	Bridge of Allan	Brown Trout	1 Apr. to 6 Oct.	Country Pursuits, 46 Henderson Street, Bridge of Allan. Tel: (01786) 834495.	Average weight of fish caught: 8–12 oz.
Crosswood Reservoir	West Calder	Brown Trout Brook Trout Rainbow Trout	1 Apr. to 30 Sep.	East of Scotland Water, Fishing Desk, 55 Buckstone Terr., Edinburgh EH10 6XH. Tel: 0131-445 6462.	Boat fishing only. 3 Boats. Double sessions: May to August. Single session Apr. and Sept. Fly fishing only.
Loch Drunkie	Aberfoyle	Brown Trout	15 Mar. to 6 Oct.	Forest Enterprize, Queen Elizabeth Forest Park Visitor Centre, Aberfoyle.	Bank fishing only.
Loch Fitty	Kingseat Dunfermline	Salmon Brown/ Rainbow Trout	20 Feb. to 19 Dec.	The Fishing Lodge, Loch Fitty, Dunfermline, Fife. Tel: (01383) 620666. Staff always on duty for help and information.	Really good fishing. Boat and bank fly fishing. Day – 10 a.m. to 5 p.m. Evenings – 5.30pm–dusk. Reductions for single anglers, retired, UB40's, father and Schoolboy son.
Gartmorn Dam Fishery	Nr. Alloa	Brown Trout	1 Apr. to 4 Oct.	Sep.–Apr.: Speirs Centre, 29 Primrose Street, Alloa FK10 1JJ. Tel: (01259) 213131. Apr.–Sep.: Visitor Centre, Gartmorn Dam Country Park, by Sauchie FK10 3AZ. Tel: (01259) 214319.	Average weight of fish caught: 1 lb 4 oz. Popular flies: Nymphs, Buzzers, Olives, Wickhams, 9 boats available. Disables anglers' wheelyboat. 2 sessions: 9am–5pm & 5pm–dusk.

Water	Location	Species	Season	Permit available from	Other information
Gladhouse Reservoir	Midlothian	Brown Trout	Mid Apr. to Sep.	East of Scotland Water, 55 Buckstone Terrace, Edinburgh EH10 6XH. Tel: 0131-445 6462.	Local Nature Reserve. Double sessions: May-Aug. Single session: Apr and Sept. Day: 8 a.m.-4.30 p.m. Evening: 5 p.m.-Sunset. Fly, boat fishing only. 5 boats.
Glencorse Reservoir	Penicuik	Brown Trout Brook Trout Rainbow Trout	Apr. to Sep.	East of Scotland Water, 55 Buckstone Terrace, Edinburgh EH10 6XH. Tel: 0131-445 6462.	Bank fishing only. 4 boats. Double sessions: May-Aug. Single session: Apr and Sept. Fly fishing only.
Glen Finglas Reservoir	By Callander	Brown Trout	15 Mar. to 27 Sep.	Morris Meikle Tel: (01786) 841692.	Average weight of fish caught 8 ton 12oz. Popular flies: Silver Butcher, Grouse & Claret, Black Pennel, Greenwell's Glory. No live bait allowed. Rowing boat available.
Loch Glow	Cleish Hills, nr. Kelty.	Brown Trout	15 Mar. to 6 Oct.	Tackle shops in Dunfermline, Cowdenbeath, Kelty and Kinross.	Fly, bait & Spinning. Regularly stocked with brown trout: some tagged fish. Further information: Mr. J. W. Mill. Tel: (01383) 722128.
Golden Loch	Nr. Grange of Lindores	Rainbow Trout		Mr Nicol, Tel: (01337) 840355.	Fly only. Boat hire. Nature walk around Farm. Will rent loch out and allow family barbecues.
Harlaw Reservoir	Balerno	Brown/ Rainbow Trout	1 Apr. to 30 Sep.	Day tickets: Fleming's Grocery Shop, 42 Main Street, Balerno. Tel: 0131-449 3833. Season Permits: Dalmeny Estate Office, South Queensferry, West Lothian.	Average weight of fish caught: 1–2 lbs. Fly fishing only. Bank fishing only. Season tickets issued by ballot – applications must be in by 1 March.
Harperrig Reservoir	West Calder	Brown Trout	1 Apr. to 30 Sep.	Bank fishing only. Permits from machine at reservoir.	Correct coins required for machine: £2, £1, 50p, 20p, 10p, denominations. Four boats and bank fishing. No Sunday fishing. Fly fishing only.
Hopes Reservoir	Gifford	Brown Trout	Apr. to Sep.	East of Scotland Water, Alderston House, Haddington EH41 3SY. Tel: (01620) 826422. Gobin Ha'Hotel Gillford. Tel: (01620) 810244	Boat fishing only. Fly fishing only. 2 boats.
Hopetoun Quarry Pond	Nr. Winchburgh	Rainbow Trout	All year (at all times)	At Hopetoun Quarry Pond. Tel: 0131- 331 5312.	Average weight of fish caught: 1.5 lbs. Any method fishing. Competitions every Sat & Sun. Competitions weekly for heaviest bag. Summer Season - April on coaching available. Stocked bait/tackle for hire or sale.
Holl Reservoir	Leslie	Rainbow/ Brown Trout	Apr. to Sept.	East of Scotland Water, Craig Mitchell House, Hemington Road, Glenrothes. Tel: (01592) 614000.	Fly Fishing only, 6 Boats, Boat fishing only. Double sessions: May-Aug. Single session: Apr. and Sept.

Water	Location	Species	Season	Permit available from	Other information
Loch Katrine	Stronach-lachar	Brown Trout	15 Mar. to 27 Sep.	Morris Meikle Tel: (01786) 841692.	Average weight of fish caught: 8 to 12 oz. Popular flies: Silver Butcher, Grouse & Claret, Black Pennel, Greenwell's Glory. No live bait allowed. Rowing boats only are available.
Lake of Menteith	Port of Menteith	Rainbow Trout	5 Apr. to 1 Nov.	Lake of Menteith Fisheries Ltd, Port of Menteith, Perthshire. Tel: (01877) 385664.	28 boats are available. No bank fishing.
Lindores Loch	Newburgh	Rainbow Trout	All Year.	Gamefishing (Lindores), by Newburgh. Tel: (01337) 810488.	Two sessions: 9am–5pm. Other sessions and times by arrangement.
Linlithgow Loch	Linlithgow	Brown/ Rainbow Trout	15 Mar. to 6 Oct.	Tel: (0831) 288291.	Average weight of fish caught: 1 lb 8 oz. Popular flies: black lures, Green Peter, Grouse & Claret, Buzzers. Fly fishing only. 12 boats are available.
Lochore	Ballingry	Brown/ Rainbow Trout	1 Mar. to 30 Nov.	Lochore Meadows Country Park, Crosshill, Lochgelly, Fife KY5 8BA. Tel: (01592) 414312.	Sessions: any 8 hours till dusk, bank. Boats: Day 9am–4.30pm. Evening 5pm–dusk. Spinning and bait fishing from bank from 1 June.
Loganlea Trout Fishery	Nr. Penicuik	Wild Brown Trout Rainbow Trout	All year	Loganlea Trout Fishery, Milton Bridge, nr. Penicuik EH26 0PP. Tel: (01968) 676328.	Average weight of fish caught: 2 lbs. Fly fishing only. Stocked twice weekly with rainbows. Boats are available. Refreshments and tackle for sale.
Loch Lomond	Balloch to Ardlui	Salmon Sea Trout Brown Trout Pike Roach Perch	11 Feb. to 31 Oct. 15 Mar. to 6 Oct. No close season	Loch Lomond Angling Improvement Assoc., C. McCrory, P.O. Box 3559, Uddingston G71 7SJ. Tel: (01506) 655063. Mobile: 0789 9751363	Boats for hire locally. No Sunday fishing. Day permits available.
	Ardlui	Salmon Sea Trout Brown Trout Pike	11 Feb. to 31 Oct. 15 Mar. to 6 Oct.	Ardlui Hotel, Loch Lomond. Tel: (01301) 704243.	Popular flies: Silver Victor, Mallard, Claret. Other baits: Toby, Rapala, Sprat. Boats are available.
	Balmaha	Salmon Sea Trout Pike	Mar. to Oct. All year	MacFarlane & Son, The Boatyard, Balmaha. Tel: (01360) 870214.	Boats and outboard motors are available. Rods available. Permits sold.
	Rowardennan by Drymen	Salmon Sea Trout Brown Trout Pike	11 Feb. to 31 Oct. 15 Mar. to 6 Oct. All year	Rowardennan Hotel, Rowardennan. Tel: (01360) 870273.	Average weight of fish caught: Salmon 9 lbs; Sea Trout 3 lbs; Brown Trout 1 lb 12 oz. Other baits: Toby for trawling.
	Inverbeg	Salmon Sea Trout Brown Trout Pike Perch	11 Feb. to 31 Oct. 15 Mar. to 6 Oct. All year	Inverbeg Caravan Park, Inverbeg. Tel: (01436) 860267.	Popular flies: March Brown, Peter Ross. Live bait allowed.

Water	Location	Species	Season	Permit available from	Other information
Markle Loch (5.5 acres)	nr. East Linton	Rainbow/ Brown Trout	All year	J. Swift, The Lodge, Markle Fisheries, Markle, East Linton EH40 3EB. Tel: (01620) 861213.	Average weight of fish caught: 2 lbs 4 oz. Popular flies: Damsel Nymphs, Buzzers, Hares Lug, mini lures, Dunkeld and dark traditional wets. Bank fishing only – no wading. Brown trout to be returned out of.
Millhall Reservoir	Polmont	Brown/ Rainbow Trout	Mar. to Oct.	Avonbank Fishing Club, c/o Mr. Ian Geran, Polmont. Tel: (01324) 714190.	Average weight of fish caught: 1.5 lbs. Fly fishing only. 2 boats are available.
Monastery Loch (2.5 acres)	Nr. East Linton	Rainbow/ Brown Trout	All year	The Lodge, Markle Fisheries, Markle, East Linton EH40 3EB. Tel: (01620) 861213.	Average weight of fish caught: 2 lbs 4 oz. Popular flies: Damsel Nymphs, Buzzers, Hares Lug, mini lures, Dunkeld and dark traditional wets. Bank fishing only – no wading. Brown trout to be returned out of season.
Morton Fishery	Mid Calder	Rainbow Trout	11 Mar. to 29 Oct.	Morton Fishery, Morton Reservoir, Mid Calder, W. Lothian. Tel: (01506) 882293.	Fly fishing only. Advance bookings. Double sessions May–Aug., 9am–5pm, 5pm–dusk. Bag limits 3–6 fish per rod.
Newton Farm Loch	Between Wormit & Gaudry on B946				Snacks and refreshments available.
North Third	nr. Stirling	Rainbow/ Brown Trout	15 Mar. to 31 Oct.	North Third Trout Fishery, 'Greathill', Cambusbarron, Stirling. Tel: (01786) 471967. Fax: (01786) 447388.	Fly fishing only. Boat and bank. Day, evening and combined permits. 23 boats. Averages 22,000 fish per year. Fishery record for rainbow trout 19 lbs 3 oz. 50-60 double figure per year. Consessions for Juniors. STB commended.
Parkley Fishery	Linlithgow	Brown/ Rainbow Trout	All year	Parkley Fishery, Edinburgh Road, Linlithgow. Tel: (01506) 842027. Mobile: (0836) 348037.	Bait and fly fishing permitted. Bank fishing only.
Raith Lake	Kirkcaldy (B925)	Wild Brown Trout Rainbow Trout American Brook Trout	All year	At Raith Lake. Tel (01592) 646466. Mobile: (0850) 532434.	Average weight of fish caught: 2 lbs. Fly fishing only. Stocked weekly. 13 boats are available.
Lochan Reoidhe	Aberfoyle	Brown Trout	15 Mar. to 6 Oct.	Forest Enterprise, Queen Elizabeth Forest Park Visitor Centre, Aberfoyle.	Fly fishing only. Limited rods. Advance bookings accepted.
Rosslynlee Reservoir	Nr. Penicuik	Brown/ Rainbow/ Brook Trout Salmon	All year	At Rosslynlee Reservoir. Tel: (01968) 679606.	Average weight of fish caught: 2 lbs. Popular flies: Buzzers, Sedges, Silver Invictas, Damsel Nymphs. Fly fishing only. 1 boat available. Bank fishing. Rods for hire. Stocked weekly.

65

Water	Location	Species	Season	Permit available from	Other information
Selm Muir Loch	Mid Calder	Rainbow Trout Brook Brown Trout	All year	Selm Muir Fishery. George Gowland Tel: (01506) 884550. Selm Muir Fishery.	Average weight of fish caught: 2 lb 2 oz. Popular flies: Montana Nymph, small black lures. Other baits: maggots, sweetcorn. No spinning or groundbaiting.
Swanswater Fishery	Stirling	Rainbow/ Brown Trout Steelhead	All year for Rainbow	Swanswater Fishery. Tel: (01786) 814805.	Average weight of fish caught: 2 lbs. Popular flies: Viva, Black Pennel. Fly fishing only. 3 boats are available. Stocked daily with top quality fish. Smokehouse and farm shop.
Threipmuir Reservoir	Balerno	Brown/ Rainbow Trout	1 Apr. to 30 Sep.	Day tickets: Flemings, Grocer, 42 Main Street, Balerno. Tel: 0131-449 3833. Season permits: Dalmeny Estate Office, South Queensferry, W. Lothian.	Average weight of fish caught: 1–2 lbs. Fly fishing only. Bank fishing only. Season tickets issued by ballot – applications must be in by 1 March.
Loch Venachar	Callander	Brown Trout	15 Mar. to 6 Oct.	J. Bayne, Main Street, Callander. Tel: (01877) 330218.	Boats for hire.
Loch Voil	Balquhidder	Brown Trout Salmon Sea Trout Char	15 Mar. to 6 Oct.	Stronvar Country House Hotel, Balquhidder FK19 8PB. Tel: (01877) 384688. Mrs C.M.Oldham, Muirlaggan, Balquhidder, Lochearnhead FK19 8PB. Tel: (01877) 384219.	Hotel's guests only. Advanced bookings necessary. Popular flies: Blae & Black, Kate McLaren, Grouse & Claret, Black Spider, Greenwell's Glory, Butcher, Professor (size 12). Other baits: spinners, rapala, toby, kynoch killer for salmon. 5 boats are available.
West Water	West Linton	Brown Trout	May to Aug.	East of Scotland Water, Fishing Desk, 55 Buckstone Terrace, Edinburgh EH10 6XH. Tel: 0131-445 4642.	Average weight of fish caught: 14 oz. Boat fishing only. 1 boat. Fly fishing only.

Angus and Dundee Tourist Board
7-12 Castle Street,
Dundee DD1 3AA.
Tel: (01382) 527527.

Perthshire Tourist Board
Chief Executive,
Administration Headquarters,
Lower City Mills,
West Mill Street,
Perth PH1 5QP.
Tel: (01738) 627958.
Fax: (01738) 630416

**Scottish Environment
Protection Agency**
1 South Street,
Perth PH2 8NJ.
Tel: (01738) 627989.

RIVERS

Water	Location	Species	Season	Permit available from	Other information
Braan	Amulree	Brown Trout	15 Mar. to 6 Oct.	Amulree Tearoom, Post Office, Amulree. Tel: (01350) 725200.	Fly fishing only.
	Cochill Burn	Brown Trout	15 Mar. to 6 Oct.	Kettles of Dunkeld, Atholl Street, Dunkeld. Tel: (01350) 727556.	Fly fishing only.
Dean	Strathmore	Brown Trout	15 Mar. to 6 Oct.	Strathmore Angling Improvement Assoc., Mrs. M.C. Milne, 1 West Park Gdns, Dundee. Tel: (01382) 667711.	Fly fishing only.
Devon	Hillfoots, Tillicoultry to Crook of Devon	Salmon Sea Trout Brown Trout	15 Mar. to 31 Oct. 15 Mar. to 6 Oct.	Country Pursuits, 46 Henderson Street, Bridge of Allan. Tel: (01786) 834495.	Fly fishing only from: 15 March to 12 April.
Dochart (Map IV C2)	Killin	Brown Trout	15 Mar. to 6 Oct.	J.H. Rough, J.R. News, Main Street, Killin. Tel: (01567) 820362. Clachaig Hotel, Killin. Tel: (01567) 820270.	All legal lures permitted.
Earn (Map IV D2)	Crieff	Salmon Sea Trout Brown Trout	1 Feb. to 15 Oct. 15 Mar. to 6 Oct.	Crieff Angling Club, Adam Boyd Newsagents, 39 King Street, Crieff. Tel: (01764) 653871.	No shrimp, prawn, diving minnow or floats. No bait before 1 May.
	By Crieff	Salmon Sea Trout Brown Trout	1 Feb. to 31 Oct. 15 Mar. to 6 Oct.	Country Pursuits, 46 Henderson Street, Bridge of Allan. Tel: (01786) 834495.	(Lower Strowan Beat) Permit available for season (day per week throughout session).
Ericht	Glenericht	Salmon Brown Trout	1 Apr. to 15 Oct. 15 Mar. to 6 Oct.	Mr R. McCosh. Tel: (01250) 875518.	Fly fishing only.
	Craighall (upper)	Salmon Brown Trout	15 Jan. to 15 Oct. 15 Mar. to 6 Oct.	A.L. Rattray, Craighall, Blairgowrie PH10 7JB. Tel: (01250) 874749 or (01250)875080.	Subject to availability.

Water	Location	Species	Season	Permit available from	Other information
Fillan	by Crianlarich	Salmon	15 Jan to 15 Oct.	Portnellan House, by Crianlarich FK20 8QS. Tel: (01838) 300284.	
		Brown Trout	16 Mar. to 16 Oct.		
Garry (Map IV C1)	Blair Atholl	Brown Trout	15 Mar. to 6 Oct.	Highland Shop, Blair Atholl. Tel: (01796) 481303.	Fly or Spinning.
Isla	Strathmore	Brown Trout	15 Mar. to 6 Oct.	Strathmore Angling Improvement Association, Mrs. M.C. Milne, 1 West Park Gardens, Dundee. Tel: (01382) 667711.	Fly fishing only on upper beats.
Lochay (Map IV C2)	Killin	Brown Trout Pike Perch	15 Mar. to 6 Oct.	J.H. Rough, J.R. News, Main Street, Killin. Tel: (01567) 820362.	Fly only on upper beat.
Lunan	Arbroath	Sea/ Brown Trout	15 Mar. to 6 Oct.	Arbroath Cycle and Tackle Centre, 274 High Street, Arbroath. Tel: (01241) 873467.	Fly, bait or spinning.
Lyon (Map IV B2)	Aberfeldy	Salmon	15 Jan. to 15 Oct.	Fortingall Hotel, Fortingall, by Aberfeldy. Tel: (01887) 830367. Coshieville Hotel. Tel: (01887) 830319 .	No Sunday fishing. Max. rods on each of 2 beats. Maps, tackle, etc. available.(6 miles single bank.) 1 beat (3 miles) North bank 6 rods Max.
	Tirinie Fishings	Salmon	15 Jan. to 15 Oct.	Coshieville Hotel, by Aberfeldy PH15 2NE.	Max. 4 rods. No bait fishing. No Sunday fishing. Boat & ghillie available for hire.
		Brown Trout	15 Mar. to 6 Oct.		
South Esk (Map III F5)	Kirriemuir	Salmon Sea Trout	16 Feb. to 31 Oct.	H. Burness, Kirriemuir Angling Club, 13 Clova Road, Kirriemuir. Tel: (01575) 573456.	No permits on Saturdays. No Sunday fishing. Fly only in parts in low water. Booking advisable. Map available.
Tay (Map IV C2)	Aberfeldy	Salmon Sea Trout	15 Jan. to 15 Oct.	Country Pursuits, 46 Henderson Street, Bridge of Allan. Tel: (01786) 834495.	(Killiechassie Beat) 4 rods maximum. Ghillie available. No prawns/ shrimps after 1Sep.
		Salmon Sea Trout	5 Jan. to 15 Oct.	Country Pursuits, 46 Henderson Street, Bridge of Allan. Tel: (01786) 834495.	(Derculich Beat) Maximum 3 rods. Ghillie available. No bait.
		Salmon Sea Trout	15 Jan. to 15 Oct.	Country Pursuits, 46 Henderson Street, Bridge of Allan. Tel: (01786) 834495.	(Lower Farleyer) 4 rods maximum. Ghillie available.
		Salmon Sea Trout	15 Jan. to 15 Oct.	Country Pursuits, 46 Henderson Street, Bridge of Allan. Tel: (01786) 834495.	(Moness Beat) Maximum 3 rods. Boat & ghillie available.
		Salmon Sea Trout	15 Jan. to 15 Oct.	Country Pursuits, 46 Henderson Street, Bridge of Allan. Tel: (01786) 834495.	(Lower Bolrocks Beat) 4 rods max. Boat & ghillie available.
		Trout	15 Mar to 6 Oct.	Tom Sharp, Laigh of Cluny, Steading, Edvadynate, Aberfeldy PH15 2JU. Tel/Fax: (01887) 840469.	(Weem Water Beat). 6 rods max 1 1/4 single bank fishing. Private beat day or weekly permits. Booking advisable.
		Salmon	15 Jan to 15 Oct.		

Water	Location	Species	Season	Permit available from	Other information
Tay cont.	Grandtully	Salmon	15 Jan. to 15 Oct.	Country Pursuits, 46 Henderson Street, Bridge of Allan. Tel: (01786) 834495.	Fly or spinning. Boat and ghillie available. Booking advisable. Rod hire and tackle. 5-rod beat.
		Brown Trout Grayling	15 Mar. to 6 Oct.		
		Salmon Sea Trout	15 Jan. to 15 Oct.	Country Pursuits, 46 Henderson Street, Bridge of Allan. Tel: (01786) 834495.	(Findyate Beat) Maximum 3 rods. Boat and ghillie available. No prawns/shrimps after 1 Sep. Good Spring beat.
		Salmon Sea Trout	15 Jan. to 15 Oct.	Country Pursuits, 46 Henderson Street, Bridge of Allan. Tel: (01786) 834495.	(Clochfoldich Beat) Maximum 3 rods. Boat & ghillie available. No prawns/shrimps after 1 Sep. Good Spring Beat.
	Dalguise	Salmon	15 Jan. to 15 Oct.	Country Pursuits, 46 Henderson Street, Bridge of Allan. Tel: (01786) 834495. Finlayson Hughes, 29 Barossa Place, Perth. Tel: (01738) 451600.	11/4 miles both banks. Boats & ghillies available.
	Dunkeld	Salmon	15 Jan. to 15 Oct.	Stakis Hotels Ltd., Dunkeld House Hotel, Dunkeld. Tel: (01350) 727771.	Two boats with two rods. Experienced ghillies. 8 bank rods. Tuition. No salmon fishing on Sundays. Booking advisable.
		Brown Trout	15 Mar. to 6 Oct.		
		Brown Trout Grayling	15 Mar. to 6 Oct.	Kettles of Dunkeld, Atholl Street, Dunkeld. Tel: (01350) 727556.	Fly fishing only. Tackle hire.
		Salmon Sea Trout	15 Jan. to 15 Oct.	Country Pursuits, 46 Henderson Street, Bridge of Allan. Tel: (01786) 834495.	(Upper Newtyle Beat) Maximum 5 rods. Boat & ghillie available.
		Salmon Sea Trout	15 Jan. to 15 Oct.	Country Pursuits, 46 Henderson Street, Bridge of Allan. Tel: (01786) 834495.	(Lower Newtyle Beat) Maximum 5 rods. Boat & ghillie available.
	Stanley	Salmon Sea Trout Brown Trout	15 Jan. to 13 Oct. 12 Mar. to 6 Oct.	Tayside Hotel, Stanley, nr. Perth. Tel: (01738) 828249. Tackle & Guns, 920 Pollokshaws Road, Glasgow. Tel: 0141-632 2005. (Jan.–May Spring salmon)	Day permits available May–Jul. Ghillies by arrangement. Advisable to book in advance.
	Perth	Salmon Sea Trout Flounder Roach	15 Jan. to 15 Oct.	Director of Leisure & Recreation, Perth & Kinross District Council, 3 High Street, Perth. Tel: (01738) 475211/12. (Monday to Friday) Tourist Information Centre, 45 High Street, Perth PH1 5TJ. Tel: (01738) 638353. Weekends & public holidays.	Advisable to book in advance. Only 20 permits per day. Only 2 permits in advance by any one person. No weekly permits.
Tilt	Blair Atholl	Salmon	End May to 15 Oct.	The Highland Shop, Blair Atholl. Tel: (01796) 481303.	(Private beat, 3 miles) Booking advised. Fly or spinning only. Max. 4 rods

Water	Location	Species	Season	Permit available from	Other information
Tummel (Map IV C2)	Pitlochry	Salmon	15 Jan. to 15 Oct.	Pitlochry Angling Club, c/o Tourist Information Centre, Pitlochry. Tel: Mr. Gardiner (01796) 472157 (evenings/weekends).	Permits available Monday to Saturday. Booking in advance is advisable.
Tummel cont.	Pitlochry to Ballinluig	Brown Trout Grayling	15 Mar. to 6 Oct.	Tourist Information Centre, Pitlochry. Mitchells of Pitlochry, 23 Atholl Road, Pitlochry. Tel: (01796) 472613. Season tickets and enquiries to: Pitlochry Angling Club, Secretary, Mr. Harriman, Sunnyknowe, Nursing Home Brae, Pitlochry Tel: (01796) 472484 (evenings and weekends).	Pitlochry angling water. Five miles of river, both banks. Maps and rules on permits. Grayling permits available in the winter.
	Moulinearn to Ballinluig	Salmon Sea Trout	15 Jan. to 15 Oct.	Pitlochry Angling Club, c/o Tourist Information Centre, Pitlochry. Tel: Mr. Gardiner (01796) 472157 (evenings and weekends).	Only available July & August.
Tummel (Upper)	Kinloch Rannoch	Brown Trout	15 Mar. to 6 Oct.	Lochgarry Cottage. Tel: (01882) 632354. Innerhadden Keeper. Tel: (01882) 632339. Local shops and hotels.	Average weight of fish caught: 12 oz. Other baits: spinning and live.

LOCHS & RESERVOIRS

Water	Location	Species	Season	Permit available from	Other information
Loch Bainnie	Spittal of Glenshee	Brown Trout	18 Mar. to 11 Aug.	Invercauld Estates Office, Braemar AB35 5XQ. Tel: (01339) 741224.	Boat available from: Mr J. Cruickshanks, Gamekeeper, Wester Binzean, Glenshee. Tel: Glenshee 206. No spinning or use of live bait.
Ben Vrackie Loch	By Pitlochry	Brown Trout	15 Mar. to 30 Sep.	Mr. Seaton, Gamekeeper's House, Baledmund Estate, Pitlochry.	Average weight of fish caught: 8 oz. Any legal method permitted.
Blair Walker Pond	Blair Atholl	(Stocked) Brown/ Rainbow Trout	15 Mar. to 6 Oct.	The Highland Shop, Blair Atholl. Tel: (01796) 481303.	Fly only.
Butterstone Loch	Dunkeld	Rainbow/ Brown Trout	20 Mar. to 22 Oct.	The Bailiff, Lochend Cottage, Butterstone, by Dunkeld. Tel: (01350) 724238.	Fly fishing only.
Castlehill Reservoir	Glendevon	Brown Trout	1 Apr. to 30 Sep.	Fife Regional Council, Craig Mitchell House, Flemington Road, Glenrothes. Tel: (01592) 754411. Glendevon Treatment Works. Tel: (01259) 781453.	Fly fishing only. Boat or bank fishing.
Loch Dochart	By Crianlarich	Salmon Brown Trout	15 Jan. to 15 Oct.	Portnellan House, by Crianlarich FK20 8QS. Tel: (01838) 300284.	Fly only. Boats available.
Dunalastair Reservoir	Kinloch Rannoch	Brown Trout	15 Mar. to 6 Oct.	Lochgarry Cottage. Tel: (01882) 632354. Dunalastair Hotel. Tel: (01882) 632323.	Six boats. No bank fishing. Fly fishing only for trout – average weight 1 lb 9 oz. 9am to dusk.

Water	Location	Species	Season	Permit available from	Other information
Loch Earn	St. Fillans/ Lochearnhead	Brown Trout Charr Rainbow Trout	15 Mar. to 6 Oct.	P.O., Drummond Arms Hotel, Four Seasons Hotel (all St. Fillans). Clachan Cottage Hotel, 45 Bar & Rest., P.O., Village shop (all Lochearnhead).	12-14 ozs - Regular stocking with brown trouts up to 3lbs. 6 boats available without board engines. Drummond Estates boat hire. Tel: (01567) 830400.
Loch Eigheach	Moor of Rannoch	Brown/ Rainbow Trout Brown Trout	Mar. to Oct. 15 Mar. to 6 Oct.	St. Fillans Post Office, St. Fillans. Rannoch & District Angling Club, John Brown, The Square, Kinloch Rannoch. Tel: (01882) 632268.	Average weight of fish caught: 12 oz–9 lbs. Loch is regularly stocked. Bank fishing only.
Errochty Dam	Nr. Blair Atholl	Brown Trout Pike	15 Mar. to 6 Oct. All year	The Highland Shop, Blair Atholl. Tel: (01796) 481303.	Any legal method.
Loch Faskally	Pitlochry	Salmon Brown Trout Pike Perch	May to 15 Oct. 15 Mar. to 6 Oct.	Mr. D. McLaren, Pitlochry Boating Station, Loch Faskally, Pitlochry. Tel: (01796) 472919/472759.	Any legal lure for salmon and trout. Boats available. Cafe facilities. Fishing tackle bait when available.
Loch Freuchie	Amulree	Brown Trout Pike	15 Mar. to 6 Oct.	Amylree Tearoom, Post Office, Amulree. Tel: (01350) 725200.	Fly fishing only. Coarse fishing.
Glendevon (Upper & Lower Reservoir)	Glendevon	Brown Trout	1 Apr. to 30 Sep.	Fife Regional Council, Craig Mitchell House, Flemington Road, Glenrothes. Tel: (01592) 754411. Glendevon Treatment Works. Tel: (01259) 781453.	Fly fishing only. No Sunday fishing. Bank fishing on Lower Glendevon.
Glenfarg	Glenfarg	Brown Trout	1 Apr. to 30 Sep.	Fife Regional Council, Craig Mitchell House, Flemington Road, Glenrothes. Tel: (01592) 754411. Glenfarg Treatment Works. Tel: (01577) 830561.	Fly fishing only. No Sunday fishing. Boat available.
Heathery-ford	Just off Junc. 6 on M90 at Kinross	Brown/ Rainbow Trout	Mid-Mar. to Dec.	Kinross Trout Fishery, office on site. Tel: (01577) 864212.	All bank fishing, top quality trout. Trout master water. Fly fishing only.
Holl	Lomond Hills	Brown Trout	1 Apr. to 30 Sep.	Fife Regional Council, Craig Mitchell House, Flemington Road, Glenrothes. Tel: (01592) 754411.	Fly fishing only. No Sunday fishing. Boat available.
Loch Lubhair	Nr. Crianlarich	Salmon Brown Trout	15 Jan. to 13 Oct.	Portnellan House, by Crianlarich FK20 8QS. Tel: (01838) 300284.	Popular flies: Black Pennel, Black & Peacock, Mullard, Claret. Any legal method. Boats available.
Loch Kinardochy	Tummel Bridge	Brown Trout	15 Mar. to 6 Oct.	Mitchells of Pitlochry, 23 Atholl Road, Pitlochry PH16 5BX. Tel: (01796) 472613.	Fly fishing from boat only. Advance booking recommended.
Lochan-na-Laraig	Killin	Trout	15 Mar. to 6 Oct.	J.H. Rough, J.R. News, Main Street, Killin. Tel: (01567) 820362.	All legal lures.
Loch Lee	Glen Esk	Brown Trout Arctic Char	1 May to 12 Aug.	Head Keeper, Invermark, Glenesk, by Brechin DD9 7YZ Tel: (01356) 670208.	Average weight of fish caught: 8 oz to 12 oz. 3 boats – 3 rods per boat. No Sunday fishing.
Loch Leven	Kinross	Rainbow/ Brown Trout	2 Apr. to 6 Oct.	Loch Leven Fisheries, The Pier, Kinross. Tel: (01577) 863407.	Fly and boat fishing.

Water	Location	Species	Season	Permit available from	Other information
Lintrathern Reservoir	Kirriemuir	Brown Trout	1 Apr. to 6 Oct.	Lintrathen Angling Club, Jack Yule, 61 Hillrise, Kirriemuir, Angus DD8 4JS. Tel: Loch (01575) 560327. Tel: Home (01575) 573816. Club bookings: Dr. Parratt, 91 Strathearn Road, Broughty Ferry, Dundee. Tel: (01382) 677305. (Not after start of season.)	20 boats & 2 disabled boats. Sunday fishing. Max. catch 15 fish per boat. Telephone for details of sessions and backwater dam. Bank fishing.
Mill of Criggie Trout Fishery	St. Cyrus, Montrose	Rainbow/ Brown Trout	All year except Xmas day.	Mill of Criggie, St. Cyrus, Montrose DD10 0DR. Tel: (01674) 850864.	Fly fishing only. Tuition (trout & salmon), courses, tackle hire. Bothy.
Monikie	Monikie	Brown Trout	Start Apr. to 6 Oct.	Tel: (01382) 370300.	Average weight of fish caught: 1 lb 4 oz. Popular flies: Bibio, Kate McLaren, Ace of Spades. Boats: (10) Island Pond, (4) North Pond, (4) Crombie. Fly only. Boat only.
Loch nan Ean	Dalmunzie	Brown Trout	18 Mar. to 11 Aug.	Invercauld Estates Office, Braemar AB35 5XQ. Tel: (01339) 741224.	No spinning or use of live bait permitted.
Loch Rannoch	Kinloch Rannoch	Brown Trout Arctic Char Pike Perch	15 Mar. to 6 Oct.	Local shops and hotels. Loch Rannoch Conservation Association, R. Legate (Sec.), Glenrannoch House. Tel: (01882) 632307.	Fly and spinners only. No live bait. Average weight of fish caught: 8 oz to 1 lb. Boats from Dunalastair Hotel. Ghillie service. Rod hire. Small tackle shop.
		Brown Trout Pike Perch	15 Mar. to 6 Oct.	Dunalaster Estate, Lochgelly House, Kinloch, Rannoch, Tel: (01882) 632314.	Average weight of fish caught: 8 oz to 1 lb. No live bait allowed.
Rescobie Loch	Forfar	Brown/ Rainbow Trout	15 Mar. to 31 Oct.	Bailiff, Rescobie Loch, South Lodge, Reswallie, by Forfar DD8 2SA. Tel: (01307) 818384.	Fly fishing only.
Sandy-knowes Fishery	Bridge of Earn	Rainbow Trout	1 Mar. to 25 Dec.	E. Christie, The Fishery Office, Sandyknowe Fishery, Bridge of Earn. Tel: (01738) 813033.	Bank fly fishing only. Session times: 10am–2pm, 2pm–6pm, 6pm–10pm. Bag limit 4 trout per session. .
Loch Tay	Killin	Brown Trout	15 Mar. to 5 Oct.	J.H. Rough, J.R. News, Main Street, Killin. Tel: (01567) 820362.	All legal lures permitted.
		Salmon	15 Jan. to 15 Oct.	Clachaig Hotel, Killin. Tel: (01567) 820270.	
	Milton Morenish	Salmon	15 Jan. to 15 Oct.	Loch Tay Highland Lodges, Milton Morenish, by Killin. Tel: (01567) 820323.	3 boats available with outboards. Sixteen boats available. Ghillie and rod hire. Special offers for midweek fishing.
		Trout	15 Mar. to 6 Oct.		
Loch Tummel	West of Pitlochry	Trout Pike Perch	Apr. to Oct.	Queen's View Visitor Centre, Strathtummel, by Pitlochry PH16 5NR.	
Loch Turret	Crieff	Brown Trout	Apr. to Sep.	East of Scotland Water, Forth Valley Division, Balmore Treatment Works, Balmore, Torrance, Glasgow G64 4AJ. Tel: (01360) 620511. Adam Boyd Newsagents, 39 King Street, Crieff. Tel: (01360) 653871.	Fly fishing only. 4 boats. Season tickets available.

Highlands of Scotland Tourist Board
Peffery House,
Strathpeffer,
Ross-shire IV14 9HA.
Tel: (01997) 421160.
Fax: (01997) 421168.
Email: info@host.co.uk.
Web site: http://www.host.co.uk.

Aberdeen and Grampian Tourist Board
Head Office,
27 Albyn Place,
Aberdeen AB10 1YL.
Tel: (01224) 822000.
Fax: (01224) 581367.
Area Office, Tel: (01224) 522452.

Kincardine and Deeside Tourist Board
Tourist Officer,
Tourist Information Centre,
Bridge Street, Banchory,
Kincardineshire AB31 2SX.
Tel: (01330) 822000.

City of Aberdeen Tourist Board
Director, City of Aberdeen Tourist Board, St.
Nicholas House,
Broad Street,
Aberdeen AB9 1DE.
Tel: (01224) 632727.

Gordon District Tourist Board,
Director,
Gordon District Tourist Board,
St. Nicholas House,
Broad Street,
Aberdeen AB9 1DE.
Tel: (01224) 632727.

Moray Tourist Board
Chief Tourist Officer,
Tourist Information Centre,
17 High Street,
Elgin,
Morayshire IV30 1EG.
Tel: (01343) 542666.

River Purification Board
North East River Purification Board
Greyhope House,
Greyhope Road,
Torry,
Aberdeen AB1 3RD.
Tel: (01224) 248338.

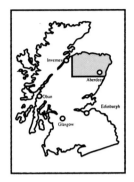

RIVERS

Water	Location	Species	Season	Permit available from	Other information
Avon (Map III E2)	Ballindalloch	Salmon Sea Trout	11 Feb. to 30 Sept.	Delnashaugh Inn, Ballindalloch, Banffshire AB37 9AS. Tel: (01807) 500255. Estates Office, Ballindalloch, Banff-shire, AB37 9AX. Tel: (01807) 500205	No prawn. Fly fishing Sep. No lead attached to fly.
	Tomintoul	Salmon Sea Trout	Feb. to end Sep.	Gordon Hotel, Tomintoul, Banffshire AB37 9ET. Tel: (01807) 580206.	No prawn. Fly fishing Sep. No lead attached to fly.
Bogie	Huntly	Salmon Sea Trout	11 Feb. to 31 Oct. 1 Apr. to 6 Oct.	Clerk of Fishings, Huntly Fishings Committee, Murdoch, McMath & Mitchell, 27/29 Duke Street, Huntly. Tel: (01466) 792291.	Permit covers Bogie, Deveron and Isla.
Carron	Stonehaven	Salmon Sea Trout Brown Trout	1 May to 31 Aug.	David's Sports Shop, 31 Market Square, Stonehaven. Tel: (01569) 762239.	Visitors' permits for Sea pool to railway viaduct. Further info: Mr. A.G. Kellas, 44 Farburn Drive, Stonehaven AB3 2 BZ. Tel: (01569) 764227.

Water	Location	Species	Season	Permit available from	Other information
Clunie	Braemar	Brown Trout	15 Mar. to 20 Sep.	Ballater Angling Association, Tourist Information Centre, Braemar.	Fly fishing only.
Cowie	Stonehaven	Sea Trout Salmon Brown Trout	1 May to 31 Aug.	David's Sports Shop, 31 Market Square, Stonehaven. Tel: (01569) 762239.	Visitors' permits for Sea pool to railway viaduct. For further information: Mr. A.G. Kellas, 44 Farburn Drive, Stonehaven AB3 2BZ. Tel: (01569) 764227.
Dee (Map III F3)	Aboyne	Salmon Sea Trout	1 Mar. to 30 Sep.	Glen Tanar Estate, Brooks House Glen Tanar, Aboyne AB34 5EU. Tel: (013398) 86451. Fax: (013398) 86047	No Sunday fishing. Day permits available.
Deveron (Map III F2)	Huntly	Salmon Sea Trout Brown Trout	11 Feb. to 31 Oct. 1 Apr. to 6 Oct.	Clerk of Fishings, Huntly Fishings Committee, Murdoch, McMath & Mitchell, 27/29 Duke Street, Huntly. Tel: (01466) 792291.	Permits cover Deveron.
		Salmon Sea Trout Brown Trout	11 Feb. to 31 Oct.	Castle Hotel, Huntly, Aberdeenshire AB54 4SH. Tel: (01466) 792696. Fax: (01466) 792641. Email: castlehot@enterprise.net	2 rods on hotel's own beat. Other private beats also available. Fly and spinning only.
		Salmon Sea Trout Brown Trout	11 Feb. to 31 Oct.	Forbes Country Matters, 47 Gordon Street, Huntly AB54 5EQ.	Huntly, Rothiemay, Bridge of Marnoch and other private beats. Daily and weekly lets. No shrimp or prawn.
	Turriff	Salmon Sea Trout Brown Trout	11 Feb. to 31 Oct.	Turriff Angling Assoc., I. Masson, The Cross, 6 Castle Street, Turriff. Tel: (01888) 562428.	No day tickets. Six weekly available to visitors. Restrictions on spinning.
Don (Map III F3)	Manar Beat	Salmon Sea Trout Brown Trout	11 Feb. to 31 Oct. 1 Apr. to 30 Sep.	J.J. Watson, 44 Market Place, Inverurie. Tel: (01467) 620321.	No worm, shrimp or prawn. Limit of 4 rods per day.
	Strathdon	Salmon Brown Trout	11 Feb. to 31 Oct.	Colquhonnie Hotel, Strathdon. Tel: (01975) 651210.	Fly and spinning only.
	Kintore	Salmon Sea Trout Brown Trout	11 Feb. to 31 Oct.	J.A. Copland, Newsagent, 2 Northern Road, Kintore. Tel: (01467) 632210.	No worm until 1 Apr. No natural minnow. No shrimp or prawn. Reductions for school children and OAPs.
	Inverurie	Salmon Sea Trout Brown Trout	11 Feb. to 31 Oct. 1 May to 30 Sep.	J.J. Watson, 44 Market Place, Inverurie. Tel: (01467) 620321.	No worm until 1 Apr to 1 May. No shrimp or prawn. Reductions for school children and OAPs. Booking advised.
	Inverurie (Keithhall & Ardmurdo Beats)	Salmon Sea Trout Brown Trout	11 Feb. to 31 Oct. 1 May to 30 Sep.	J.J. Watson, 44 Market Place, Inverurie. Tel: (01467) 620321.	No worm 1 Apr to 1 May. No shrimp or prawn. Reductions for school children and OAPs. Booking advised. Saturday - members only.

Water	Location	Species	Season	Permit available from	Other information
Dulnain (Map III D3)	Grantown-on-Spey	Salmon Sea Trout Brown Trout	11 Feb. to 30 Sep. 15 Mar. to 30 Sep.	Strathspey Angling Assoc., Mortimer's, 3 High Street, Grantown-on-Spey. Tel: (01479) 872684.	Visitors resident in Grantown, Cromdale, Duthill, Carrbridge, Dulnain Bridge and Nethy Bridge areas. 12 miles of river.
Findhorn (Broom of Moy Beat) (Map III D2)	Forres	Salmon Sea Trout	11 Feb. to 30 Sep.	J. Mitchell, Springbank, Findhorn, Forres. Tel: (01309) 690406.	Popular flies: all shrimp. Stoats Tail, Dunkeld, Munro Killer. Spinning or worming allowed. Let by the week. Some day rods in early part of season.
Gairn	Nr. Ballater	Brown Trout	15 Mar. to 20 Sep.	Ballatet Angling Association. Countrywear, Bridge Street, Ballater.	Fly fishing only.
Glen of Rothes	By Elgin	Rainbow Brook Brown Trout	All year (Except browns)	Glen of Rothes Trout Fishery, Glen of Rothes, Rothes, Moray AB38 7AG. Tel: (01340) 831888.	Average weight of is 2lb. Lures conventional, wet flies, dry flies, advice available on site. Additional loch for bait fishing. Bank fishing only.
Isla	Huntly	Salmon Sea Trout Brown Trout	11 Feb. to 31 Oct. 1 Apr. to 6 Oct.	Clerk of Fishings, Huntly Fishings Committee, Murdoch, McMath & Mitchell, 27/29 Duke Street, Huntly. Tel: (01466) 792291.	Permit covers Isla, Deveron and Bogie.
Muckle Burn	By Forres	Salmon Sea Trout	11 Feb. to 30 Sep.	I. Grant, Tackle Shop, 97D High Street, Forres. Tel: (01309) 672936.	Reductions for juniors.
Spey (Map III D3)	Aberlour	Salmon Sea Trout Brown Trout	11 Feb. to 30 Sep.	J.A.J. Munro, 93–95 High Street, Aberlour. Tel: Aberlour 871428.	3 tickets per hotel (Aberlour, Lour & Dowans or 6 day tickets, first come first served). One fish above bridge (9am–5pm), one fish below bridge (9am–midnight), other fish sold for club funds. No day tickets on Saturdays or local holidays.
	Ballindalloch	Salmon Sea trout	11 Feb. to 30 Sept.	Estates Office, Ballindalloch, Banff-shire AB37 9AX. Tel: (01807) 500205.	Fly fishing only.
	Grantown-on-Spey	Salmon Sea Trout Brown Trout	11 Feb. to 30 Sep. 15 Mar. to 30 Sep.	Strathspey Estate Office, Old Spey Bridge Road, Grantown -on-Spey. Moray PH26 3NQ. Tel: (01479) 872529.	7 miles both banks. No prawn. No Sunday fishing. Visitors must reside in Grantown, Cromdale, Duthill, Carrbridge, Dulnain Bridge or Nethy Bridge.
	Nethy Bridge Boat of Garten	Salmon Sea Trout Brown Trout	11 Feb. to 30 Sep.	Abernethy Angling Improvement Assoc., Boat of Garten. Allen's, Deshar Road, Boat of Garten. Tel: (01479) 831372.	6.25 miles both banks. No Sunday fishing. Visitors should reside in Boat of Garten, Nethy Bridge, Carrbridge or Dulnain Bridge. No shrimp or prawn allowed.
	Boat of Garten	Salmon Sea Trout Brown Trout	11 Feb. to 30 Sep. 15 Mar. to 30 Sep.	Allen's, Deshar Road, Boat of Garten. Tel: (01479) 831372.	

Water	Location	Species	Season	Permit available from	Other information
		Salmon Sea Trout	11 Feb. to 30 Sep.	Strathspey Estate Office, Old Spey Bridge Road, Grantown -on-Spey. Moray PH26 3NQ. Tel: (01479) 872529.	No live bait. Fly only from May 1.
	Aviemore	Salmon Sea Trout Brown Trout	11 Feb to 30 Sept.	Rothiemurchus Estate, Inverdruie, Aviemore PH22 1QH. Tel: (01479) 810703. R.J. Campbell, Kinrana, Aviemore. Tel: (01479) 811292. The Rowan Tree Restaurant & Guesthouse. Tel: (01479) 810207.	Beats on River Spey.
		Salmon Sea Trout Brown Trout	11 Feb. to 30 Sep.	Abernethy Angling Improvement Assoc., Speyside Sports, 64 Grampian Road, Aviemore. Tel: (01479) 810656.	Day tickets & weekly tickets available. No Sunday fishing.
	Kincraig	Brown Trout Salmon Sea Trout	11 Feb. to 30 Sep.	Alvie Estate Office, Kincraig, by Kingussie. Tel: (01540) 651255/651249. Dalraddy Caravan Park, by Aviemore. Tel: (01479) 810330.	Fly fishing or spinning.
Ugie (Map III G1)	Peterhead	Salmon Sea Trout Brown Trout	11 Feb. to 31 Oct.	Dicks Sports, 54 Broad Street, Fraserburgh. Tel: (01346) 514120. Robertson Sports, 1–3 Kirk Street, Peterhead AB4 6RT. Tel: (01779) 472584.	Bag limit 4 fish per day. Fly, spinning or worm entire season. No shrimps, prawns or illegal baits.
Ury	Inverurie	Salmon Sea Trout Brown Trout	11 Feb. to 31 Oct. 1 May to 30 Sep.	J.J. Watson, 44 Market Place, Inverurie AB5 3XN. Tel: (01467) 620321.	No worm 1 Apr to 1 May. No natural minnow. No shrimp or prawn. Reductions for school children and OAPs. Sunday fishing – trout only.
Ythan (Map III G2)	(Estuary) Newburgh	Salmon Sea Trout	11 Feb. to 31 Oct.	The Ythan Fishery, Mrs. Forbes, 3 Lea Cottages, Newburgh, Ellon, Aberdeenshire AB41 0BN. Tel: (01358) 789297.	Limited fishing available. Details from Mrs. Forbes.
	Fyvie	Salmon Sea Trout	11 Feb. to 31 Oct.	Fyvie Angling Assoc., Sec. J.D. Pirie, Prenton South Road, Old Meldrum AB51 0AB. Tel: (01651) 872229.	No shrimps or prawns. No worming May to August.

LOCHS & RESERVOIRS

Water	Location	Species	Season	Permit available from	Other information
Aboyne Loch	Aboyne	Pike Perch		The Warden, Aboyne Loch, Holiday Park. Tel: (01339) 886244.	Fishing parties restricted on Sat. and Sun.
Loch Alvie	Aviemore	Brown Trout Pike	15 Mar. to 6 Oct. All year	Alvie Estate Office, Kincraig,Kingussie. Tel: (01540) 651255/651249. Dalraddy Caravan Park, by Aviemore. Tel: (01479) 810330.	1 boat. Fly fishing or spinning only.
Avielochan	Aviemore	Rainbow/ Brown Trout Wild Brown Trout Rainbow Trout	1 Apr. to 30 Sep.	Mrs. MacDonald, Avielochan, Aviemore. Tel: (01479) 810847. Allen's, Deshar Road, Boat of Garten. Tel: (01479) 831372. Speyside Sports, Aviemore. Tel: (01479) 810656.	Boat available. Fly fishing only. Sunday fishing 9am–5pm, 5pm–10pm. Fly fishing only. Stocked rainbow trout up to 7lbs.

Water	Location	Species	Season	Permit available from	Other information
Loch of Blairs	Forres	Brown/ Rainbow Trout	30 Mar. to 30 Sep.	I. Grant, Tackle Shop, 97D High Street, Forres. Tel: (01309) 672936.	Average weight of fish caught: 1 lb 8 oz. Popular flies: lures, conventional wet flies, dry flies. Two sessions. Boat fishing. Sunday fishing. 3 boats available.
Brucklay Fishery	Maud	Rainbow Trout	1 Apr. to 30 Sep.	Brucklay Estate Office, Shevado, Maud AB42 8QN. Tel: (01771) 613263.	6 acre loch with bank and boat fishing. Average weight of fish caught: 2 lbs 8 oz. Fly fishing only.
Crimon-mogate Loch	Fraserburgh	Brown/ Rainbow Trout	All year	Crimonmogate, Lonmay, Fraserburgh. Tel: (01374) 224492.	Average weight of fish caught: 2 lbs 8 oz. Fly and lure fishing.
Loch Dallas	Boat of Garten	Brown/ Rainbow Trout	1 Apr. to 30 Sep.	Mortimer's, 3 High Street, Grantown-on-Spey. Tel: (01479) 872684. Allan's Store, Boat of Garten. Tel: (01479) 831372.	Fly fishing only (10am–6pm). Boat fishing. No Sunday fishing. 1 boat (2 rods).
Loch Ericht	Dalwhinnie	Brown Trout	15 Mar. to 6 Oct.	Badenoch Angling Assoc., Loch Ericht Hotel, Dalwhinnie. Tel: (01528) 522257.	Bank fishing only.
Glenlatterach Reservoir	By Elgin	Stocked Brown Trout	1 May. to 30 Sep.	.The Warden, Millbuies Lochs, Longmorn, Elgin. Tel: (01343) 860234.	Fly fishing only. 3 boats available. Bank fishing.
Lochindorb	Between Forres & Grantown	Brown Trout	1 May to 30 Sep.	Frank & Wendy Anderson, Underkeeper's Cottage, Lochindorb, Grantown-on-Spey, Tel: (01309) 651270.	One boat. Boat fishing only. Fly fishing or spinning.
Loch Insh	Kincraig	Salmon Sea Trout Brown Trout Char Pike	11 Feb. to 30 Sep. 15 Mar. to 6 Oct. All year	Alvie Estate Office, Kincraig, Kingussie. Tel: (01540) 651255/651249. Dalraddy Caravan Park, by Aviemore. Tel: (01479) 810330.	Free fishing boat from bank. Boats available during the season.
		Salmon Sea Trout Brown Trout Arctic Char Pike	May to Sep.	Loch Insh Watersports, Boat House, Kincraig. Tel: (01540) 651272.	Boats are available.
Loch Laggan	Laggan	Brown Trout	15 Mar. to 6 Oct.	Loch Ericht Hotel, Dalwhinnie. Tel: (01528) 522257.	Bank fishing.
Loch of Logie	Fraserburgh	Brown/ Rainbow Trout	All year	Crimonmogate, Lonmay, Fraserburgh. Tel: (01374) 224492.	Average weight of trout caught: 2 lbs 8 oz. Fly and lure fishing.
Loch McLeod	Nr. Grantown on-Spey	Stocked Rainbow Trout	1 Apr. to 30 Sep.	Strathspey Estate Office, Old Spey Bridge Road, Grantown -on-Spey. Moray PH26 3NQ. Tel: (01479) 872529.	Bank fishing only. No fishing on Sundays. 2 rods per day. Fly fishing only (10am–6pm).
Millbuies Loch	By Elgin	Brown/ Rainbow Trout	Late Mar. to mid-Oct.	The Warden, Millbuies Loch, Longmorn, Elgin. Tel: (01343) 860234.	Boat fishing. Fly fishing only. Four boats available.

Water	Location	Species	Season	Permit available from	Other information
Loch Mor	Dulnain Bridge	Brown/ Rainbow Trout	Apr. to Sep.	Mortimer's, 3 High Street, Grantown-on-Spey. Tel: (01479) 872684.	Fly fishing only.
Loch Na Bo	Lhanbryde	Brown Trout	1 Apr. to 30 Sep.	D. Kinloch, Gardener's Cottage, Loch-na-Bo, Lhanbryde, Elgin. Tel: (01343) 842214.	Fly fishing only.
Pitfour Lake	Nr. Peterhead	Rainbow/ Brown Trout Tench, Carp Perch	All year (except for Browns)	Saplinbrae House Hotel, Old Deer, nr. Peterhead. Tel: (01771) 623515. Pitfour Sporting Estates, Pitfour, Old deer nr. Mintlow, Peterhead. Tel: (01771) 624448.	7 boats, bank fishing, fly only for trout. No spinning. No dogs.
Rothie-murchus Estate (Fish farm lochs)	Aviemore	Rainbow Trout Brown Trout Pike	Check with manager, Aviemore.	Rothiemurchus Fishery, by Aviemore PH22 1 QH. Tel: (01479) 810703.	Stocked rainbow trout loch. Open all year except when frozen. Additional private lochs available.
Loch Saugh	Fettercairn/ Drumtochty Glen	Brown Trout	15 Mar. to 6 Oct.	Brechin Angling Club, W.G. Balfour, 9 Cookston Crescent, Brechin DD9 6BP. Tel: (01356) 622753. Ramsay Arms Hotel, Fettercairn. Tel: (01561) 340334. Drumtochty Arms Hotel, Auchenblae AB30 1XR. Tel: (01561) 320210. David Rollston-Smith, Fishing Tackle, Guns & Sport, 180 High Street, Montrose. Tel: (01674) 672692. G. Carroll Angling Supplies, Brechin.	Fly fishing only from bank.
Glen Tanar Loch	Glen Tanar	Rainbow Trout	Mar. to Dec.	Glen Tanar Estate, Brooks House, Glen Tanar, Aboyne AB34 5EU. Tel: (013398) 86451. Fax: (013398) 86047.	3 boats. Boat fishing by day or evening.
Loch Vaa	Aviemore	Brown/ Rainbow Trout	1 Apr. to 30 Sep.	Mortimer's, 3 High Street, Grantown-on-Spey. Tel: (01479) 872684.	Boat fishing only. 2 boats - 2 rods per boat. Fly fishing only. No Sunday fishing. Fishing 10am–6pm only.
Loch Vrotichan	Cairnwell	Brown Trout	18 Mar. to 11 Aug.	Ballater Angling Association, 10 Golf Road, Ballater. Tel: (01339)7 55365.	Fly fishing only.

Highlands of Scotland Tourist Board
Peffery House,
Strathpeffer,
Ross-shire IV14 9HA.
Tel: (01997) 421160.
Fax: (01997) 421168.
Email: info@host.co.uk.
Web site: http://www.host.co.uk.

River Purification Board
Highland River Purification Board
Graesser House,
Fodderty Way,
Dingwall.
Tel: (01349) 62021.

RIVERS

Water	Location	Species	Season	Permit available from	Other information
Brogaig	North Skye	Sea Trout Brown Trout	1 Mar. to 31 Oct.	Jansport, Wentworth Street, Portree, Skye. Tel: (01478) 612559.	
Croe (Map 11C5)		Salmon Brown Trout	1 Mar. to 30 Sep.	National Trust for Scotland, Morvich Farm, Inerinate, by Kyle. Tel: (01559) 511231.	Fly fishing only.
Farrar (Map 11E4)	Struy	Salmon Brown Trout	Jun. to 15 Oct. 15 Mar. to 30 Sep.	Culligran Estate, Glen Strathfarrar, Struy, nr. Beauly IV4 7JX. Tel/Fax: (01463) 761285.	Fly fishing only.
Garry (upper) (Map 11D6)	Garry Gualach to Poulary Bridge	Salmon Sea Trout Brown Trout	15 Mar. to 14 Oct. 15 Mar. to 6 Oct.	Mr. Isaacson, Garry Gualach Country Holidays, Invergarry.	Fly only 1 May to end of season.
Glass (map 11E4)	Struy	Salmon Brown Trout	Jun. to 15 Oct. 15 Mar. to 30 Sep.	Culligran Estate, Glen Strathfarrar, Struy, nr. Beauly IV4 7JX. Tel/Fax: (01463) 761285.	Fly fishing only.
Kilmaluag River	North Skye	Salmon Sea Trout	1 Mar. to 31 Oct.	Jansport, Wentworth Street, Portree, Skye. Tel: (01478) 612559.	
Lealt	North Skye	Salmon Sea Trout Brown Trout	1 Mar. to 31 Oct.	Jansport, Wentworth Street, Portree, Skye. Tel: (01478) 612559.	Fly only. Short (approx. 5 miles) spate river.

Water	Location	Species	Season	Permit available from	Other information
Moidart (Map 11B7)	West of Fort William	Salmon Sea Trout	11 Feb. to 31 Oct.	Mrs. N. Stewart, Kinlochmoidart House, Kinlochmoidart, nr. Fort William.	Fly and spinning only.
Moriston	Glenmoriston Estuary beat	Salmon	15 Jan. to 15 Oct.	Vincent Tait, Head Gamekeeper. Tel: (01320) 351219.	Fly and spinning only.
	Dundreggan Beat	Salmon Brown Trout	1 May to end Sep. Mar. to Sep.	Vincent Tait, Head Gamekeeper. Tel: (01320) 351219.	
Nairn (Map 111 F4)	Nairn/ Culloden Moor	Salmon Sea Trout	11 Feb. to 7 Oct.	Nairn Angling Association, P. Fraser, High Street, Nairn. Tel: (01667) 453038. Clava Lodge Holiday Homes, Culloden Moor, Inverness IV1 2EJ. Tel: (01463) 790228.	
Ness (Map 11 F4)	Inverness Town Water	Salmon Sea Trout	15 Jan. to 15 Oct.	Graham's Tackle, 37 Castle Street, Inverness. Tel: (01463) 233178.	3 miles of river immediately above the tide.
Nevis (Map II D7)	Fort William	Salmon Sea Trout		Rod & Gun Shop, 18 High Street, Fort William. Tel: (01397) 702656.	Spinning permitted in afternoon only.
Polloch	Strontian	Salmon Sea Trout	1 May. to 31 Oct.	Post Office, Strontian.	Average weight of fish caught: Salmon 6 lbs, Sea Trout 1 lb, Brown Trout 1 lb. Popular flies: dark flies. Worm and spinning allowed. No prawn fishing.
Sligachen	South Skye	Salmon Sea Trout	1 Mar. to 31 Oct.	Jansport, Wentworth Street, Portree, Skye. Tel: (01478) 612559.	
Snizort	Skye	Salmon Sea Trout Brown Trout	1 Jul. to 15 Oct.	Skeabost House Hotel, Skeabost, Isle of Skye. Tel: (01470) 532202.	Discounts for residents.
Spean (Map II E7)	Nr. Fort William	Salmon Sea Trout Brown Trout	15 Jan. to 15 Oct.	Rod & Gun Shop, 18 High Street, Fort William. Tel: (01397) 702656.	Major tributary of the Lochy.
Staffin	North Skye	Salmon Sea Trout	1 Mar. to 31 Oct.	Jansport, Wentworth Street, Portree, Skye. Tel: (01478) 612559.	
Strontian	Strontian	Salmon Sea Trout Brown Trout	1 May. to 31 Oct.	Post Office, Strontian.	Average weight of fish caught: Salmon 6 lbs to 10 lbs, Sea Trout 1 lb. Popular flies: Blue Charm, Hair Fly. Worm (if river in spate) and spinning. No prawns.

LOCHS & RESERVOIRS

Water	Location	Species	Season	Permit available from	Other information
Ardtornish Estate Waters	Morvern	Salmon Sea Trout Brown Trout	Apr. to Oct.	Ardtornish Estate Office, Morvern, by Oban, Argyll. Tel: (01967) 42128	Six boats for hire.
Loch Arkaig	Fort William	Sea Trout Brown Trout Salmon (occasional) Pike	Mar. to Oct.	Lochiel Estate Fishings, 33 High Street, Fort William. Tel: (01397) 702433.Rod & Gun Shop, 18 High Street,Fort William. Tel: (01397) 702656. Mrs Yates, No. 2 Clunes, Achnacarry. Tel: (01397) 712719.	

Water	Location	Species	Season	Permit available from	Other information
Loch Dochfour	Inverness	Brown Trout	15 Mar. to 6 Oct.	Dochfour Estate Office, Dochgarroch, by Inverness. Tel: (01463) 861218. Dochgarrod Shop & P.O.	No Sunday fishing. Bank fishing only. Fly only.
Loch Doilet	Strontian	Salmon Sea Trout Brown Trout	1 May to 31 Oct.	General Store, Strontian. Post Office, Strontian.	Average weight of fish caught: Salmon 6 lbs, Sea Trout 1 lb. Popular flies: black flies. Worm and spinning available. No prawns. Boats available from: Jim Bannerman, Tel: (01967) 402408 or (01967) 402412.
Glen-moris-ton Hill Lochs (21)	Glenmoriston	Brown Trout	May to Oct.	Vincent Tait (Gamekeeper), Levishie, Glenmoriston. Tel: (01320) 351219 (Eve.).	1 boat available.
Guisachan Hill Lochs	Tomich	Brown/ Rainbow Trout	Apr. to Sep.	Tomich Hotel, Tomich, by Beauly. Tel: (01456) 415399.	Fly fishing only. Brown trout, Rainbow Trout on 8 lochs.
Loch Inchlaggan & Loch Garry	Invergarry	Brown Trout Arctic Char	May to Sep.	Mr. P. Thomas, Ardochy Lodge, Glengarry, Invergarry PH35 4HR. Tel: (01809) 511232.	Boats available. Loch Inchlaggan fly only.
Loch Insh	Kincraig	Salmon Trout Arctic Char Pike	May to Sep.	Loch Insh Watersports, Boat House, Kincraig. Tel: (01540) 651272.	Boats are available. Bank and Boat fishing. Small children stock. Lochan with brown and rainbow trout. Ghillie available. Rods for hire. Tackle for sale.
Loch Lundrava	Nr. Fort William	Brown Trout	15 Apr. to 30 Sep.	Mrs. A. MacCallum, Lundavra Farm, Fort William. Tel: (01397) 702582.	Average weight of fish caught: 8 oz. Fly fishing only. 2 boats available. Bank fishing.
Loch Mealt	North Skye	Brown Trout Arctic Char	15 Mar. to 30 Sep.	Jansport, Wentworth Street, Portree, Skye. Tel: (01478) 612559.	
Loch Morar (and hill lochs)	Morar	Salmon Sea Trout Brown Trout Arctic Char	15 Mar. to 6 Oct.	The Morar District Salmon Fishery Board, Superintendent, Viv de Fresnes. Tel: (01687) 462388.	Fly fishing only. Boat for hire. No bank fishing. Contact: Ewan M'Donald (01687) 462520
Loch Ness	Glenmoriston	Salmon Sea Trout		Vincent Tait (Gamekeeper), Levishie, Glenmoriston. Tel: (01320) 450279 (Eve.)	Fly fishing only. 4 boats. No bank fishing.
Loch Ruthven	Farr	Brown Trout	15 Mar. to 6 Oct.	J. Graham & Co., 37/39 Castle Street, Inverness. Tel: (01463) 233178.	1 boat available.
Loch Sheil	Glenfinnan	Salmon Sea Trout	Apr. to Oct.	The Prince's House, Glenfinnan. Tel: (01397) 722246.	Fly fishing only.
South Skye Fishings (various lochs)	South Skye	Sea Trout Brown Trout Arctic char	Apr. to Oct.	Hotel Eilean Iarmain at weekends. Tel: (01471) 833332.	4 boats available with outboards. Advance bookings only. Fishing on approx. 20 lochs both wild and stocked, also two small spate rivers.

Water	Location	Species	Season	Permit available from	Other information
Storr Lochs (and hill lochs)	North Skye	Brown Trout	1 Apr. to 30 Sep.	Jansport, Wentworth Street, Portree, Skye. Tel: (01478) 612559.	Further information: Sec., Portree Angling Assoc., Hillcroft, Treaslane, by Portree.
White-bridge Lochs (Knockie, Bran & Killin)	Whitebridge	Brown Trout	Mar. to Oct.	Whitebridge Hotel, Stratherrick, Gorthleck, Inverness-shire. Tel: (01456) 486226.	Boats available. Fly fishing only.

Highlands of Scotland Tourist Board
Peffery House,
Strathpeffer,
Ross-shire IV14 9HA.
Tel: (01997) 421160.
Fax: (01997) 421168.
Email: info@host.co.uk.
Web site: http://www.host.co.uk.

Sutherland Tourist Board
Area Tourist Officer,
Tourist Information Centre,
The Square,
Dornoch,
Sutherland IV25 3SD.
Tel: (01862) 810400.

Ross and Cromarty Tourist Board
Area Tourist Officer,
Information Centre,
North Kessock,
Black Isle, Ross-shire IV5 1XB.
Tel: (01463) 730505.

Scottish Purification Agency (SEPA)
Graesser House,
Fodderty Way,
Dingwall IV15 9XB.
Tel: (01349) 862021.

RIVERS

Water	Location	Species	Season	Permit available from	Other information
Alness (Map I D5)	Alness	Salmon Sea Trout	15 May to 16 Oct.	Novar Estates, Estate Office, Evanton, Ross-shire. Tel: (01349) 830208.	Fly fishing only. 6 beats on rotation. 4 rods per beat.
Beauly (Map II E4)	Muir of Ord	Salmon Sea Trout Brown Trout	May to Sep.	Ord House Hotel, Muir of Ord. Tel: (01463) 870492.	River and loch fishing available.
Blackwater	Strathpeffer	Salmon Sea Trout	Apr. to end Sep.		Further info. from: Craigdarroch Lodge Hotel, Contin, by Strathpeffer. Tel: (01997) 421265.
Borgie (Map I D2)	Tongue	Salmon	12 Jan. to 30 Sep.	Borgie Lodge Hotel, Skerray, Tongue, Sutherland. Tel/Fax: (01641) 521332.	Fly fishing only. Average weight 8lbs. 3 rotating beats of 2 rods. Day ticket water for 3 rods and tackle hire.
Brora (Lower) (Map I E4)	Brora	Salmon Sea Trout	1 Feb. to 15 Oct.	Mr. & Mrs. Hammond, Sciberscross Lodge, Strath Brora, Rogart. Tel: (01408) 641246.	Popular flies: Orange, black, red Waddingtons, Willie Gunn.
Carron (Map II C4)	Various beats upstream from Ardgay	Salmon Sea Trout	11 Jan. to 30 Sep.	Finlayson Hughes, 29 Barossa Place, Perth PH1 5EP. Tel: (01738) 630926.	Fly only. Finlayson Hughes handle fishing on five subst-antial and productive beats.
Cassley (Map I C4)	Glencassley Water	Salmon Sea Trout	May to 30 Sep.	Bell Ingram, Bonar Bridge, Sutherland IV24 3EA. Tel: (01863) 766683.	Fly only. Approx. 9 miles of the upper river (left bank only).
	Glenrossal Beat	Salmon Sea Trout	11 Jan. to 30 Sep.	Glenrossal Estate, Rosehall, Sutherland IV27 4BG. Tel: (01549) 84203.	Fly only. 2.5 miles of left bank of the lower river.

Water	Location	Species	Season	Permit available from	Other information
Conon (Map II E3)	Rosehall	Salmon Sea Trout	11 Jan. to 30 Sep.	Achness Hotel, Rosehall, Sutherland IV27 4BD. Tel: (01549) 84239.	Fly only. Over a mile of very productive double bank fishing.
	Upper Cassley Beats 1 & 2	Salmon Sea Trout	May to 30 Sep.	Bell Ingram, Bonar Bridge, Sutherland IV24 3EA. Tel: (01863) 766683.	Fly only. 2 extensive beats (right bank only) of the upper river.
	Maryburgh	Brown/ Rainbow Trout Pike	15 Mar. to 6 Oct.	Seaforth Highland Estate, Brahan, Dingwall. Tel: (01349) 861150.	Stocked pond. Loch fishing and river in the lower, middle and upper Conon. Fishing available in the stocked pond and loch all year round.
	Muir of Ord	Salmon Sea Trout Brown Trout	May to Sep.	Ord House Hotel, Muir of Ord. Tel: (01463) 870492.	River and loch fishing available.
	Strathpeffer	Salmon Brown Trout	1 Apr. to 30 Sep.		Further information from: Craigdarroch Lodge Hotel, Contin, by Strathpeffer. Tel: (01997) 421265.
	Dingwall	Salmon Sea Trout	25 Jan. to 30 Sep.	The Sports & Model Shop, High Street, Dingwall. Tel: (01349) 862346.	Popular flies: Greenwell's Glory, Peter Ross, Black Pennel. Fly fishing only. Thigh waders only.
Lower Conon	Contin	Salmon Sea Trout	26 Jan. to 30 Sep.	Dingwall & District A.C., c/o Sports & Model Shop, High Street, Dingwall. Tel: (01349) 862346.	Fly only. Waist waders only.
Doinard (Map I C2)	Durness	Salmon Sea Trout		Cape Wrath Hotel, Durness, Sutherland. Tel: (01971) 511274.	Please phone in advance. especially in high season.
Glass	Evanton	Brown Trout	15 Mar. to 6 Oct.	Novar Estates, Estate Office, Evanton, Ross-shire. Tel: (01349) 830208.	Fly fishing only.
Halladale (Map I E2)	Forsinard	Salmon	11 Jan. to 30 Sep.	Miss A. Imlach, The Strath Halladale Partnership, Bunahoun, Forsinard, Sutherland KW13 6YU. Tel/Fax: (01641) 571271.	Fly fishing only (spate river).
	Tongue	Salmon	11 Jan. to 30 Sep.	Borgie Lodge Hotel, Skerray, Tongue, Sutherland. Tel/Fax: (01641) 521332.	Fly fishing only. 4 rotating beats, 3 rods per beat. Tackle hire.
Helmsdale (Map I E3)	Helmsdale	Salmon Sea Trout	11 Jan. to 30 Sep.	Strathullie Crafts & Fishing Tackle, Dunrobin Street, Helmsdale KW8 6AH. Tel: (01431) 821343.	Association beat. Fly fishing only.
Kirkaig (Map I B4)	Lochinver	Salmon	1 May to 15 Oct.	Inver Lodge Hotel, Lochinver IV27 4LU. Tel: (01571) 844496.	
Oykel (Map I C4)	Sutherland	Salmon Sea Trout	End June to 30 Sep.	Inver Lodge Hotel, Lochinver IV27 4LU. Tel: (01571) 844496.	2 top beats only (3 miles).
Thurso (Map I F2)	Thurso/ Halkirk	Salmon Trout	11 Jan. to 5 Oct.	Thurso Fisheries Ltd., Estate Office, Thurso East, Thurso. Tel: (01847) 893134.	Fly fishing only. Twelve 2 rod beats in rotation.
Wester	By Wick	Salmon Sea Trout Brown Trout	1 Mar. to 31 Oct.	Mrs. G. Dunnet, Auckhorn Lyth, by Wick KW1 4UD. Tel: (01955) 631208. Hugo Ross Tackle Shop, 56 High Street, Wick. Tel/Fax: (01955) 604200.	

Water	Location	Species	Season	Permit available from	Other information
Wick (Map I G2)	Wick	Salmon Sea Trout Brown Trout	11 Feb. to 21 Oct.	Hugo Ross Tackle Shop, 56 High Street, Wick. Tel/Fax: (01955) 604200.	Fly/worm fishing. Spate river with good holding pools.

LOCHS

Water	Location	Species	Season	Permit available from	Other information
Loch A'chroisg	Achnasheen	Pike Perch Brown Trout	No close season	Ledgowan Lodge Hotel, Achnasheen. Tel: (01445) 720252.	Free to customers.
Loch a'Ghriama	Overscaig	Brown Trout	30 Apr. to 30 Sep.	Overscaig Lochside Hotel, Loch Shin, by Lairg IV27 4NY. Tel: (01549) 431203.	Boats available. No Sunday fishing.
Loch an Ruthair	By Kinbrace	Brown Trout	Apr. to 30 Sep.	Head Keeper, Achentoul Estate, Kinbrace. Tel: (01431) 831227.	Average weight of fish caught: 8 to 12 oz. Popular flies: Soldier Palmer, Black Pennel. Bait fishing and spinning allowed. 2 boats available.
Lochs Airigh Leathaid	By Westerdale, Halkirk	Brown Trout	Apr. to Sep.	Ulbster Arms Hotel, Halkirk. Tel: (01847) 831206.	Fly only. Average weight: 1 lb 2 oz.
Loch Ascaig	Helmsdale	Salmon Sea Trout Brown Trout	1 Jun. to 30 Sep. 15 Mar. to 6 Oct.	M. Wigan, Borrobol, Kinbrace KW11 6UB. Tel: (01431) 831264.	Popular flies: Loch Ordie, Soldier Palmer. Fly fishing only. 3 boats available.
Loch Badagyle	Nr. Achiltibuie	Sea Trout Brown Trout Arctic Char	1 Apr. to 30 Sep.	Polly Estates Ltd., Inverpolly, Ullapool IV26 2YB. Tel: (01854) 622452.	Fly fishing only. Boats with or without motors are available.
Loch Badanloch (& other hill lochs)	Kinbrace	Brown Trout	15 Mar. to 6 Oct.	Brian Lyall, Badanloch, Kinbrace, Sutherland. Tel: (01431) 831232.	Average weight of fish caught: 8 oz. 9 boats. Fly only. Sunday fishing. Private beat at top of River Helmsdale for 2 rods per day.
Loch Beannach	Lairg	Brown Trout	30 Apr. to 30 Sep.	Boat permits: R. Ross (Fishing Tackle), Main Street, Lairg IV27 4DB. Tel: (01549) 402239.	Average weight of fish caught: 1 lb. Popular flies: Kate McLaren, Loch Ordie. Strictly fly fishing only. Boats available from R. Ross.
Loch Bad na H-Achlaise (Green Loch)	Nr. Achiltibuie	Brown/Sea Trout	1 Apr. to 30 Sep.	Polly Estates Ltd., Inverpolly, Ullapool IV26 2YB. Tel: (01854) 622452.	Fly fishing only.
Loch Bad na h'Erba	Sciberscross	Wild Brown Trout	1 Apr. to 30th Sept.	Mr. & Mrs. Hammond, Sciberscross Lodge, Strath Brora, Rogart IV28 3YQ. Tel: (01408) 641246.	Average weight of fish caught: 12 oz.. Popular flies: Black Pennel, Ke-He, Loch Ordie, Dunkeld. Boats are available.
Black Loch	Nr. Achiltibuie	Brown Trout	1 Apr. to 30 Sep.	Polly Estates Ltd., Inverpolly, Ullapool IV26 2YB. Tel: (01854) 622452.	Fly fishing only. Boat available.

Water	Location	Species	Season	Permit available from	Other information
Borgie & Skerray Hill Lochs (Mapl D2)	Tongue	Brown Trout	15 Mar. to 6 Oct.	Borgie Lodge Hotel, Stkerray, Tongue, Sutherland. Tel/Fax: (01641) 521332.	8 - 10 ozs, fish up to 4lbs. Fly only. Bank and boat fishing.
Loch Borralan	Ledmore	Brown/ Rainbow Trout Arctic Char	15 Mar. to 6 Oct.	Te Alt Bar, The Altnacealalgach, Ledmore, by Lairg. Tel: (01854) 666220.	Any legal method permitted. Boat fishing.
		Brown Trout Arctic Char	1 Apr. to 30 Sep.	Ledmore Estate, Blarmhor, Elphin, by Lairg. Tel: (01854) 666207.	Baits: Any legal mathod permitted. Boats available with outboards.
Loch Borralie	Durness	Brown Trout	Apr. to end Sep.	Cape Wrath Hotel, Durness, Sutherland. Tel: (01971) 511274.	Limestone loch. Fly fishing only. Boats available. Please phone in advance, especially in high season.
Loch Broom (Map II D2)	By Ullapool	Salmon Sea Trout	Apr. to Oct.	Ullasport, West Argyle Street, Ullapool. Tel: (01854) 612621.	
Loch Brora	Brora	Salmon Sea Trout Brown Trout	Apr. to Oct.	Rob. Wilson Rods & Guns, Rosslyn Street, Brora. Tel: (01408) 621373.	Boats available. Fly only. Ghillies available.
		Salmon Sea Trout Brown Trout Char	1 May to 15 Oct.	Mr. & Mrs. Hammond, Sciberscross Lodge, Strath Brora, Rogart IV28 3YQ. Tel: (01408) 641246.	Popular flies: General Practitioner, Stoats Tail, Dunkeld. Boat available with outboard, if required.
Loch Cam	Ledmore	Brown Trout Arctic Char	1 Apr. to 30 Sept.	Ledmore Estate, Blarmhor, Elphin, By Lairg. Tel: (01854) 666207.	Any legal method permitted. Boats available with outboards. Bank fishing available.
Loch Caladail	Durness	Brown Trout	Apr. to end Sep.	Cape Wrath Hotel, Durness, Sutherland. Tel: (01971) 511274.	Limestone loch. Fly fishing only. Boats available. Please phone in advance, especially in high season.
Loch Calder	Thurso	Brown Trout	15 Mar. to 6 Oct.	Harper's Fishing Tackle, 57 High Street, Thurso. Tel: (01847) 893179. Fax: (01847) 893179.	Average weight of fish caught: 12 oz to 1 lb (fish up to 7 lbs). Popular flies: Bibio, Black Pennel, Kate McLaren. Spinning and bait fishing permitted, but fly fishing preferred. Boats available.
Cape Wrath & hill lochs (30-plus)	Durness	Brown Trout	Apr. to end Sep.	Cape Wrath Hotel, Durness, Sutherland. Tel: (01971) 511274	Please phone in advance, especially in high season.
Cherigal Loch	By Wester- dale Halkirk	Brown Trout	Apr. to Sep.	Ulbster Arms Hotel, Halkirk. Tel: (01847) 831206.	Fly only. Average weight: 12 oz. Average weight of fish caught: 8 oz. Popular flies: Loch Ordie, Black Spider, Black Pennel. Fly fishing only.
Col Loch Beg		Wild Brown Trout	1 Apr. to 15 Oct.	Garvault Hotel, by Kinbrace. Tel: (01431) 831224.	
Col Loch Mhor		Wild Brown Trout	1 Apr. to 15 Oct.	Garvault Hotel, by Kinbrace. Tel: (01431) 831224.	Average weight of fish caught: 8 oz. Popular flies: Loch Ordie, Black Spider, Black Pennel. Fly fishing only.

Water	Location	Species	Season	Permit available from	Other information
Loch Craggie	Tongue	Wild Brown Trout (occ. Salmon) Brown Trout	15 Mar. to 6 Oct. Mar. to Sep.	Ben Loyal Hotel, Tongue. Tel: (01847) 611216. Post Office, Tongue. Tel: (01847) 611201. Altnaharra Hotel, by Lairg IV27 4UE.	Fly fishing available. Boat available. Average weight of fish caught: 8 oz. to 1 lb. Popular flies: Pennel, Goats Toe, Zulu.
		Salmon Sea Trout Brown Trout	15 Mar. to 6 Oct.	Borgie Lodge Hotel, Skerray, Tongue, Sutherland. Tel/Fax: (01641) 521332.	8 oz. Fly, spinning, trolling. Dapping good for salmon. 1 boat with outboard and outriggers.
Loch Croispol	Durness	Brown Trout	Apr. to end Sep.	Cape Wrath Hotel, Durness, Sutherland. Tel: (01971) 511274.	Limestone loch. Fly fishing only. Boats available. Please phone in advance, especially in high season.
Loch Culag (and numerous other lochs)	Lochinver	Brown Trout	Mid-May to 6 Oct.	Inver Lodge Hotel, Lochinver, Sutherland. Tel: (01571) 844496.	7 lochs with boats. 2 lochs for residents of hotel only. (Check for details).
Loch Doir na H-Airb (Stac Loch)	Nr. Achiltibuie	Brown/Sea Trout	1 Apr. to 30 Sep.	Polly Estates Ltd., Inverpolly, Ullapool IV26 2YB. Tel: (01854) 622452.	Fly fishing only.
Dornoch & District A.C. (7 lochs)	Dornoch	Salmon Sea Trout Brown Trout	15 Mar. to 6 Oct.	Dornoch & District A.A., William A. McDonald, Castle Street, Dornoch. Tel: (01862) 810301.	No Sunday fishing. Fly fishing only. 7 boats available.
Dornoch Lochans	Dornoch	Rainbow Trout	All year	M. & B. MacGillivray, Davochfin, Dornoch IV25 3RW. Tel: (01862) 810600.	Open all year: 10am to dusk. Sundays: 2–6pm. 2 lochans fly only. 2 for bait (provided). Instruction and tackle available. Popular flies: Ace of Spades, Black Pennel, Nymphs, etc.
Lochan Dubh na H-Amaite	Sciberscross	Wild Brown Trout	1 Apr. to 30th Sept.	Mr. & Mrs. Hammond, Sciberscross Lodge, Strath Brora, Rogart IV28 3YQ. Tel: (01408) 641246.	Average weight of fish caught: 1 lb. Popular flies: Black Pennel, Ke-He, Loch Ordie, Dunkeld. Boat available.
Dubh-nan-Geodh	Westerdale Halkirk	Brown Trout	Apr. to Sep.	Ulbster Arms Hotel, Halkirk. Tel: (01847) 831206.	Fly only. Average weight of fish caught: 1 lb 10 oz.
Dunnet Head Loch	Dunnet Head (B855)	Brown Trout	May to Oct.	Dunnet Head Tearoom, Brough Village, Dunnet Head. Tel: (01847) 851774.	Loch well stocked. Fly from bank only. No Sunday fishing. Sea fishing from rocks.
Eileanach Loch	By Westerdale, Halkirk	Brown Trout	Apr. to Sep.	Ulbster Arms Hotel, Halkirk. Tel: (01847) 831206.	Fly only. Average weight: 9 oz.
Eun Loch	By Westerdale, Halkirk	Brown Trout	Apr. to Sep.	Ulbster Arms Hotel, Halkirk. Tel: (01847) 831206.	Fly only. Average weight: 1 lb 8 oz.
	Kyle of Tongue	Salmon Sea Trout Sea Bass	11 Feb. to 31 Oct.	Ben Loyal Hotel, Tongue. Tel: (01847) 611216. Post Office, Tongue. Tel: (01847) 611201.	No Sunday fishing. Bank fishing only.

Water	Location	Species	Season	Permit available from	Other information
Gainimh Loch	By Westerdale, Halkirk	Brown Trout	Apr. to Sep.	Ulbster Arms Hotel, Halkirk. Tel: (01847) 831206.	Fly only. Average weight: 7 oz.
Loch Ganneigh		Wild Brown Trout	1 Apr. to 15 Oct.	Garvault Hotel, by Kinbrace. Tel: (01431) 831224.	Average weight of fish caught: 8 oz. Popular flies: Loch Ordie, Black Spider, Black Pennel. Fly fishing only.
Loch Glascarnoch	Aultguish	Brown Trout Pike	Mar. to Sep. All year	Free Fishing.	
Loch Glass	Head of River Glass	Brown Trout	15 Mar. to 6 Oct.	Novar Estates, Estate Office, Evanton, Ross-shire. Tel: (01349) 830208.	Bank fishing only. Any legal method.
Golspie A.C. Waters (Lochs: Brora, Lundie, Horn, Buidhe)		Salmon Sea Trout Brown Trout	1 Apr. to 15 Oct.	Golspie A.C., Lindsay & Co., Main Street, Golspie. Tel: (01408) 633212.	Fly fishing only. Bank and boat fishing. No Sunday fishing.
Loch Heilan	Castletown	Brown Trout	May to Sep.	H.T. Pottinger, Greenland Mains, Castletown, Thurso. Tel: (01847) 821210.	Bank and boat fishing.
Loch Hempriggs	South of Wick	Brown Trout	14 Mar. to 14 Oct.	Thrumster Filling Station. Tel: (01955) 651252. Hugo Ross Fishing Tackle Shop, 56 High Street, Wick. Tel/Fax: (01955) 604200.	Average weight of fish caught: 12 oz to 1 lb.
Hill Lochs (32)	Around Assynt	Brown Trout	15 Mar. to 6 Oct.	Tourist Information Centre, Lochinver. Tel: (01571) 844330.	Mainly fly fishing. There are 6 lochs where spinning or bait can be used. Bank fishing only.
Loch Hope (Map I D2)	Nr. Tongue	Salmon Sea Trout	Mid-Apr. to Sep. Jun. to Sep.	Altnaharra Hotel, by Lairg IV27 4UE. Tel: (01549) 411222.	Average weight of fish caught: Salmon 8 lbs, Sea Trout 3 lbs. Popular flies: Salmon - Invicta, Pennel. Sea Trout - Peter Ross. Fly only. 6 boats are available.
Lochs Kernsary Tournaig Goose	Gairloch	Brown Trout	15 Mar. to 6 Oct.	National Trust for Scotland, Inverewe Visitor Centre, Poolewe, Ross-shire. Tel: (01445) 781229.	
Kyle of Tongue & local lochs	Tongue & Farr	Salmon Sea Trout Brown Trout		Tongue Stores & Post Office, Main Street, Tongue. Tel: (01847) 611201.	Sunday fishing for brown trout only. Boats available from: Ben Loyal Hotel, Tongue.
	Tongue	Salmon Sea Trout Sea Bass	11 Feb. to 31 Oct.	Borgie Lodge Hotel, Skerray, Tongue, Sutherland. Tel/Fax: (01641) 521332.	Tackle hire. Bank and boat fishing.
Leckmelm Hill Lochs	Ullapool	Brown Trout	May to Aug.	Leckmelm Holiday Cottages, Leckmelm, Ullapool. Tel: (01854) 612471. N. & D.Wynne, Navidale Estate, Helmsdale, Sutherland KW8 6JS. Tel: (01431) 821257.	Bank fishing only. No Sunday fishing.

Water	Location	Species	Season	Permit available from	Other information
Loch Loyal	Tongue	Salmon Sea Trout Wild Brown Trout Ferox	15 Mar. to 6 Oct.	Ben Loyal Hotel, Tongue. Tel: (01847) 611216. Post Office, Tongue. Tel: (01847) 611201.	Fly fishing only. Bank or boat fishing, spinning, worming and trolling.(2 boats available).
		Brown Trout	Mar. to Sep.	Altnaharra Hotel, by Lairg IV27 4UE. Tel: (01549) 411222.	Average weight of fish caught: 8 oz to 1 lb. Popular flies: Pennel, Goats Toe, Zulu. 1 boat available.
		Salmon Sea Trout Brown Trout Ferox	15 Mar. to 6 Oct.	Borgie Lodge Hotel, Skerray, Tongue, Sutherland. Tel/Fax: (01641) 521332.	8 oz. Fly, spinning, worming and trolling. Outriggers available one with outboard.
Loch Lurgainn	Nr. Achiltibuie	Brown/Sea Trout	1 Apr. to 30 Sep.	Polly Estates Ltd., Inverpolly, Ullapool IV26 2YB. Tel: (01854) 622452.	Fly fishing only. Boats with or without motors available.
Loch Maree	Wester Ross	Salmon Sea Trout Brown Trout	May to Oct.	Loch Maree Hotel, Achnasheen IV22 2HL. Tel: (01445) 760288.	Several boats available.
				Kinlochewe Holiday Chalets, c/o Castlegate House, Castlegate. Tel: (01445) 760256.	2 boats available. Fly only end June onwards.
Loch Meadie (Map I E1)	By Westerdale, Halkirk Tongue	Brown Trout	Apr. to Sep.	Ulbster Arms Hotel, Halkirk. Tel: (01847) 831206.	Fly only. Average weight: 10 oz.
		Brown Trout	Mar. to Sep.	Altnaharra Hotel, by Lairg IV27 4UE. Tel: (01549) 411222.	Average weight of fish caught: 8 oz to 1 lb. 1 boat available.
		Brown Trout	15 Mar. to 6 Oct.	Borgie Lodge Hotel, Skerray, Tongue, Sutherland. Tel/Fax: (01641) 521332.	8 oz. Fly only. Bank or boat fishing. Average basket 20 fish.
Loch Merkland	Overscaig	Brown Trout	30 Apr. to 30 Sep.	Overscaig Lochside Hotel, Loch Shin,by Lairg IV27 4NY. Tel: (01549) 431203.	Boat available. Fly only. No Sunday fishing.
Loch Migdale	By Bonar Bridge	Brown Trout	May to 31 Oct.	Dunroamin Hotel, Bonar Bridge, Sutherland. Tel: (01863) 766236.	1 boat available.
More Loch	By Westerdale, Halkirk	Brown Trout	Apr. to Sep.	Ulbster Arms Hotel, Halkirk. Tel: (01847) 831206.	Fly only. Average weight: 9 oz.
Loch Morie	Head of River Alness	Brown Trout	15 Mar. to 6 Oct.	Novar Estates, Estate Office, Evanton, Ross-shire. Tel: (01349) 830208.	Bank fishing only. Any legal method.
Loch na Dail (Polly Loch)	Nr. Achiltibuie	Brown/Sea Trout	1 Apr. to 30 Sep.	Polly Estates Ltd., Inverpolly, Ullapool IV26 2YB. Tel: (01854) 622452.	Fly fishing only. Boat available.
Loch nan Clar		Wild Brown Trout	1 Apr. to 15 Oct.	Garvault Hotel, by Kinbrace. Tel: (01431) 831224.	Average weight of fish caught: 8 oz. Fly fishing only.

Water	Location	Species	Season	Permit available from	Other information
Loch Naver		Salmon Brown Trout	Mar. to end Sep.	Altnaharra Hotel, by Lairg IV27 4UE. Tel: (01549) 411222.	Average weight of fish caught: Salmon 9 lbs, Brown Trout 8oz. 3 boats available. Sea Trout 1½ lbs.
Loch Palm		Wild Brown Trout	1 Apr. to 15 Oct.	Garvault Hotel, by Kinbrace. Tel: (01431) 831224.	Average weight of fish caught: 8 oz. Fly fishing only.
Loch Rangag	Latheron	Brown Trout	1 Apr. to 30 Sep.	John Anderson, Lochend Cottage, Latheron, Caithness. Tel: (01593) 741230.	Average weight of fish caught: 12 oz. Fly fishing only. Boats are available.
Rhiconich (50 lochs)	Nr. Kinlochbervie	Salmon Sea Trout Brown Trout	15 Feb. to 15 Oct.	Rhiconich Hotel, Kinlochbervie. Tel: (01971) 521224.	Fly fishing only. 7 boats available.
Loch Rhifail		Wild Brown Trout	1 Apr. to 15 Oct.	Garvault Hotel, by Kinbrace. Tel: (01431) 831224.	Average weight of fish caught: 8 oz. Fly fishing only.
Loch Rhimsdale		Wild Brown Trout	1 Apr. to 15 Oct.	Garvault Hotel, by Kinbrace. Tel: (01431) 831224.	Average weight of fish caught: 8 oz. Fly fishing only.
Loch Rossail		Wild Brown Trout	1 Apr. to 15 Oct.	Garvault Hotel, by Kinbrace. Tel: (01431) 831224.	Average weight of fish caught: 8 oz. Fly fishing only.
Loch St. Johns	Caithness	Wild Brown Trout	7 Apr. to 30 Sep.	Hugo Ross Fishing Tackle, 56 High Street, Wick. Tel/Fax: (01955) 604200.	Boats are available from Hugo Ross.
Sarclet Loch	Thrumster	Brown Trout	15 Mar. to 14 Oct.	Thrumster Filling Station. Tel: (01955) 651252. Hugo Ross, Fishing Tackle Specialists, 56 High Street, Wick. Tel/Fax: (01955) 604200.	Average weight of fish caught: 8 oz to 1 lb plus. Popular flies: Cocky Bundu, Soldier Palmer, Loch Ordie, Black Pennel.
Scourie Lochs	N.W. Sutherland	Salmon Sea Trout Brown Trout	1 May to 15 Oct.	Scourie Hotel, Scourie IV27 4SX. Tel: (01971) 502396.	Fly fishing only. Boats available.
Loch Sgeirach		Wild Brown Trout	1 Apr. to 15 Oct.	Garvault Hotel, by Kinbrace. Tel: (01431) 831224.	Average weight of fish caught: 8 oz. Fly fishing only.
Loch Shin (Map I D4)	Overscaig	Brown Trout Ferox Trout	30 Apr. to 30 Sep.	Overscaig Lochside Hotel, Loch Shin, by Lairg IV27 4NY. Tel: (01549) 431203.	Boats and outboards available.
	Lairg	Brown Trout Char	15 Apr. to 30 Sep.	Sutherland Sporting company, Main Street, Lairg IV27 4AR. Tel: (01549) 402229.	Average weight of fish caught: 7 oz. Popular flies: Kate McLaren. Spinning and worming permitted, fly preferred. Boats and engines available from boathouse from 1 June.
Loch Sionascaig (& 9 other lochs)	Ullapool	Brown Trout	1 Apr. to 30 Sep.	Polly Estate Office, Inverpolly, Ullapool IV26 2YB. Tel: (01854) 622452.	Boats and outboards available. No Sunday fishing. Fly fishing only, trawling for ferox permitted. Noted for large ferox.
Loch Skerray (Map I D2) Skyline Loch	Tongue	Brown Trout	15 Mar. to 6 Oct.	Borgie Lodge Hotel, Skerray, Tongue, Sutherland. Tel/Fax: (01641) 521332.	1 lb. Fly only. Boats available. Trout up to 4 lbs but hard to catch.

Water	Location	Species	Season	Permit available from	Other information
	Forsinard	Brown Trout	1 May to 30 Sep.	Forsinard Hotel, Forsinard, Sutherland. Tel: (01641) 571221.	Popular flies: Black Zulu, Silver Butcher.
Loch Slain (Map 1 D2)	Tongue	Salmon Sea Trout Brown Trout Char	15 Mar. to 6 Oct.	Borgie Lodge Hotel, Skerray, Tongue, Sutherland. Tel/Fax: (01641) 521332.	12 oz to 1 lb. Fly fishing only. 1 boat. No bank fishing.
Loch Stack	N.W. Sutherland	Salmon Sea Trout Brown Trout	1 May to 15 Oct.	Scourie Hotel, Scourie IV27 4SX. Tel: (01971) 502396.	Fly fishing only. Boats are available. Ghillie mandatory on loch.
Loch Staink	Tongue	Brown Trout	Mar. to Sep.	Altnaharra Hotel, by Lairg IV27 4UE. Tel: (01549) 411222.	Average weight of fish caught: 8 oz to 1 lb. 1 boat available.
Loch Stemster	Latheron	Brown Trout	1 Apr. to 30 Sep.	John Anderson, Lochend Cottage, Latheron, Caithness. Tel: (01593) 741230.	Average weight of fish caught: 12 oz. Fly fishing only. Boats are available.
Tarvie Lochs	By Contin	Brown/ Rainbow Trout		Sports & Model Shop, High Street, Dingwall. Tel: (01349) 862346.	Main loch: Fly fishing only. Boat available. Troutmaster water. Small loch only: coarse methods.
Loch Tarvie	By Strathpeffer	Brown Trout Rainbow Trout	15 Mar. to 6 Oct. All year	The Tarvie Lochs Trout Fishery, Tarvie, by Strathpeffer IV14 9EJ. Tel: (01997) 421250.	Average weight of fish caught: Rainbow 2 lbs 4 oz, Brown 1 lb 12 oz - Troutmaster water. Fly fishing only. Boat fishing only. Open all year, except Xmas. Tuition and tackle hire available.
Loch Uidh Tarraigean (Upper Polly Lochs)	By Achiltibuie	Brown Trout	1 Apr. to 30 Sep.	Polly Estates Ltd., Inverpolly, Ullapool IV26 2YB. Tel: (01854) 622452.	Fly fishing only.
Loch Tofingall	Caithness	Wild Brown Trout	1 May to 30 Sept.	Hugo Ross, Fishing Tackle Specialist, 56 High Street, Wick. Tel/Fax: (01955) 604200.	
Ulbster Estate Lochs (9 hill lochs)	Halkirk	Brown Trout	15 Mar. to Sep.	Ulbster Arms Hotel, Halkirk, Caithness. Tel: (01847) 831206.	No Sunday fishing. Fly fishing only. 1 boat on each of 5 lochs.
Loch Urigill	Ledmore	Brown Trout Arctic Char	1 Apr. to 30 Sept.	Ledmore Estate, Blarmhor, Elphin, By Lairg. Tel: (01854) 666207.	Baits: Any legal mathod permit-ted. Boats available with outboards. Bank fishing available.
Loch Vegatie	Ledmore	Brown Trout Arctic Char	1 Apr. to 30 Sept.	Ledmore Estate, Blarmhor, Elphin by Lairg. Tel: (01854) 666207.	Any legal method permitted. Boats available with outboards. Bank Fishing available.
Loch Watenan	Ulbster	Brown Trout	1 Mar. to 30 Sep.	Mr. J. Swanson, Aspen Bank, Banks Road, Watten. Tel: (01955) 621208.	Fly fishing only. 1 boat available.
Loch Watten	Watten Village	Brown Trout	1 May to 30 Sep.	Hugo Ross Fishing Tackle, 56 High Street, Wick. Tel/Fax: (01955) 604200.	Boats for hire from tackle shop. Fish min. size 10". No Sunday fishing. Fly only.

Water	Location	Species	Season	Permit available from	Other information
		Brown Trout	1 May to 1 Oct.	J.A. Barnetson, Lynegar Farm, Watten. Tel: (01955) 621205/621308. Harpers Fishing Tackle, 57 High Street, Thurso. Tel/Fax: (01847) 893179.	Average weight of fish caught: 12 oz. 3 boats available. Boats for hire.
	(A882) Between Wick & Thurso	Stocked Brown Trout	1 May to 30 Sep.	John F. Swanson, Aspen Bank, Banks Lodge, Watten. Tel: (01955) 621326/621208.	Average weight of fish caught: 12 oz to 1 lb. Fly fishing only. 4 boats available.
Loch Wester	By Wick	Salmon Sea Trout Brown Trout	1 Mar. to 31 Oct.	Mrs. G. Dunnet, Auckhorn Lyth, by Wick KW1 4UD. Tel: (01955) 631208. Hugo Ross Fishing Tackle Specialists, 56 High Street, Wick. Tel/Fax: (01955) 604200.	Fly fishing only. Boats available 1 Jul. to 31 Oct.
Yarrows Loch	Thrumster	Brown Trout	15 Mar. to 14 Oct.	Thrumster Filling Station. Tel: (01955) 651252. Hugo Ross Fishing Tackle Specialists, 56 High Street, Wick. Tel/Fax: (01955) 604200.	Average weight of fish caught: 12 oz to 1 lb Boats are available – ask Thrumster Filling Station.

Area Tourist Boards
Western Isles Tourist Board
Area Tourist Officer,
Western Isles Tourist Board,
26 Cromwell Street,
Stornoway,
Isle of Lewis PA87 2XY.
Tel: (01851) 703088.

River Purification Authority
Western Isles Island Area
No formal board constituted.

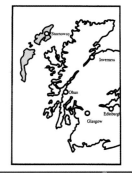

RIVERS

Water	Location	Species	Season	Permit available from	Other information
LEWIS River Blackwater	13 miles West of Stornoway	Salmon Sea Trout Brown Trout	1 Jul. to 14 Oct. 15 Mar. to 30 Sep.	The Manager, Garynahine Estate Office, Isle of Lewis. Tel: (01851) 621314.	Fly fishing only from bank.

LOCHS

Water	Location	Species	Season	Permit available from	Other information
LEWIS Beag-Na-Craoibhe	Stornoway	Brown Trout	15 Mar. to 6 Oct.	Sportsworld, 1–3 Francis Street, Stornoway. Tel: (01851) 705464.	Bank fishing only. 1 boat available.
Loch Bruiche Breivat	Nr. Stornoway	Brown Trout Arctic Char	15 Mar. to 30 Sep.	Estate Office, Scaliscro, Timsgarry, Isle of Lewis. Tel: (01851) 672325.	Popular flies: Brown Muddler, Invicta, Soldier Palmer. Boats are available.
Breugach	Stornoway	Brown Trout	15 Mar. to 6 Oct.	Sportsworld, 1–3 Francis Street, Stornoway. Tel: (01851) 705464.	Bank fishing. Two boats available.
Loch Coirigeroid	Nr. Stornoway	Brown Trout Arctic Char	15 Mar. to 30 Sep.	Estate Office, Scaliscro, Timsgarry, Isle of Lewis. Tel: (01851) 672325.	Popular flies: Brown Muddler, Invicta, Soldier Palmer. Boats are available.
Loch Fhir Mhaoil	Nr. Stornoway	Salmon Sea Trout Brown Trout	Jun. to 15 Oct.	Estate Office, Scaliscro, Timsgarry, Isle of Lewis. Tel: (01851) 672325.	Spinning and worm fishing permitted. Boats are available.
Keose (and other lochs in Keose Glebe fishings)	10 miles South of Stornoway	Brown Trout	15 Mar. to 30 Sep.	M. Morrison, 'Handa', 18 Keose Glebe, Lochs, Isle of Lewis HSQ 9JX. Tel: (01851) 830334. Sportsworld, 1–3 Francis Street, Stornoway. Tel: (01851) 705464. Tourist Office, 26 Cromwell Street, Stornoway. Tel: (01851) 703088.	Boat and equiptment available.
Loch Langavat	Nr. Stornoway	Salmon Sea Trout Brown Trout Arctic Char	15 Mar. to 15 Oct.	Estate Office, Scaliscro, Timsgarry, Isle of Lewis. Tel: (01851) 672325.	Spinning and worming permitted. Boats are available.

Water	Location	Species	Season	Permit available from	Other information
Loch MacLeod	Nr. Stornoway	Salmon Sea Trout Brown Trout	1 Jul. to 14 Oct. 15 Mar. to 30 Sep.	The Manager, Garynahine Estate Office, Isle of Lewis. Tel: (01851) 621314.	
Loch na Craoibhe	Achmore	Brown Trout	15 Mar. to 6 Oct.	Sportsworld, 1–3 Francis Street, Stornoway. Tel: (01851) 705464.	Bank fishing. 1 boat available.
Loch nam Falcag	Achmore	Brown Trout	15 Mar. to 6 Oct.	Sportsworld, 1–3 Francis Street, Stornoway. Tel: (01851) 705464.	Bank fishing. 1 boat available.
Loch nan Culaidhean	Nr. Stornoway	Salmon Sea Trout Brown Trout	1 Jul. to 14 Oct. 15 Mar. to 30 Sep.	The Manager, Garynahine Estate Office, Isle of Lewis. Tel: (01851) 621314.	
Lochs Sgibacleit, Shromois, Airigh Thormaid	Nr. Stornoway	Salmon Sea Trout Brown Trout	May to 30 Oct.	Estate Office, Scaliscro, Timsgarry, Isle of Lewis. Tel: (01851) 672325.	Spinning and worm fishing permitted. Boats are available.
Loch Tarbart	Nr. Stornoway	Salmon Sea Trout Brown Trout	1 Jul. to 14 Oct. 15 Mar. to 30 Sep.	The Manager, Garynahine Estate Office, Isle of Lewis. Tel: (01851) 621314.	
Loch Tungavat	Nr. Stornoway	Brown Trout	15 Mar. to 15 Oct.	Estate Office, Scaliscro, Timsgarry, Isle of Lewis. Tel: (01851) 672325.	Average weight of fish caught: 6 to 8 oz. Popular flies: Soldier Palmer, Butcher, Invicta. Boats are available.
Vatandip	Stornoway	Brown Trout	15 Mar. to 6 Oct.	Sportsworld, 1–3 Francis Street, Stornoway. Tel: (01851) 705464.	Bank fishing. 1 boat available.
BEN-BECULA Loch Eilean Iain	Benbecula	Brown Trout	Mar. to Sep.	South Uist Estates Ltd., Estate Office, South Uist.	Average weight of fish caught: 1 to 3 lbs. Popular flies: Soldier Palmer, Black Pennel, Ke-He. Worm. Fly. 1 boat available.
Loch Hermidale	Benbecula	Brown Trout		South Uist Estates Ltd., Estate Office, South Uist. Colin Campbell Sports, Benbecula. Tel: (01870) 602236. Bornish Stores, Bornish, South Uist. Tel: (01878) 710366.	Average weight of fish caught: 12 oz to 1 lb. Popular flies: Black Spider, Blue Zulu, Peter Ross, Invicta. 1 boat is available.
South Langavat (Heorovay-Olavat) and numerous other lochs	Benbecula	Brown Trout	15 Mar. to 30 Sep.	Bornish Stores. Tel: (01878) 710366. Colin Campbell Sports Ltd., Balivanich. Tel: (01870) 602236.	Fly only. Boats available.
Loch Olavat (East, West, North)	Benbecula	Brown/Sea Trout		South Uist Estates Ltd., Estate Office, South Uist.	Popular flies: Black Pennel, Invicta, Peter Ross, Grouse & Claret. 2 boats are available.

Water	Location	Species	Season	Permit available from	Other information
SOUTH UIST Loch Druim an Lasgair	South Uist	Brown Trout	15 Mar. to 6 Oct.	South Uist Estates Ltd., Estate Office, South Uist.	Average weight of fish caught: 12 oz to 1 lb. Popular flies: Soldier Palmer, Butchers, Black Spider.
East Loch Bee	South Uist	Brown Trout	Mar. to Sep.	South Uist Estates Ltd., Estate Office, South Uist. Colin Campbell Sports, Benbecula. Tel: (01870) 602236. Bornish Stores, Bornish, South Uist. Tel: (01878) 710366.	Average weight of fish caught: 12 oz to 1 lb 8 oz. Popular flies: Black Pennel, Ke-He, Bloody Butcher. 2 boats are available.
All hill and Machair lochs	South Uist	Salmon / Sea Trout / Brown Trout	Jul. to mid Oct. / Jul. to Oct. / Apr. to Sept.	Resident Manager, Lochboisdale Hotel, Lochboisdale, South Uist. Tel: (01878) 700332. South Uist Estates Ltd., Estate Office, South Uist.	14 boats available on lochs. Fly fishing only.
Loch Snaid	South Uist	Brown Trout		South Uist Estates Ltd., Estate Office, South Uist.	Average weight of fish caught: 12 oz to 1 lb. Popular flies: Grouse & Claret, Black Pennel, Black Spider, Butchers.
NORTH UIST Lochs & Sea Pools in North Uist		Salmon / Sea Trout / Brown Trout	25 Feb. to 15 Oct. / 15 Mar. to 31 Oct. / 15 Mar. to 30 Sep.	The Manager, Lochmaddy Hotel, North Uist. Tel: (01876) 500331.	Average weight of fish caught: Salmon 5 lbs 5 oz, Sea Trout 2 lbs 5 oz, Brown Trout 8 oz. Fly fishing only. No Sunday fishing. Boats are available on most lochs.
ISLE OF HARRIS Laxdale System	Isle of Harris	Salmon / Sea Trout / Brown Trout	15 Mar. to 15 Oct.	Tony Scherr, Borve Lodge Estates, Isle of Harris. Tel: (01859) 550202.	Fly fishing only. Permits cannot be reserved in advance.

NORTHERN ISLES - LOCHS

Area Tourist Boards
Orkney Tourist Board
Information Centre,
6 Broad Street,
Kirkwall,
Orkney KW15 1NX.
Tel: (01856) 872856.

Tourism
Shetland Islands Tourism
Area Tourist Officer,
Δ12
Shetland Islands Tourism,
Information Centre,
Market Cross, Lerwick,
Shetland ZE1 0LU.
Tel/Fax: (01595) 693434.

LOCHS

Water	Location	Species	Season	Permit available from	Other information
ORKNEY **Board-house**	Mainland	Brown Trout	15 Mar. to 6 Oct.	None required.	Boats available locally. All legal methods permitted. Anglers are recommended to join Orkney Trout Fishing Association, Kirkwall, who make facilities available to visitors.
Harray	Mainland	Brown Trout	15 Mar. to 6 Oct.	None required.	See Orkney for further information.
Hundland	Mainland	Brown Trout	15 Mar. to 6 Oct.	None required.	See Orkney for further information.
Kirbister	Mainland	Brown Trout	15 Mar. to 6 Oct.	None required.	See Orkney for further information.
Stenness	Mainland	Sea Trout	25 Feb. to 31 Oct.	None required.	See Orkney for further information.
		Brown Trout	15 Mar. to 6 Oct.		
Swannay	Mainland	Brown Trout	15 Mar. to 6 Oct.	None required.	See Orkney for further information.
SHETLAND	Shetland Islands	Sea Trout	25 Feb. to 31 Oct.	Rod and Line Tackle Shop, Harbour St., Lerwick. Tel: (01595) 695055.	Average weight of fish caught: Brown Trout 12oz. Popular flies: all dark flies, Black Pennel, Grouse &
		Brown Trout	15 Mar. to 6 Oct.	Shetland Islands Tourism, Market Cross, Lerwick. Tel: (01595) 693434.	Claret, Ke-He, Invicta, Blue Zulu (Sizes 10 & 12). Other baits: spinning where permitted with mepps spoons and toby lures. Boats available on 5 popular lochs:

Water	Location	Species	Season	Permit available from	Other information
Various	Yell Island	Brown Trout	15 Mar. to 6 Oct.	No permit required.	Average weight of fish caught: 8 oz to 8 lbs plus. Popular flies: Bibio, Silver Invicta. Spinning permitted.
Loch Benston	East Mainland	Brown Trout	15 Mar. to 6 Oct.	Rod and Line Tackle Shop, Harbour St., Lerwick. Tel/Fax: (01595) 695055.	Average weight of fish caught: 1 1/2 lb. Fly fishing only. A boat is available. Tackle for hire/sale in town. A good loch early in the season.
Loch Girlsta	East Mainland	Brown Trout Ferox Char	15 Mar. to 6 Oct.	Rod and Line Tackle Shop, Harbour St., Lerwick. Tel/Fax: (01595) 695055.	Average weight of fish caught: 1 to 2 lbs. Fly and spinning. The loch is at its best late in the season around July and August.
Huxter Loch	Isle of Whalsay	Brown Trout	15 Mar. to 6 Oct.	Brian J. Poleson, Sheardaal, Huxter, Symbister, Whalsay.	Average weight of fish caught: 12 oz. Fly fishing only. 1 boat available.
Ibister Loch	Isle of Whalsay	Brown Trout	15 Mar. to 6 Oct.	Brian J. Poleson, Sheardaal, Huxter, Symbister, Whalsay.	Average weight of fish caught: 10 to 12 oz. Fly fishing only. 1 boat available.
Loch Spiggie	South Mainland	Sea/ Brown/ Brook Trout	1 Apr. to 30 Sep.15 Mar. to 6 Oct.	Rod and Line Tackle Shop, Harbour St., Lerwick. Tel/Fax: (01595) 695055.	Strictly fly fishing only. A boat is available. Certain areas of the loch have restricted access.

FISHERIES FOR FEROX TROUT

The Highlands of Scotland have many lochs containing "ferox", a large predatory trout, much prized by anglers. Although in the past believed to be a genetically distinct species, ferox are now regarded as just one of many forms of the European brown trout (Salmo trutta L.), a highly variable species, capable of adopting a wide range of life history traits and morphological appearance. Some trout live entirely in headwater burns where their growth is stunted by lack of space and food availability, yet they are often highly coloured and well-marked little fish. Others migrate from natal spawning burns into rivers, or lochs, or even the sea, where food is more plentiful and growth opportunity much better, before returning to their birthplace to spawn. Trout found in the shallow water around the loch margins are often deep-bodied, with yellow flanks and red spots, while the ones that inhabit the open water tend to be more silvery, with many black and red spots. Fresh from the marine environment, sea trout are highly-silvered, but they darken with time spent in fresh water once they return from the sea to spawn. Ferox trout themselves vary greatly in appearance even in a single loch. Older specimens can be dark and highly-spotted fish, while younger, immature ones can be almost as silvery as seat trout. There seems to be no set rule. Living out their mysterious lives in the depths of large, cold, nutrient-poor lochs such as Rannoch, Tay, Awe, Arkaig and Quoich, ferox can reach the formidable size of a large salmon. In "The Art of Angling as practised in Scotland" (1835), Stoddart describes a Salmo ferox weighing 30 lbs caught in Loch Rannoch around 1800 by Baron Norton. In "The Anglers Companion" (1853), the same author tells us that a Major Cheape, also fishing in Rannoch, caught twenty-five of these fish on trolling tackle in 1849. Obviously a devotee of ferox fishing in Rannoch, the gallant Major caught one weighing 12 lbs there with a spoon bait in 1867, according to Hardie in "Ferox and Char" (1940). In his fascinating and highly recommended book "Ferox Trout and Arctic Charr" (1995), our former colleague Ron Greer argues strongly in support of the validity of a trout of 39.5lbs from Loch Awe which was caught by W. Muir in 1866 and was later disputed.

These were the days when the landed gentry with an interest in fishing had the ready services of thick-armed ghillies prepared to row them up and down the large and often stormy lochs for a sniff from a bottle of whisky. However, even these times must have been inflationary, for Colonel Thornton advises in "A Sporting Tour" (1896) that gentlemen should make a previous agreement before embarking on a loch with a Highlander, for "many of them have but one idea, which is that an Englishman is a walking mint, and they are never satisfied...". Not surprisingly, interest in ferox fishing gradually waned as it became more difficult to find suitably philanthropic ghillies and anglers had to resort to rowing for themselves.

Outboard motors have changed all that. On the large lochs with ferox, the modern equivalents of the Highland ghillies have fancy foreign names like Yamaha, Honda and Suzuki. Yet the principles of the sport of fishing for ferox remain essentially the same as before. You sit in a boat and troll artificial lures, or natural fish dead baits, around at various depths for hours and hours and generally catch nothing but

A Brown Trout caught, adipose clipped and released in Loch Rannoch in September 1994 weighing 3lb 8oz. (photo: A. Thorne)

some fresh air and scenery. Success can be very elusive and, for the weak-willed, life is simply too short. However, when your chance does arrive, what excitement! Suddenly the rod is alive and bucking all too easily will leap from the boat to plummet into the murky depths. With luck, you grasp it and are attached through a strong line and set of keenly sharpened hooks to a large, angry, double-figure trout, possibly even one of a record size. Often, of course, you are out of luck and the leviathan manages to shed the hooks and escape or, on capture, it turns out to be much smaller than expected, a mere few pounds in weight. No matter, it is still likely to be much larger than the normal size caught by fly-fishing in the same waters and who knows how big will be the next one!

The fact is that giant ferox like those caught by Major Cheape and perhaps even Mr Muir are not confined to history. Far from it; the current authenticated British rod-caught record wild brown trout was a ferox measuring 96.5cm in length and weighing 25lbs 6 oz, which was caught in Loch Awe as recently as 1997. Seven years earlier, an even larger, but damaged specimen, authentically measured at 100cm, was found dead below the Barrage at the outflow from the Loch. We can only speculate over its possible live weight. Ron Greer (1995) cites the dimensions of several monster brown trout, including one of 37.5lbs from a lake in northern Sweden which measured 105cm and a Norwegian specimen, weighing 39.6lbs and measuring 104cm. In our opinion and that of Ron Greer, a British rod-caught record in excess of 30lbs is a realistic prospect at Loch Awe and 20 pounders probably exist in several Scottish lochs.

That ferox still occur at all may be more a tribute to the resilience of Salmo trutta as a species than to human intervention. The natural desire is for people to want to escape from the frantic conurbations in the south to holiday homes, or retirement, in quiet, scenic surroundings. Thus, an ever-increasing proportion of the catchments of accessible Highland lochs is being developed for housing and tourist infrastructure and there is an inevitable build-up of water abstraction, low-grade pollution and boating activity. Ferox trout urgently require our protection, like their main prey the Ice-Age relic, deepwater fish, the Arctic charr, Salvelinus alpinus L.

4 lochs, stocked daily with prime hard fighting Rainbows. Rod and net hire, Casting and Fishing Tuition.
Beginners most welcome......................

Self Catering Cottages, Shop & Tearoom
Salmon Fishing also available.
Inverawe, Nr Taynuilt, Argyll. PA35 1HU
Tel: 01866 822446 Fax: 01866 822274

MORTON FISHERY
Mid-Calder, West Lothian
1999 SEASON

A well established Fishery of 22 acres which is proving to be increasingly popular with Anglers. We place great emphasis on the quality of the Rainbow Trout which are stocked at least twice weekly throughout the Season. 10 boats are available for all Sessions plus good Bank Fishing.

Booking and further information:
Tel: (01506) 882293

REGULATIONS
Absolutely no trawling.
All catch/release permits must be on barbless hooks.
No netting or misshandling of fish allowed.
Fly fishing only.

TACKLE &GUNS

GUNSMITHS & FISHING TACKLE SPECIALISTS
920 Pollokshaws Road, Glasgow G41 2ET

Permits for local fisheries and rivers
Experienced local knowledge
Abu, Daiwa, Mitchell, Shimano, Century
Live and frozen bait available
PHONE FOR DETAILS OF OUR SPECIAL OFFERS

ESTABLISHED OVER 20 YEARS
OUR PERSONAL ATTENTION &
KNOWLEDGE ARE THERE TO SHARE
Fully stocked GUN ROOM with accessories
for all country pursuits

COMPETITIVE PRICES-REPAIR SERVICE
Open Mon-Sat 10am-6pm
Telephone/Fax: 0141-632 2005
e-mail: tackle.guns@virgin.net

But how can this be achieved? We know a lot about the ecological requirements of brown trout in general, but very little about those of ferox. We don't know whether they have different preferences for depth and temperature during the diel and seasonal cycles, whether they are always solitary fish, or sometimes hunt in groups. More important, very little is known about their spawning sites and nothing about the numbers that live in individual lochs. Nor do we know for certain whether, as in Lough Melvin in Ireland, ferox are genetically distinct from other trout living in the same waters. There are still more questions than answers about these intriguing fish.

Working in conjunction with the Freshwater Fisheries Laboratory, the Ferox 85 Group of anglers is gradually accumulating some of the necessary information. Since 1994, twenty-nine of the large trout they have caught in Loch Rannoch have been released alive. Each

The same brown Trout recaptured in May 1998 weighing 14lb 4oz. Note the identical series of spots on the gill cover. (photo: J. Bailey)

was anaesthetised and carefully unhooked, photographed, measured, weighed and sexed, a sample of scales was removed for age determination, the adipose fin was removed for genetic analysis and then it was allowed to recover in clean water and released. Details of the date, time and place of capture, based on a grid system, were noted in a computer data-base. Since June 1995, twenty-two have also been tagged and this is already paying dividends as three adipose-clipped ferox were reported recaptured during 1998. One of the tagged fish was caught again only four weeks after first capture. Another one which was at liberty for three years showed evidence of having lost its tag. The remaining fish was adipose-clipped, but not tagged, in September 1994, at which time it weighted 3.5lbs. It was then recaptured by the Ferox 85 Group in May 1998, when it weighed 14.25lbs. This superb trout was identified in two ways. First, growth characteristics shown by its scales under low-power microscopy narrowed the search down to a small number of released fish. Secondly comparison of the archives of photographs of captured ferox showed a unique likeness between the September 1994 and May 1998 fish, based on an identical pattern of spots present on their gill covers (Plates 1 and 2). There was no doubting that these were photographs of the same male fish, separated by a time gap of nearly four years, during which it had grown in weight to nearly 11lbs.

These early results from the Ferox 85 Group study suggest that rod-caught ferox can be released with a reasonable expectation of their survival and substantial growth. Also, recaptures of tagged specimens are helping to validate age determinations by scale reading when the dates of release and capture are compared against the two sets of scales. On the other hand, only limited information can be gained about the movements of the ferox through conventional tagging. Two of the recaptures from Loch Rannoch were made several kilometres away from the places where they were originally caught, one having crossed the loch, but no information is available on their movements prior to these times. The use of radio emitting tags would allow tracking of the movements of individuals, although the locational information they provide is only precise in shallow water and becomes poorer with depth. Acoustic or ultrasonic tags would be better if the fish swim deep. Modern data-storage tags can even be used to log depth and water temperature details and can then be downloaded to a computer if the fish can be recovered by netting, which may be possible if their location in the loch is being tracked at the same time. Used in conjunction with modern acoustic survey techniques, this information could provide answers to some of the questions we ask about the daily lives of these fascinating creatures. Unfortunately, research like this is expensive and would also depend on a ready source of ferox for tagging. In the meantime, until suitable funding can be found, many anglers may wish to adopt the precautionary approach to ferox conservation by photographing and releasing alive any that they catch.

By Andy Walker and Alistair Thorne
Fisheries Research Services
The Freshwater Fisheries
Laboratory
Pitlochry, Perthshire.

Angling - Shetland. (Photo by Jim McLanaghan)

USEFUL ADDRESSES FOR VISITING FISHERMEN

Western Isles Fisheries Trust,
Contact: Mark Bilsby,
Creed Lodge,
Marybank, Stornoway.
Isle of Lewis HS2 9JN.
Tel/Fax: (01851) 701526.
Email: m.bilsby@btinternet.com

West Sutherland Fisheries Trust,
Contact: Dr Shona Marshall,
Gardener's Cottage,
Scourie by Lairg,
Sutherland IV27 4SX.
Tel/Fax: (01971) 502259.
Shona@WSFT.Demon.co.uk

Wester Ross Fisheries Trust,
Contact: Dr James Butler,
Rose Cottage,
Eilean Darach Estate,
by Garve,
Wester Ross IV23 2QN.
Wk Tel/Fax: (01854) 633349.
EMail: james@wrftrust.demon.co.uk

Lochaber & District Fisheries Trust,
Contact: Dr. Jon Watt,
Arieniskill Cottage,
Lochailort,
Inverness-shire PH38 4LZ.
Tel/Fax: (01687) 470350.
EMail:ldftrust@zetnet.co.uk

Awe Fisheries Trust,
Contact: Dr. Colin Bull,
The Ardchonnel Old Schoolhouse,
Eredine,
by Dalmally,
Argyll PA33 1BW.
Tel/Fax: (01866) 844293.
Email: c.bull@zetnet.co.uk

West Galloway Fisheries Trust,
Contact: Callum Sinclair,
12A Victoria Street,
Newton Stewart DG8 6BT.
Tel: (01671) 403011.
Fax: (01671) 402248.
EMail: wgft@btinternet.com

**River Clyde Fisheries
Management Trust,**
Contact: Jim MacAloon,
12 Chalmers Crescent,
Murray 7,
East Kilbride G75 0PE.
Tel: (01355) 221724.

THE ANGLERS CREEL

SCOTLAND'S AIRFLO DIRECT DEALER

Quality tackle from leading companies at competitive prices.

Fly tying tools and materials a speciality.

Airflo, Ashima, B Church, Craftye, Eagle Claw, Emvee, Ewing Feather, Firefly, Fly Rite, Griffin, G Griffiths, Hoffman, Kamasan, Keogh, Louper Innovations, Lureflash, Metz, Niche, Owdy Lane, Partridge, Scorpion, Sparton, Sprite, Steker, Tiemco, Veniard, Drennan, Shakespear, Leeda, Penn.

A large selection of materials are available on the premises.

IF NOT IN STOCK IT CAN BE GOT

The Anglers Creel, 33 Exchange Street, Dundee, Angus DD1 3DJ.
Tel/Fax: (01382) 205075   Proprietor - Ian Wilson

Ian is a past International Fly Fisherman who has represented Scotland at World, Commonwealth, Home and British Rivers Championships. He has fished extensively throughout Britain, Southern Ireland, Tasmania and Canada.

Whilst his favourite sport is fly fishing, he also dabbles with sea, salmon and coarse angling.

The question most often asked by anglers is "Where do you fish?" and like most fanatics his answer is "Anywhere there are Fish!"

Some of his favourite waters are Lochore Meadows (the Meedies), Lindores Loch and having returned to river fishing several years ago the River Tummel at Pitlochry.

He has been known to say that "If you can catch fish on the Tummel, you can catch fish anywhere"

The ANGLERS CREEL caters for all types and ages of anglers. It specialises in fly tying tools and materials. Ian is particularly keen on helping people who want to start tying their own flies, and is always ready to help with any difficulties or problems that they may have in this field.

You will always find a warm welcome and good crack when you go to "the Creel".

Scottish Tourist Board
23 Ravelston Ter,
Edinburgh
EH4 3EU.
Tel: 0131-332 2433.

Scottish Office Department of Agriculture, Environment & Fisheries for Scotland (S.O.A.E.F.D.)
Pentland House,
47 Robb's Loan,
Edinburgh
EH14 1TY.
Tel: 0131-244 6015.

Inspector of Salmon and Freshwater Fisheries
Pentland House,
(Room 407)
47 Robb's Loan,
Edinburgh
EH14 1TY.
Tel: 0131-244 6227.

S.O.A.E.F.D.
Officer in Charge,
Freshwater Fisheries
Laboratory, Faskally,
Pitlochry
PH16 5LB.
Tel: (01796) 472060.
Fax: (01796)473523.

S.O.A.E.F.D.
Marine Laboratory
P.O. Box 101,
Victoria Rd,
Aberdeen
AB11 8DB.
Tel: (01224) 295511.

Scottish Environment Protection Agency
1 South St,
Perth PH2 8NJ.
Tel: (01738) 627989.

Scottish Sports Council
Caledonia House,
South Gyle,
Edinburgh
EH12 9DQ.
Tel: 0131-317 7200.

Scottish Natural Heritage
12 Hope Terrace
Edinburgh
EH9 2AS.
Tel: 0131-447 4784.

Forestry Commission
William Cairns,
Senior Information
Officer,
231 Corstorphine Rd,
Edinburgh
EH12 7AT.
Tel: 0131-334 0303.

Scottish Hydro-Electric plc
10 Dunkeld Rd,
Perth PH1 5WA.
Freephone:
0800 300000.

Scottish Anglers' National Association
Administrative Office,
Caledonia House,
South Gyle,
Edinburgh
EH12 9DQ.
Tel: 0131-339 8808.

Federation of Highland Angling Clubs
K. MacDonald,
Secretary,
13 Swanston Ave,
Inverness IV3 8QW.
Tel: (01463) 240095.

Institute of Ecology and Resource Management, REIM (Forestry),
University of
Edinburgh,
Darwin Buildings,
The Kings Buildings,
Mayfield Rd,
Edinburgh
EH9 3JU.
Tel: 0131-650 5430.

Institute of Aquaculture
University of Stirling,
Stirling FK9 4LA.
Tel: (01786) 473171.

CLUB	SECRETARY
Aberfeldy Angling Club	V. Hackel, P.O. Box 2000, Aberfeldy.
Airdrie Angling Club	Jimmy Potter, Sharp Avenue, Coatbridge, Lanarkshire.
Berwick & District Angling Association	D. Cowan, 129 Etal Road Tweedmouth, Berwick. Tel: (01289) 306985.
Blairgowrie, Rattray & District Angling Association	W. Matthew, 9 Mitchell Square, Blairgowrie, Perthshire. Tel: (01250) 873679.
Castle Douglas & District Angling Association	Stanley Kaye, 2 Cairnsmore Road, Castle Douglas, Kirkcudbrightshire. Tel: (01556) 502695.
Craigdarroch Fishing Club	Brian Thompson, Tel: (01848) 200467.
Dalbeattie Angling Association	J. Moran, 12 Church Crescent, Dalbeatttie DG5 4BA. Tel: (01556) 502292.
Devon Angling Association	R. Breingan, 33 Redwell Place, Alloa, Clackmannanshire FK10 2BT. Tel: (01259) 215185.
Dumfries & Galloway Angling Association	L. Chalmers, 50 Brooms Road, Dumfries. Tel: (01387) 267647.
Dunkeld & Birnam Angling Association	Mr . A. Steele, 21 Willowbank, Little Dunkeld, Perthshire. Tel: (01350) 727428.
Dunoon & District Angling Club	A. H. Young, "Ashgrove", 28 Royal Crescent, Dunoon PA23 7AH, Tel: (01369) 705732.
Eckford Angling Association	The Buccleugh Estates Ltd., Estate Office, Bowhill, Selkirk. Tel: (01750) 20753.
Eye Water Angling Club	W. S. Gillie, 2 Tod's Court, Eyemouth, Berwickshire. Tel: (01890) 750038.
Fyvie Angling Association	J.D. Pirie, Prenton, South Road, Oldmeldrum, Aberdeenshire AB51 0AB. Tel: (01651) 872229.
Galashiels Angling Club	Mr. S. Grzybowski, 3 St. Andrew Street, Galashiels. Tel: (01896) 755712.
Goil Angling Club	Mr. Ian Given, 'Bonnyrigg', 25 Churchill Drive, Bishopton, Renfrewshire,
Gordon Fishing Club	J. Fairgrieve, Burnbrae Eden Road, Gordon TD3 6JU. Tel: (01573) 410357.
Greenlaw Angling Club	Mr. T. Waldie, 26 East High Street, Greenlaw, Berwickshire, TD10 6UF. Tel: (01361) 810542.
Hawick Angling Club	D. Smith, (Secretary) "Wellogate Bank", Wellogate Brae, Hawick, TD9 9NE. Tel: (01450) 373142.
Inverness Angling Club	Mr. K. MacDonald, Swanston Avenue, Inverness IV3 8QW. Tel: (01463) 240095.
Jedforest Angling Association	J. Tait, 9 Boundaries, Jedburgh TD8 6EX. Tel: (01835) 863871.
Kelso Angling Association	Euan Robson, 33 Tweedsyde Park, Kelso TD5 7RF. Tel: (01573) 225279.

CLUB	SECRETARY

Killin, Breadalbane Angling Club — J. H. Rough,. J.R.News, Main Street, Killin, Perthshire FK21 8UJ. Tel: (01567) 820362.

Kilmaurs Angling Club — T. C. McCabe, 8 East Park Crescent, Kilmaurs, Ayrshire. Tel: (01563) 538652.

Kyles of Bute Angling Club — A. H. Richardson, Allt Beag, Tignabruaich, Argyll PA21 2BE. Tel: (01700) 811486.

Ladykirk & Norham Angling Association — Mr. R. G. Wharton, 8 St. Cuthbert's Square, Norham, Berwick-upon-Tweed, TD15 2LE. Tel: (01289) 382467.

Lairg Angling Club — J. M. Ross, St. Murie, Church Hill Road, Lairg, Sutherland IV27 4BL. Tel: (01549) 402010.

Lauderdale Angling Associated Waters — D. M. Milligan, The Torrs, Portling, Dalbeattie, Kirkcudbrightshire DG5 4PZ.

Loch Keose & Associated Waters — M. Morrison, Handa, 18 Keose Glebe, Lochs, Isle of Lewis, HS2 9JX. Tel: (01851) 830334.

Loch Lomond Angling Improvement Association — Richard Legate, Glenrannoch House, Kinloch Rannoch. Tel: (01882) 632307.

Morebattle Angling Club — D.Y. Gray, 17 Mansfield Avenue, Morebattle, Kelso TD5 8QW. Tel: (01573) 440528.

New Galloway Angling Association — A. Carnie, Carsons Knowe, New Galloway, Tel: (01644) 420760.

Peeblesshire Salmon Fishing Association — Blackwood & Smith W. S., 39 High Street, Peebles. Tel: (01721) 720131.

Peebleshire Trout Fishing Association — D.G. Fyfe, 39 High Street, Peebles. Tel: (01721) 720131.

Perth & District Anglers' Association — Mr D. Brand, "Langholme"' Braehead, Almondbank, by Perth PH1 3LN. Tel/Fax: (01738) 583288.

Pitlochry Angling Club — R. Harriman, Sunnyknowe, Nursing Home Brae, Pitlochry, Perthshire. Tel: (01796) 472484.

Rannoch & District Angling Club — J. Brown, The Square, Kinloch Rannoch, Perthshire. Tel: (01882) 632268.

River Almond Angling Association — H. Meikle, 23 Glen Terrace, Deans, Livingston, West Lothian. Tel: (01506) 411813.

St. Andrews Angling Club — Peter F. Malcolm, 54 St. Nicholas St., St. Andrews, Fife. Tel: (01334) 476347.

St. Marys Loch Angling Association — Mr. N. MacIntyre, "Whincroft", 8 Rosetta Road, Peebles EH45 8JU. Tel: (01721) 722278.

South West Fishermans Association — D Carse Chairman, 24 Port Street, Annan DG12 6BN. Tel: 01461 204733. Social evenings 1st and 3rd Tuesday of each month at Annan & District Ex-Svs Club. Visitors welcome.

Stormont Angling Club — Mrs. Shirley Wood, Scone Estates Office, Scone Palace, Perth PH2 6BD. Tel: (01738) 552308.

Turriff Angling Association — I. Masson, 6 Castle Street, Turiff AB53 7BJ. Tel: (01888) 562428.

MOUSSELINE OF SOLE

Serves 4
8¾ ozs (250g) Sole Fillet
1 Whole egg
1 Egg white
Scant pint Cream
Salt (1 level teaspoon)
Juice of half a lemon

Method

1   Work sole to a paste in processor, add salt.
2   Add egg and egg white, work together.
3   Add cream, blend thoroughly.
4   Pass mixture through a sieve to remove any membrane pr piece of skin etc.
5   Add lemon juice, check seasoning, adjust if necessary. Cover bowl refrigerate until needed.

NOTE: other white fish can be used for this recipe but if using lobster or scallops increase quantity of fish to 12½ ozs (325g).

Recipes courtesy of David Wilson - celebrated proprietor and chef of the acclaimed Peat Inn in Fife

A Tag 'goes in' prior to releasing a 200lb+ Porbeagle.

It never ceases to amaze me how the man in the street still has a perception of sea angling as being a sport of billiard cue rods, huge centre pin reels and feathers with huge weights being the perfect outfit. Well, nothing could be further from the truth and a look at the modern sea angler's tackle and techniques would show that he is evolving and adapting to modern trends at a far greater rate that his freshwater brethern. Oh yes, there is a still the need for some hefty tackle but it is now half the weight, twice the power and surprisingly, since most were designed in America, they suit the British angler perfectly. To get some idea of how techniques have evolved, let's take a look at some popular applications and how things have advanced.

More years back than I care to remember, I started experimenting with spoons as attractors and my mainstay was the old metal flounder spoon which I later evolved into plastic and had enormous success with. These were – and still are – superb for catching ling, conger, cod and of course flatties. They had literally and metaphorically one big drawback and that

was due to their size 2"-3". they caused a lot of drag and necessitated large weights to keep them on the bottom – and they only came in chrome or white! Enter the Americans, and a source was found for small light metal spoons such as are used in MEPPS spinning lures and, glory, glory, they came in several shapes, sizes and dozens of colours. Also available were devices to fit them onto the line and ensure free spinning movement and in one fell swoop we could fish lighter, more colourfully and more effectively. As a bonus it was hugely more sporting. These new lightweight spoons, allied to fluorescent beads, now play a huge part in the boat angler's repertoire and their success can be judged by the numbers used during competitions. Indeed, so successful have spoons become in fish catching that during competitions colours and bead combinations are experimented with and successful rigs are much copied. The rods and reels to match are now fine tuned to such a degree that lines 8-15lbs are regularly used and rods in the 12lbs class are common with spinning rods being used by more experienced anglers now – even in competition. Lighter spoons

Big Skate - Big Mouth - Keep fingers well clear

are of greater use in drift conditions when the extra movement gives the added flutter to entice the predators and over rough ground can result in substantial bags. A sink and draw style of approach helps give additional movement and lessen losses as the baits literally bounce over underwater snags.

At anchor, larger brighter spoons can be deadly for ling and even totally static bait will have conger and rays being attracted by spoons. Even the modern uptider will benefit from a small spoon, which, if worked across the tide, is extremely effective for flatties.

Almost twenty years ago I was asked to field test an American lure system which had a hook whose eye was bent at 90 degrees to the shank in the same plane as the bend and a small lead ball had been moulded onto the hook. A very soft latex rubber eel with a curly tail was then fed up onto the hook which, when used always

A healthy tope goes back. - The modern attitude to conservation.

Short and extremely powerful - both Rod and Angler!!!

swam with the hook point uppermost, away from snags. This system was called MR TWISTER with jigheads. These lures were – and still are – deadly for pollack, coalfish and cod and these also form a large part of a sea angler's gear but it is the lead jighead which has seen the greatest changes – certainly in Scotland where its use has developed into almost a cult.

When people realised the fish-catching potential of this system, demand outstripped supply for the eels and stocks ran out, so the next best thing was ragworm and these proved even more deadly, particularly for pollack. One problem, however, was that the lead jigheads were fairly small (quarter to half an ounce) so in order to cast them, light

The smile says it - Lures work!

the jigheads up to 2oz and these are also used with spinning rods but carrying two additional hooks above, paternoster style. This is generally a competition rig since it can get just a bit hectic if more than one fish is hooked at a time! A final work on competitions, since multiple fish may be hooked, more powerful rods and reels must be considered.

When we start comparing rods, there really is no comparison. Our modern tackle is light years ahead from what I started with. My first shark rod was 7'6" long and made of solid fibre glass and weighed a few ounces short of a ton. It certainly tamed sharks but it was some handful – it gave me as much stick as I

spinning rods had to be used with such success that they are now considered the definitive pollack gear in shallow waters. One skipper, TONY WASS, working out of Girvan, has perfected this style of angling and on his trips to Ailsa Craig and the rocky headlands to the south, the lures (plus ragworms) are used almost exclusively. The sport he provides can be very hectic but he is absolutely insistent that pollack and wrasse are returned alive. Cod can be kept for the pot – naturally. The big plus side for conservationists is that being a lure, almost all fish are lip hooked and thus unhooking presents no problem. Rods and lines must match the size of the expected catch since a double figure pollack is almost unstoppable in its first dive and if it gets home to the kelp beds, well, it's goodnight Vienna!

To allow them to fish in deeper water, some anglers have made moulds to take

Ladies get it on the Tope act too -
with superb results.

SEA ANGLING TACKLE ADVANCES

have the sharks. Its modern counterpart – once again designed in America – is a fairly short stubby creature, 2 feet shorter, half the weight and incredibly powerful. Made from various combinations of carbon, kevlar, boran and glass, it is so much more comfortable to use. By coincidence it was designed as a stand-up rod where the angler could get up and walk around the boat, which is the only way we fight big fish in Britain, so it is tailor made for our angling styles. The shorter length also means we expend less energy for more power – a big bonus as the years creep on! What with carbon, kevlar and boron, our rods and reels are getting lighter and easier to use giving us more enjoyment and I believe catching

more fish in the process. These materials are used in all our angling rods including the spinners.

Fishing in deep water or in very strong tides has always presented its own brand of hassle for the sea angler trying to hold bottom. In the past the only effective means was wire or heavy leads, both with their attendant and potentially dangerous problems. Now we have the new breeds of line, extremely fine nylon, dynabraid and finest of all spiderwire, something to suit everyone.

As ever, with expanding technology, we must adapt our techniques to match and since finer lines are harder to knot, greater care must be taken. One example is spiderwire which I use. It is 30lbs breaking

An evening Tope Battle

strain but is as thin as thread – literally – or 8lb nylon. I now have to use smaller swivels and since it has NO stretch, I have to temper my strikes when hitting into large fish like tope or I have a break. I also have gone onto smaller, sharper hooks so the process is endless but very exciting.

With so many advances in tackle it is difficult to see how our modern gear can be improved but it will be fun finding out.

Yes – like most modern sea anglers, I am completely sold on modern methods and tackle. Well, maybe not completely. I still regularly use, and would never change it, an old ABU CARDINAL 77 – unbeatable. Heck, nobody's perfect!!!

Jim McLanaghan

Lures - The modern bait.

HOW TO COOK YOUR CATCH

FRIED COD FILLET WITH SPRING GREENS AND SMOKED FISH

Serves 4 (as a starter portion)

1lb (500g) Cod Fillet (Skin off)	Salt/Pepper
4oz (100g) Smoked Fish	Olive Oil
8oz (200g) Spring Cabbage	Coriander
	Vinaigrette Dressing

To Cook Salmon

1   Remove the leaves from the cabbage, cut out the central rib, blanch in boiling salted water.

2   Dice the smoked fish in pieces about ⅜" (24mm) thick.

3   Cut the unskinned cod fillets into 4 by 4oz pieces. Check to ensure no small pin bones have been left, if so remove with tweezers.

4   Put olive oil in pan, when beginning to smoke sprinkle sea salt on skin of cod then place cod fillets skin side down in pan, cook for about 5 minutes, depending on thickness of cod (skin should be crisp and golden brown) then turn over and cook for just 1 minute on the other side.

5   Cut cabbage into strips put in pan with a little olive oil then add diced smoked fish, heat through, season then add at last minute the coriander leaves.

6   Arrange cabbage and smoked fish in a soup bowl or deep plate, place cod fillet on top and spoon a little vinaigrette around edge.

BORDERS

The Scottish Borders provide some of the best sea angling in the UK. Based on Eyemouth, which has the largest fishing fleet in the South of Scotland, and the smaller fishing villages of Burnmouth and St Abbs, the clear unpolluted waters are well stocked with a wide variety of seafish. So clear is the water that one of the first Marine Reservations has been established off Eyemouth. The rugged coastline with its unique fauna make a spectacular background to your day's fishing. It should be noted that sea angling is not permitted off St. Abbs Head National Reserve (Petticowick-Long Carr). Eyemouth is only nine miles north of Berwick-upon-Tweed, just off the A.1. Its colourful boats, fish auction and sandy beach make it a popular resort during the summer. Well known for its excellent rock fishing, the town is also a useful point of access to the north and south. Boat fishing has developed over the years due to the efforts of Eyemouth Sea Angling Club who now run a number of shore and boat competitions throughout the season.

The club operates the coast from Burnmouth harbour in the south to the harbour at St Abbs in the north.

Types of fish: Shore - cod, mackerel, coalfish, flounder, plaice, sole, haddock,whiting, catfish, ling and wrasse. Boat - the same species can be caught as on shore but larger specimens.

Boats: A large number of fishing boats are usually available from Eyemouth, St Abbs and Burnmouth for parties of anglers at weekends.

DUMFRIES AND GALLOWAY

Solway Firth to Isle of Whithorn

The area is renowned for its strong tides which can create difficulties for boat angling in the wrong conditions. Local advice should be sought before sailing and as a further safety measure the Coastguard should be advised of any intended trips. If a boat trip is cancelled or an angler prefers shore fishing, the coastline abounds with excellent shore marks which produce a great diversity of species. Summer months are undoubtedly the most productive but the winter cod fishing can also be very good with many large fish being taken.

Kippford

Better known as a yachting centre Kippford still offers good angling opportunities.

Shore marks around Kippford yield bags of flatfish and dogfish in the summer with the occasional bass. The area excels in the winter with catches of big cod. The Scottish shore caught record cod came from here. Boat fishing during the summer tends to give more variety with mackerel, thornback and dogfish, both spur and spotted featuring in the catches.

Bait: Lug and ragworm can be dug locally and cockles and mussels picked from the shore.

Season: May to September for comfort and variety. November to February for big cod but wrap up well!

Kirkcudbright

About 5 miles from the open sea on the Dee estuary, Kirkcudbright is at the centre of an excellent shore fishing area. Rocky points in Kirkcudbright bay along the Dundrennan shore to the east and Borgue to the west, give good varied fishing especially during the summer. Dogfish feature heavily in local club matches with the occasional conger, bull huss and thornback. Settled conditions and clear water give good bags of pollack and garfish, and mullet are attracted to ground bait. The estuary produces bags of plaice, dabs flounders, eels and coalfish giving good sport at the harbour. The bay also fishes well for cod and whiting in the winter. Boat fishing can be good with launching sites at the harbour, Ross Bay and Brighouse but these are restricted by the tides. One charter boat operates from Kirkcudbright. Boat catches are as varied as the shore, but there is always the chance of a tope.

Bait: Lug and ragworm are available locally along with cockles and mussels. Mackerel and herring can be bought in the town.

Tackle: A limited amount available from: Watson Mckinnel in Kirkcudbright.

A better selection from: "Patties", 109 Queensberry Street, Dumfries, "Reel em In", Friars Vennel, Dumfries.

Charter Boat: "Howzat" Howard Williams. Tel: (01557) 330367.

Further Information: Information Centre, Kirkcudbright. Tel: (01557) 330494.

Garlieston & The Isle of Whithorn

Situated on the east side of the Machars Peninsula, the area is sheltered from the prevailing westerly winds giving good shore and boat fishing. Rock marks give good bags of dogfish, pollack and wrasse with conger and mullet also being taken. Burrow Head gives good fishing when the weather is fine. The summer months are the best for both shore and boat fishing. Boats can be launched from both harbours on a suitable tide and charter boats operate from the Isle of Whithorn. The biggest attraction for boat anglers is tope which can· sometimes be caught in numbers. Some big fish are caught every year and most are released. Spurdog and thornback sometimes take bate meant for tope.

Tackle: Some available locally from: A. McGhie, Radio Shop, George Street, Whithorn. J.M. William, Grocer & Harbour Master, The Harbour, Isle of Whithorn. Tel: (01988) 500246.

Bait: Lug, rag and shellfish available locally.

Boats: Craig Mills, Main Street, Isle of Whithorn DG8 8LN. Tel: (01988) 500393 - (Manu Kea). Rab McCreadie - (Crusader).

Local Clubs: Kirkcudbright & District SAC, Stuart Ross, "Fanore", 53 St. Cuthbert Street, Kirkcudbright. Tel: (01557) 330845. Peever Sea Anglers, Jack McKinnel,20 Merse Strand, Kirkcudbright. Tel: (01557) 331505.

Luce Bay

There are some good shore marks, namely Sandhead Sands for Flatfish, Dogfish and Bass in season. Terrally Bay for these species plus Codling, Whiting, Spurdogfish. Around East and West Tarbet bays at the Mull of Galloway good rock fishing may be had for Lesser Spotted Dogfish, Bull Huss, Spurdogfish, Conger Eels, Wrasse, Whiting, Pollack,

Coalfish, Flatfish and Mackerel in season, normally from late April to December.

Boats: W. Carter, Castle Daly Angling Centre, Auchenmalg, Glenluce. Tel: (01581) 500250. (Self drive boats for hire & hotel accommodation).

Bait: Lug can be dug in most sandy bays around Luce Bay, especially at Sandhead. Some shellfish available, mussels and cockles with razorfish on spring tides.

Launching Sites: Difficult to launch without four wheel drive vehicle.

Sites: Yacht Club at Drummore high water only. Cailiness Road picnic site. Back of harbour Drummore. East Tarbet Bay usually necessary to rope the trailer over shingle. £3 charge at local farm.

Safety: Dinghy anglers should be aware of the strong tides in the area, especially around the Mull of Galloway area.

Port William

Port William is situated on the east side of Luce Bay and has a good, though tidal harbour. It is the starting point for many anglers wishing to fish the lower part of Luce Bay. The once famous shore mark of Monreith Bay, still a good bass beach, lies just to the south of Port William.

Types of fish: Tope, spurdog, rays, cod, pollack, flatfish from boats. Bass wrasse, codling and pollack from the shore.

Tackle: Available in village.

Bait: Lugworm, shellfish and molluscs along beach. Mackerel in bay.

Season: May-October.

Drummore

Drummore, the main port for

anglers wishing to fish the western side of Luce Bay lies 5 miles north of the Mull of Galloway. Hotels and guest houses cater for anglers. There are many good shore marks on sandy beaches north of Drummore, while the Mull of Galloway provides excellent shore fishing over rocky ground. The Mull, the most southerly point of Scotland, is an area of very strong tides and is not recommended as a fishing area to anglers with small boats incapable of at least 10 knots, especially during ebb tides.

Types of fish: Pollack, wrase from rocky shores, flatfish, bass, mullet and rays from sandy beaches. Pollack, coalfish, cod, whiting, wrasse, lesser spotted dogfish, bull huss, spurdog, tope, rays, conger from boats.

Boats: "On yer Marks" Ian or Sue Burrett, Cardrain Cottage, Drummore. Tel: (01776) 840346.

Charter Boats: Stuart Aylott - Tel: (01776) 840226.

Bait: All types available on shore at low tide. Mackerel from Mull of Galloway shore marks.

Port Logan

Port Logan is the small community which is situated abut 7.5 miles north of the Mull of Galloway on the west side of the Galloway Peninsula. An area with many good shore marks both to the north and south of the village. It is one of the few relatively easy launching sites on this coastline south of Portpatrick. A good alternative for the angler with his own boat when easterly winds prevent fishing in Luce Bay. Like the Mull of Galloway an area of strong ties, especially off Crammoc Head, to the south of Port Logan Bay.

Types of fish: As for the southern part of Luce Bay with occasional haddock. Herring in June and July. Ideal to launch dinghies at Port Logan from concrete slipway onto hard sand where two wheel drive vehicles can run onto beach. Slack water occurs one and a half hours before high and low water.
Boats: Ian Burrett, Cardrain Cottage, Drummore.
Tel: (01776) 840346.

Portpatrick
The small fishing port and holiday resort of Portpatrick lies on the west coast of Wigtownshire, 8 miles from Stranraer. There is good shore fishing from the many rocky points north and south of the resort, the best known being the Yellow Isle, half a mile north of the harbour. Sandeel Bay, a little further north, and Killintringan Lighthouse are also worth fishing. Small slipway only used at high tide.
Types of fish: Pollack, coalfish, plaice, flounder, codling, mackerel, dogfish, conger, wrasse and tope occasionally.
Boats: Brian Tyreman, Pinminnoch Cottage, Portpatrick DG9 9AB.
Tel: (01776) 810468 "Cornubia".
Bait: None sold locally. Lugworm and some ragworm can be dug east of the railway pier, Stranraer.
Season: May-December.
Further Information from:
Mr. R. Smith, 24 Millbank Road, Stranraer. Tel: (01776) 703691.

Stranraer & Loch Ryan
Stranraer, at the head of Loch Ryan, offers the angler, as a rail and bus terminal, a good stepping off point for many sea angling marks and areas in this part of Scotland, with Sandhead on Luce Bay (8 miles) to the south, Portpatrick (8 miles) to

the west and Lady Bay (8 miles) on the west side of Loch Ryan with Cairnryan (6 miles) and Finnart Bay (10 miles) on the opposite side of the loch. Best Shore marks being Cairnryan Village, South of Townsend Thoresen ferry terminal. Old House Point and Concrete Barges north of Cairnryan Village, Finnart Bay on East Mouth of Loch, Wig Bay, Jamiesons Point and Lady Bay on west side of Loch Ryan. Boats may be launched at Wig Bay Slipway, Lady Bay and at Stranraer Market Street.
Access Safety: Most landowners will grant permission to cross lands to fish if this is requested and will advise best routes to avoid crossing crops. Most rock marks are safe but caution is needed in wet conditions as they may become slippy. In Loch Ryan anglers fishing from rocks or beaches should be aware of the wash from ferries and seacat as these can be dangerous if caught in the drive up the beaches or rocks. **Please note:** No fishing is allowed on the jetty at Cairnryan at any times and the owners are going to take legal action against anglers who break through the boundary fence to obtain access. The jetty is unsafe and no insurance is in force.
Types of fish: taken from shore pollack, codling, coalfish, plaice, dabs, wrasse, whiting, conger eel, lesser spotted dogfish, flounder, with spurdog, thornback ray and bull huss at times. Occasional tope. Taken from boat: Pollack, codling, coalfish, plaice, dabs, wrasse, whiting, conger eel, lesser spotted dogfish, flounder with spurdog thornback ray and bull huss at times. Turbot, monkfish and spotted and cuckoo ray in the deeper water.

Boat: Mike Watson, Main Street, Stranraer. Tel: (01776) 853225.
Tackle: The Sports Shop, George Street, Stranraer. Tel: (01776) 702705, (frozen bait stocked).
Bait: Lugworm can be dug in most sandy bays, with the cockle shore at Stranraer the most popular. Loch Ryan Sea Angling Association has a lease on the cockle shore at Stranraer to restrict bait digging and the conditions are that anglers are only allowed to dig sufficient bait for one day's fishing. Ragworm can be dug in places. Cultured ragworm on sale at sports shop in Stranraer along with a good assortment of frozen baits. Mussels can be obtained on most beaches. Mackerel are caught from shore and boat in season.
Season: Sea fishing is carried out all year but from May to October the best for daylight with a lot of night fishing giving better results.
Local Clubs: Loch Ryan Sea Angling Association, Paul Paterson, 46 Antrim Avenue, Stranraer Tel: (01776) 703529. Sealink S.A.C., Niven Dickson, Seabank Road, Stranraer.
Tel: (01776) 704895.
Further information from above or: Mr. R. Smith, 24 Millbank Road, Stranraer Tel: (01776) 703691.

STRATHCLYDE SOUTH

Loch Ryan to Ardrossan
The angling potential of much of the coast between Loch Ryan and Girvan remains unknown, the many rocky shores, small headlands and sandy beaches probably only attracting the anglers in an exploratory mood, or those seeking solitude in pursuit of their hobby.

Girvan

Girvan has a sheltered port and is a family holiday resort. From the end of the pier good fishing can be had for fair-sized plaice, flounders and spotted dog. Night fishing is good for rock cod. Just one mile to the south of the town lies the noted Horse Rock, only about 50 yards from the main Stranraer road. Access to the rock may be gained from about half tide. Except during very high tides and during storms it is a good shore mark providing access to water of about 20 feet on the sea-side even at low tide.

Types of fish: Plaice, codling, rays, flounder, pollack and ling, whiting, gurnard (mostly from boat) and tope, however very few people fish for them. (Mullet in the harbour during the summer months).

Boats: M. McCrindle, 7 Harbour Street, Girvan KA26 9AJ.
Tel: (01465) 713219. Tony Wass, 22 Templand Road, Dalry KA24 5EU. Tel: (01294) 833724.

Baits: Lugworm and ragworm can be dug at beach nearby or fresh mackerel from boat.

Tackle: Available from Girvan Chandlers, 4 Knockcushon Street, Girvan KA26 9AG.

Season: March to October.

Further information from: Brian Burn (S.F.S.A.). Tel: (01292) 264735.

Ayr

Ayr is a popular holiday town on the estuaries of the Rivers Ayr and Doon, 32 miles south-west of Glasgow. Good shore fishing can be had on the Newton Shore, north of the harbour for flounders and the odd doggie during the summer months with a few coallies, codling and whiting throughout the winter, especially

when there is a good storm. Some flounders and eels are taken from the harbour and at times excellent mullet can be caught from the tidal stretches of the river Ayr. Boat fishing in the bay can be very productive for mackerel and herring from May to October. Usually from July to November the boat fishing improves with the arrival of codling, pollack, ling, coallies, plaice, dabs, sea scorpions and spotted dogs.

Tackle: Available from Gamesport, 60 Sandgate, Ayr.

Bait: Lug and rag can be dug at the Newton Shore with Doonfoot beaches producing lug and peeler crab during summer months.

Boats: Ayr Sea Angling Centre Tel: (01292) 285297. There is also a good public slipway for dinghies to launch. Difficulty can be had on exceptionally low tides at low water.

Further information: Brian Burn (S.F.S.A.). Tel: (01292) 264735.

Prestwick & Troon

Just north of Ayr, Prestwick and Troon offers some reasonable shore fishing at certain times of the year. Prestwick beaches fish for codling, flounders and coallies from usually November to January especially on evening tides. Flounders, the odd coallie and spotted dog can be caught throughout the summer months. The Ballast Bank at Troon can produce conger, pollock, doggies, wrasse and the odd codling throughout the summer months with the better chance of a few codling and coallies during the winter. Troon pier is a favourite mark for herring and mackerel during the summer and there is always the chance of a conger or two from this area.

Bait: Lug and rag can be dug on Prestwick shore and mussels beds also at Troon and Barassie beaches.

Boats: Jimmy Wilson, 27 Wallace Avenue, Troon. Tel: (01292) 313161. Dinghies can be launched from Troon Marina, however there is a launching charge.

Further information: John Fitchett Tel: (01292) 314057.

Irvine

Irvine is Scotland's only "New Town" by the sea. The harbour which is situated at the mouth of the River Irvine and River Garnock is no longer used by commercial shipping. There is plenty to do for the non angling members of the family in the nearby Magnum Leisure Centre, Maritime Museum and shopping centre. The long sandy beaches to the north and south of the harbour are good for flounders, dabs and eels especially evening flood tides. Irvine Bay is a good boat fishing area with several reefs of varying sizes within easy reach of the harbour. The sandy stretches can often produce good bags of flatfish. Further afield from Irvine is Troon wreck and Lady Isle where good pollack can be caught.

Type of fish: Cod, ling, pollack, flatties, L.S.D. and of course mackerel and herring.

Tackle: Irvine Angling World. Tel: (01294) 313336. Young and Son, Saltcoats. Tel: (01294) 605344.

Bait: Lugworm and ragworm can be dug in the harbour. Frozen baits can be bought from local Tackle shops.

Boats: Norrie Mason, New Town Marine, c/o 19 Grange Road, Stevenston,Ayrshire KA21 3EA. Tel: (01294) 605524.

Season: All year round.

Saltcoats & Ardrossan

Saltcoats with the neighbouring towns of Stevenston and Ardrossan, is situated on the Ayrshire coast 30 miles south-west of Glasgow. Shore fishing is possible in the South Bay and around the harbours.
Approximately 3 miles north is Ardneil Bay which can produce a few codling over the rough ground.

Types of fish: Pollack, wrasse, doggies, eels, cod, saithe, flatties and herring.

Further information: Please obey any private fishing signs within the area and remember dinghy anglers. No fishing within 50 meters of Ore terminal at Hunterston.

Boats: Robert Reid- Tel: (01294) 601844.

Bait: Ragworm available from Saltcoats Harbour, Fairlie Pier. Lugworm from Ardrossan north shore and Farlie sand flats.

Tackle: Light tackle is all you require for most species in the area. Fixed spool or multiplier, light rod - 8- 10lb line, spinning or bait .

Season: May to October Local Club Ardrossan & District Sea Angling Club.

Further Information from: Bud McClymont, 41 Come Crescent, Saltcoats KA21 6JL.
Tel: (01294) 461830.

Largs

Largs is within easy reach of several good fishing banks, including the Piat Shoal, the Skelmorlie Patch and the east shore of Cumbrae.

Types of fish: Dogfish, flounders, gurnard, dragonets, pollack, mackerel, plaice, coalfish and dabs.

Boats: Are readily available from local hirers.

Tackle: Hastie of Largs Ltd, Department Store, 109 Main Street, Largs. Tel: (01475) 673104

Bait: Lug, rag, cockles and mussels are available from Fairlie Flats. Sea trout are caught regularly on the shore.

Gourock

The coastline from Largs to Greenock was probably the most popular area in Scotland for shore angling, with many anglers from the Midlands of England and beyond making regular trips north. Now the fishing is generally poor. At Wemyss Bay, angling is not permitted from the pier, but odd good catches can still be had to the south, and the Red Rocks, about a mile to the north, are noted for odd codling and other species. At Inverkip there is a sandy beach around the entrance to the marina where flounders, odd dabs and eels can be taken. Cloch Point, where the Firth turns east, is well known for its fishing potential, although the current can be fierce, and because of the rough bottom, relatively heavy lines are necessary. The coastline from Cloch along Gourock Promenade to the swimming pool car park provides fair fishing and is easily accessible. Further inland at Greenock Esplanade, flounders, dabs, eels and coallies are among the species available, although the water here is shallower, and this area is more productive at night. This stretch of coastline provides the dinghy angler with easy access to many of the Clyde marks, including the Gantocks, where outsize cod and coalfish were taken many years ago, mainly on pirks. The bay beside the power station holds

flatfish and the ground off Greenock Esplanade is popular for coallies, some pollack and dabs. Dinghy owners should note that no anchoring is permitted in the main navigation channels, and several other regulations must also be adhered to.

Types of fish: Coalfish (known locally as saithe), odd codling, conger eel, dab, dogfish, flounder, occasional ling, plaice, pollack (lythe), pouting, whiting and wrasse. Grey mullet, herring and mackerel can also be caught during the summer months.

Tackle: Inversports, 27a Kempock Street, Gourock, Brian Peterson & Co., 12 Kelly Street, Greenock. Findlay & Co., 58 Lynedoch Street, Greenock.

Bait: Lug, rag, mussels, cockles and crabs can all be obtained from the shoreline.

Boats: J Crowther, Inverclyde Boat Owners Association, 164 Burns Road, Greenock.
Tel:(01475) 634341 can advise.

Isle of Arran

The island of Arran, lying in the outer Firth of Clyde, may be reached from the mainland by ferries running from Ardrossan to Brodick, the largest community on the island. Good shore fishing is found around the whole of the island, much of which remains unexplored.

Lamlash

Lamlash is the main centre for sea angling on the island, probably because of its situation on the shores of Lamlash Bay, the large horse-shoe shaped bay which is almost landlocked by the Holy Isle. This gives excellent protection to the bay from easterly winds. Lamlash is also the starting point for boat trips to the excellent fishing grounds of Whiting Bay and those around Pladda to the south.

Types of fish: Codling, whiting, coalfish, pollack, conger, rays, flatfish, mackerel, dogfish, plaice, dabs, gurnard, wrasse and odd haddock.

Bait: Obtainable from many beaches.

Season: March-November.

Corrie

Corrie is situated on the north east coast of the island.

Types of fish: Codling, haddock, conger, rays, dogfish, ling, pollack, gurnard, garfish, mackerel and wrasse.

Whiting Bay

This bay, which takes its name from the whiting, is very open to the sea. There are excellent fishing banks from Largiebeg Point to King's Cross Point.

Boats: Dinghies can be hired from the Jetty, Whiting Bay or by arrangement with Jim Ritchie, Tel (01770) 700382.

Bait: Cockles, mussels, lugworm, ragworm, limpets and crabs are abundant on the banks from half tide.

Lochranza

Lochranza is situated at the northern end of the island. The loch is surrounded by hills opening out on to Kilbrannan Sound. Types of fish: Cod, conger, wrasse and pollack from the shore. Codling, conger, some haddock, plaice and dabs from boat.

Tackle: Available from boat hirers.

Bait: Mussels, cockles, lugworm and ragworm obtainable.

Brodick

Good fishing in Brodick Bay from Markland Point to Clauchlands Point.

Types of fish: Codling, plaice and other flatfish, conger, wrasse and pollack can be had from the shore while cod, conger, rays, dogfish, ling, pollack, gurnard, garfish and other round fish can be fished from boats.

Bait: Mussels are obtainable from the rocks around Brodick Pier or may be purchased from boat hirers.

Isle of Cumbrae, Millport

There is good fishing at a bank between the South East Point of Millport Bay (Farland Point) and Keppel Pier, Fintry Bay and Piat Shoal provide good sport. West of Portachur Point in about 15/ 20 fathoms and in Dunagoil Bay. S.W. Bute are good. Fairlie Channel directly seaward of Kelburn Castle is about 12/15 fathoms. East shore northwards about 10 fathoms line.

Types of fish: Saithe, conger, coalfish, dogfish, mackerel and flatfish.

Tackle: Available locally from boat hirers.

Bait: Mussels, worms, etc., on shore Boat hirers and local shops provide bait.

STRATHCLYDE NORTH

Helensburgh

Helensburgh is a small seaside town on the Firth of Clyde at the southern end of the Gareloch, easily reached by train or car.

Types of fish: Shore and boat flounder, coalfish, conger, dogfish, whiting, dab, pollack and mackerel.

Tackle: Lochside Bait + Tackle, 112A East Princes Street, Helensburgh . Tel: (01436) 677796.

Bait: Ragworm, lugworm, may be dug locally. Mussels and crabs can be gathered from the shore. Fresh & frozen bait can be purchased from Lochside Bait & Tackle, 112A East Princes Street, Helensburgh. Tel:(01436) 677796.

Season: All year.

Further information from: Mr M.J. Partland, Drumfork S.A.C., 142 East Clyde Street, Helensburgh G84 7AX. Tel: (01436) 671937.

Garelochhead

Garelochhead is the village at the head of the Gareloch, with the whole shoreline within easy reach. Upper and lower loch Long and Loch Goil are only a few miles away.

Types of fish: Coalfish, pollack, dab, flounder, plaice, whiting, pouting, mackerel, and lesser spotted dogfish.

Tackle: Lochside Bait & Tackle, 112A East Princes Street, Helensburgh. Tel: (01436) 677796.

Bait: Garelochhead - cockles and mussels. Roseneath - lugworm, ragworm and cockles. Rhuragworm. Kilcreggan - ragworm. Coulport - cockles. Fresh & frozen bait can be bought from: Lochside Bait & Tackle, 112A East Princes Street, Helensburgh. Tel: (01436) 677796.

Season: All year.

Further information from: Mr M.J. Partland, Drumfork S.A.C.,142 East Clyde Street.Helensburgh G84 7AX. Tel: (01436) 671937.

Arrochar, Loch Long

The village lies at the northern end of the loch, and has waters sheltered by the high surrounding hills.

Types of fish: Shore conger, pollack, coalfish. Boat - whiting, dabs, conger, pollack, coalfish, mackerel, dogfish and odd rays.

Tackle: Lochside Bait & Tackle,

112A East Princes Street, Helensburgh. Tel: (01436) 677796.
Bait: Fresh herring and mackerel, mussels and cockles usually available from the pier. Artificial baits, lures etc., available from shops in village. Fresh and frozen bait can be bought from Lochside Bait & Tackle, 112A East Princes Street, Helensburgh. Tel: (01436) 677796.
Season: All year.
Further information from: Mr M.J.Partland, Drumfork S.A.C., 142 East Clyde Street, Helensburgh G84 7AX . Tel: (01436) 671937.

Clynder
Clynder is the fishing centre on the sheltered west side of the Gareloch and one mile north of the popular Rhu Narrows.
Types of Fish: Conger, rays, plaice, flounders, dogfish, whiting, pouting and mackerel.
Tackle: Lochside Bait + Tackle, 112A East Princes Street, Helensburgh Tel (01436) 677796.
Boats: C Moar (01436) 831336.
Bait: Cockles, mussels, lug, ragworm, can be dug. Fresh & frozen bait can be bought from Lochside Bait & Tackle, 112A East Princes Street, Helensburgh. Tel: (01436) 677796. **Season:** All year.
Further information from: Mr M.J. Partland, Drumfork, S.A.C., 142 East Clyde Street, Helensburgh G84 7AX.
Tel: (01436) 671937.

Isle of Bute, Rothesay
The holiday resort of Rothesay, situated on the island of Bute, only a 30 minute crossing by roll on / roll-off ferry from Wemyss Bay, is sheltered from the prevailing south - westerly winds. Several boat hirers cater for sea anglers.

There are also many excellent shore marks. The deep water marks at Garroch Head can be productive for both shore and boat anglers.
Types of fish: Shore - cod, coalfish , pollack, plaice, mackerel, wrasse. Boat - cod, pollack, plaice. mackerel, conger, coalfish, wrasse, whiting and ling.
Tackle: Available from Bute Arts and Tackle, 94-96 Montague Street, Rothesay, Isle of Bute, Tel: (01700) 503598.
Bait: Lugworm, ragworm, cockles and mussels can be obtained from beaches around the island, and no angler should set forth without feathers or tinsel lures and a few good heavy spinners. Herring is also useful bait.
Season: July-October.

Kilchattan Bay
Sheltered bay waters at the south end of the Isle of Bute renowned for its good all year round fishing.
Types of fish: Cod, pollack, plaice, mackerel, conger, dogfish, wrasse, whiting.
Bait: Worm, fresh cockle available locally.
Season: July to October.

Mainland Ardentinny
Ardentinny is a small unspoiled village picturesquely situated on the west shore of Loch Long, 12 miles from Dunoon by car.
Types of fish: Cod, mackerel from the shore. Cod, conger, haddock, ray, plaice, flounder, whiting, coalfish and mackerel from boats.
Bait: Cockles, mussels, lug and ragworm easily dug in bay .
Season: All year, winter for large cod.

Dunoon
Types of fish: Most of the

shoreline around Dunoon provides catches of cod, coalfish, pollack, flounder, mackerel, plaice. Using ragworm & lugworm, cockle, mussel, razorfish and peeler crab. Boat fishing takes mostly cod, pollack, coalfish dogfish, dabs, plaice, flounder. Also conger over wrecks or rough ground at night.
Boats: Gourock skippers fish Dunoon waters. Approx 3 miles from Dunoon is Holy Loch.
Bait: Can be bought at shops most of the year or obtained in East Bay shore.
Further information from: John Murray, Tel: (01475) 738241.

Tighnabruaich & Kames
Tighnabruaich, on the Kyles of Bute, is famed for its beauty and Highland scenery. Access to some good fishing banks on the west side of the Bute and around the Kyles.
Types of fish: Mackerel and coalfish from the shore, flatfish, whiting, dogfish, pollack, gurnard and several species of wrasse. Conger fishing can be arranged.
Bait: Supplies of fresh bait (lug, cockle, mussel, clams etc.,) are locally available.
Boats: Motor dinghies available for hire. Local fisherman can take parties of anglers by arrangement.
Contact: Andy Lancaster, Kames Hotel. Tel; (01700) 811489.
Season: Spring to Autumn.

Loch Fyne
This is the longest sea-loch in Scotland, penetrating into the Highlands from the waters of the lower Firth of Clyde. The depth of the water within the loch varies enormously with depth of around 100 fathoms being found not only at the seaward end but also at the head of the loch of Inveraray.

Much of the shore angling potential remains unknown although access to both shores is made relatively easy by roads running down each side. Boat launching facilities are less easy to find because of the rugged shoreline. Best side is Inveraray to Furnace. Quarry is now out of bounds.

Types of fish: Mackerel, codling, pollack, flatfish, conger (at night).

Inveraray

Inveraray stands on its west shore near the head of Loch Fyne.

Types of Fish: Mackerel, pollack, codfish, ling, dogfish, conger eel and plaice.

Bait: Mussels and worms available from shore at low tide.

Season: June-September.

Tarbert (Loch Fyne)

The sheltered harbour and the adjacent coast of the loch near the lower end of the loch on the west shore are good fishing grounds for the sea angler.

Types of fish: Mackerel, coalfish and sea trout from the shore. Mackerel, cod, coalfish and whiting from boats.

Boats: Evening out with the boats of the herring fleet can be arranged.

Tackle: Local shops.

Bait: There is an abundance of shellfish and worms on the mud flats.

Season: June, July and August.

Oban

Good catches can be occasionally be taken in Kerrera Sound near the Cutter Rock and the Ferry Rocks. Fishing is much better off the south and west coasts of Kerrera Island and Shepherds Hat, Maiden Island and Oban Bay give good

mackerel fishing in July and August. These places are very exposed and should only be attempted in good settled weather. Many large skate, up to 200lbs average, are regularly taken from the Firth of Lorn.

Best shore marks: Salmore Point, North Connel at road bridge, Bonawe Quarry, rail bridge at Loch Cerran, Easdale Rocks.

Types of fish: Boat & Shore Tope, conger, whiting, codling, cod, pollack, coalfish, skate, thornback, ray, spurdog, dogfish, mackerel, ling, wrasse and gurnard.

Tackle requirements: From light spinning to beachcasters. Boat rods mainly 20lbs class, but for skate 50lbs class. All sea and game anglers necessities stocked at "The Anglers Corner."

Boats: Ronnie Campbell, 14 Kenmore Cottages, Bonawe, Argyll. Tel: (01631) 750213 (launching for Loch Etive best at Oban).

Bait: Mussels and lugworm etc. can be dug from the Kerrera beaches. Frozen and preserved baits can be bought from The Angler's Corner, 2 John Street, Oban. Tel: (01631) 566374 or from Binnie Bros. Fishmongers, 8 Stevenson Street, Oban. Tel: (01631) 566374.

Season: May-November.

Boats: Launching is available at Oban and 2 miles south at the Puffin Dive Centre.

Further information from: Ross Binnie. Tel: (01631) 566734.

Isle of Islay

This is the southernmost of the islands. Several of the larger communities like Port Ellen and Port Askaig have good harbours.

Types of fish: Boat - cod, haddock, whiting, mackerel, dogfish, flounder, conger, rays.

Tackle: Available from J. Campbell, Sub-Post Office, Bridgend.

Bait: Lugworm plentiful on most beaches. Clam skirts from fish factory waste. Bait can be purchased from fishing boats at the piers.

Season: June-October.

Further information from: Bowmore Tourist Office. Tel: (01496) 810254.

Isle of Mull (Salen)

Salen is situated on the east coast of Mull facing the sound of Mull in a central position, 11 miles from Craignure and 10 miles from Tobermory. The village is sited between Aros River and a headland forming Salen Bay. The Sound of Mull is one of the main skate marks in the Argyll area. Many 100lbs., plus skate have now been taken. One of the contributing factors is the sheltered nature of the Sound, which can allow practically uninterrupted angling. This area has also yielded a number of fine tope, the largest of which was a specimen of 50lbs. It is worth noting that cod and haddock seldom frequent the sound and should not be expected. This is an area recommended for dinghy owners.

Type of fish: Coalfish, pollack, wrasse, flounder, mullet sea trout and mackerel from the shore. Ray, skate, ling, pollack, coalfish, spurdog, tope, conger, gurnard and odd codling from boats.

Tackle: Available from the Tackle and Books, Main Street, Tobermory, 10 miles away.

Bait: Easily obtainable from shoreline. Mackerel bait from Tackle and Books, Main Street, Tobermory.

Season: March-November.
Further information from: Mr. Duncan Swinbanks, Tackle and Books, 10 Main Street, Tobermory.

Isle of Mull (Tobermory)
The principal town on Mull, it is situated on a very sheltered bay at the north eastern tip of the island. Apart from hitting the headlines in the national press with its treasure, Tobermory has been extensively covered in the angling press. It is Scotland's most popular centre for skate fishing. Every year and average of 50 ton-up specimens are caught, tagged and returned alive. It is this thoughtful conservation that has maintained the quality of fishing in the area. Large tope of between 35lbs. and 45lbs., can be numerous. Ten Scottish records, red gurnard, grey gurnard, blonde ray, spotted ray, spurdogfish, angler fish, turbot, common skate and two wrasse have come from these Mull waters. Every year catches of migratory fish can be made. Coalfish, whiting, haddock and cod are encountered.
Types of fish: Tope, skate, rays, pollack, coalfish, ling, conger, gurnard, spurdog, cod, haddock, flatfish (plaice, dabs and turbot) and whiting from boats. Coalfish, pollack, cod, wrasse, flounder, grey mullet, sea trout, conger, thornback and mackerel from the shore.
Boats: Andrew Jackson, Laggerbay, Acharacle, Argyll PH36 4JW. Tel: (01972) 500208, has a purpose built 38 ft. sea angling boat for fishing parties with boat rods and reel available. There are 14-16 ft. dinghies for hire for fishing in and around the bay.
Tackle: A tackle shop, with a complete range of stock is on the Main Street.

Bait: Herring and mackerel available from Tackle and Books, Tobermory. Mussels and lugworms are easily obtainable from the shoreline.
Season: May-November.

Further information from: Mr. Duncan Swinbanks, Tackle and Books, 10 Main Street, Tobermory.

Isle of Coll
Coll is one of the smaller islands seaward of Mull. Fishing vessels concentrate on the Atlantic side, but good sport can be had on the Mull side and even at the mouth of Arinagour Bay where the village and hotel lie and the mail steamer calls. Fishing from rocks at several spots round the island can give good results.
Types of fish: Mackerel, coalfish, pollack, cod, conger, haddock, skate and flounder.
Boats: Dinghies with or without outboard engines can be hired from local lobster fishermen.
Tackle: Visitors are advised to bring their own.
Bait: Mussels, worms and small crabs can be readily be obtained at low tide in Arinagour Bay.
Season: May to September and later depending on weather.

FORTH AND LOMOND (EAST COAST)

Anglers going afloat from Fife and Forth Harbours are advised to contact the coastguard at Fifeness for weather information. Tel: (01333) 450666 (day or night). All harbours under Forth Port Authorities may charge a launching fee.

Tayport
Tayport, on the Firth of Tay

opposite Dundee, in the northernmost part of Fife, enjoys good shore fishing in sheltered waters. There are no hotels but there is a modern caravan and camping site with showers, laundry etc.
Types of fish: Cod, flounder and plaice from shore, with occasional sea trout (permit required).
Bait: Lugworm, ragworm, mussels, cockles and crabs available locally at low water.
Season: April-January.

St. Andrews
St. Andrews is a leading holiday resort with sea angling as one of its attractions. Fishing is mainly from boats, but good sports can be had from the rocks between the bathing pool and the harbour.
Tackle: Messrs J. Wilson & Sons (Ironmongers), 169-171 South Street, St. Andrews KY16 9EE. Tel: (01334) 472477.
Bait: Excellent supplies of Lugworm, ragworm and large mussels can be gathered on the beach.

Boarhill and Kings Barns
Good beach fishing for cod and flatfish.

Anstruther
It is a fishing village with plenty of good boat and beach fishing. A very rocky coastline but can be very rewarding with good catches of cod, saithe, flounder, wrasse and whiting. Be prepared to lose tackle.
Types of fish: Cod, saithe, wrasse, flounder, ling, conger and mackerel.
Boats: Plenty charter boats with local skippers who know all the hot spots.

Bait: Lug, rag, white rag, cockle, crab, mussel which can be dug locally.
Season: Boat - May-October. Beach - September-January.

Pittenweem
The nerve centre of the East Neuk with a large deep water harbour which boats can enter or leave at any stage of the tide. The European Cod Festival is now held there each year and produces large catches of cod. The harbour wall is very popular with young and old alike, with some good catches.
Types of fish: Cod, saithe, flounder, wrasse, ling, conger, whiting, mackerel from boats. Cod, saithe, flounder, wrasse and whiting from beach.
Bait: Lug and rag can be dug locally.
Season: Beach - September-January.

Leven
A holiday resort with about 2 miles of lovely sandy beaches. Beach fishing is very popular with some very good catches.
Types of fish: Flounder, cod, bass, mullet, saithe.
Boats: No charter boats.
Bait: Lug available locally.
Season: July-January.

Buckhaven
A small town on the north side of the Firth of Forth, which is renowned for its boat and beach fishing. The Scottish Open Beach Competition is fished from Buckhaven to Dysart each year with large entries from all over Scotland.
Types of fish: Cod, saithe, flounder, whiting, mackerel from beach. Cod, saithe, flounder, whiting, ling, mackerel and wrasse from boat.

Bait: Lug available at Leven.
Boats: No charter hire.
Season: Boat - June-November. Beach - October-January.

Kirkcaldy
Beach fishing at east and west end of town.
Types of fish: Cod, flatfish, saithe and mackerel.
Bait: Beach off promenade.

Pettycur and Kinghorn
Rock and beach fishing off Pettycur Harbour and Kinghorn Beach.
Types of fish: Saithe and flatfish.
Boats: Small boats can be launched from beaches.
Bait: Plenty locally. Local caravan sites.

Burntisland
Permission required to fish the beach from harbour to swimming pool.
Types of fish: Saithe, flatfish, small cod.
Boats: None locally
Bait: Lug available locally.

South Queensferry
A picturesque burgh overshadowed by the Forth Bridges, There are 3 launching slips in the area, but currents can be dangerous and local advice should be obtained before setting out in dinghies.
Types of fish: Cod, whiting, coalfish, mackerel, flounder from boat and shore in season.
Bait: Lugworm, ragworm, mussel, cockle, clams and crabs at low water in this area.
Season: May-October.

Edinburgh
Scotland's capital city, on the south of the Forth estuary, has

several miles of shoreline. Most of this is sandy, and can produce good catches of flatfish, although codling, Ray's bream, whiting, eels and mackerel can be taken in season from the shore. Best marks are at Cramond, round the mouth of the River Almond, and the Seafield to Portobello area.
Bait: Lugworm, ragworm, mussels cockles and clams from most beaches at low water.
Season: All year round.

Musselburgh
This town stands on the estuary of the River Esk, 6 miles to the east of Edinburgh, overlooking the Firth of Forth. It has a small but busy harbour at Fisherrow, catering mainly for the pleasure craft.
Boats: Enquiries should be made at the harbour. Best shore marks range from Fisherrow harbour to the mouth of the Esk.
Bait: Lugworm, ragworm, mussels, cockles and clams at low water.

Cockenzie
Mullet can be caught around the warm water outfall to the east of Cockenzie Power station and around the harbour. Other species include flatfish, codling and mackerel.

North Berwick
There is good boat fishing out of North Berwick and the coastline between the town and Dunbar is good for shore fishing.
Types of fish: Cod, haddock, plaice, mackerel and coalfish.
Bait: Mussels, crabs and shellfiish of various types available at low water.
Further information from:
Information Centre, Quality Street, North Berwick. Tel: (01 620) 892197 January - December.

SEA ANGLING (cont'd)

Dunbar

The coastline from Dunbar to
Eyemouth is very popular for rock
and beach fishing.
Types of fish: Cod, haddock,
flounder, coalfish, mackerel,
wrasse and whiting.
Boats: Details can be obtained
from The Tourist Information
Centre, Dunbar.
Bait: Mussels, lug and ragworm
available at low water, and also
from tackle dealers.
Season: Best April to October.
Further information from:
Information Centre, Town House.
High Street, Dunbar. Tel: (01368)
863353 January - December.

TAYSIDE

Arbroath

Situated on the east coast of
Angus, 17 miles north-east of
Dundee, Arbroath is easily
accessible by road and rail. It is
the centre for commercial fishing,
and famous for its smokies.
Pleasure boats ply for short cruises
to local sea cliffs and caves, from
the harbour. There are about 10
boats between 15ft and 35ft used
for lobster and crab fishing, taking
out parties for sea angling.
Types of fish: Cod, coalfish,
mackerel, flounder, conger, plaice,
haddock and pollack.
Boats: Available through local
fishermen and part time lobster
and crab fishermen at reasonable
prices.

Dundee

Dundee is situated on the estuary
of the River Tay and has sea
fishing in the city centre, while
Broughty Ferry, a suburb of
Dundee, Easthaven and
Carnoustie, all within easy reach
by road and rail, have sea fishing

from rocks, piers or from boats.
There are good marks around the
Bell Rock about 12 miles offshore.
Types of fish: Cod, flatfish from
shore plus cod, haddock, coalfish,
ling, pouting and plaice from
boats.
Bait: Available locally.
Season: All year.

NORTH EAST AND
SPEY VALLEY

Moray Firth

The Moray Firth has always been
famous for its fishing grounds and
most of the towns along the south
coastline depend largely on
commercial fishing for their
prosperity; cod, haddock, flatfish
of many kinds, pollack, coalfish
and mackerel being landed.

Nairn

Nairn is set on the pleasant
coastal plain bordering the
southern shore of the Moray Firth.
There is a beautiful stretch of
sands to the east. Most fishing is
done from two small piers at the
entrance to the tidal harbour.
Types of fish: Mackerel, small
coalfish, pollack, dab and cod.
Boats: One or two, privately
owned, will often take a
passenger out. Enquiries should be
made at the harbour.
Tackle: P. Fraser, 41 High Street,
Nairn.Tel: (01667) 453038.
Bait: Lugworm available on the
beach at low water. Mackerel etc.,
mostly taken on flies.

Lossiemouth and Garmouth

Lossiemouth, a small prosperous
town, is a unique combination of
white fish centre, seaside, shops
and hotels. The angler will find
unlimited sport of a kind probably
new to him, for off the east and

west beaches sea trout and finnock
abound, and spinning for these into
the sea, especially into the
breakers, is a magnificent sport.
Types of fish: Sea trout, conger
from the pier, coalfish, flatfish, 6.5
miles of shore fishing. Haddock ,
cod, plaice and coalfish from
boats. Shore fishing - sea trout
between harbour and Boar's Head
Rock and at the old cement works
Garmouth.
Bait: Lugworm on the west beach
and the harbour at low water. Also
plenty of mussels to be collected.
Spinners, Pirks.
Season: Migratory fish season,
October. Best months late July,
early August.

Buckie

Buckie is a major commercial
fishing port on the eastern side of
Spey Bay. It has become
increasingly popular over the last
few years as a tourist area and is
well supplied with hotels, golf
courses and caravan sites. It offers
a varied coastline in the form of
sandy beaches and quite
spectacular rugged cliff
formations.
Types of fish: Cod, coalfish,
conger, pollack, mackerel,
haddock, whiting and flatfish.
Bait: Lugworm, ragworm, mussels
, cockles and crabs freely available
along the shoreline eastwards.
Season: April-October. Winter
months best for cod.

Cullen

M. V. Rosenberg is a 30ft long,
twin-engine cruiser providing
pleasure trips and catering for sea
anglers (tackle for hire or for sale).
The boat is licensed by the
Department of Transport and, as
such, meets all its survey
requirements annually. The vessel,

which has all modern aids to navigation, has a certificated skipper. Details may be had from Cullen Marine Services, 27 North Deskford Street, Cullen. Tel: (01542) 840323.

Portknockie
Portknockie is a quaint little fishing village to the west of Cullen Bay. The small harbour is used by two small mackerel boats.
Types of fish: Excellent rock fishing here for cod, coalfish, and some mackerel from the piers. Good boat fishing for haddock, ling and gurnard.
Boats: There are no boats for hire as such, although it is possible to get out in two small (18ft) mackerel boats.
Bait: Lugworm and mussels in the harbour at low water.
Further information from:
Tourist Information Centre, 17 High Street, Elgin IV30 1EG. Tel: (01343) 542666/543388.

Portsoy
One of the numerous small towns that line the Banffshire coast. It is a former seaport but the harbour is silting up.
Types of fish: Coalfish and mackerel from the small pier and some good rock fishing east and west for cod. From boats, mackerel, cod, haddock, plaice, coalfish and dab.
Bait: Some lugworm at low water mark.

Gardenstown and Crovie
These are traditional fishing villages. Mackerel are plentiful, June- September. Anglers would be well advised to follow local boats which are fishing commercially.
Types of fish: From shore,

coalfish, pollack flatfish conger. From boats - mackerel, cod, haddock, flounder, plaice, conger, dab, catfish, gurnard and ling.
Bait: Available on beach, but local people prefer to use flies.

Fraserburgh
Situated on the north-east shoulder of Scotland, Fraserburgh has the Moray Firth to the west and north and the North Sea to the east. The Burgh was primarily given over to the herring and white fish industry, but has developed as a holiday resort with the decline of commercial fishing in the North Sea. Tickets and permits for game fishing from the beaches can be had at Weelies, Grocer, College Bounds.
Types of fish: Shore- cod, coalfish and mackerel. Boat - as shore.
Bait: Mussels and lugworm can be dug from the beach.
Season: May-October.

Peterhead
Peterhead is an important fishing port situated north of Buchan Ness, the most easterly point of Scotland. Excellent breakwaters, 1900ft and 2800ft long, are the main shore marks for holiday anglers. Access to the breakwaters is dependent on weather conditions and can be restricted when vessels are being worked. A safety access procedure has been agreed with the North Breakwater Sea Angling Society to whom further queries should be directed. However passengers are at times taken out by private boats.
Types of fish: From the pier - mackerel, coalfish, dab and cod. From boats- cod, haddock, dabs, ling, coalfish and mackerel.
Boats: There are a number of privately owned boats which will

sometimes take out passengers. Enquiries should be made at the harbour.
Tackle: Available from Robertsons Sports, 1 Kirk Street, Peterhead. Tel : (01779) 472584
Bait: Lugworm can be dug from shore at low water while mussels can be gathered from the rocks.

Stonehaven
Stonehaven is a holiday resort 15 miles south of Aberdeen on main road and rail routes. Magnificent catches of cod and haddock are taken regularly by boat. Anglers obtain great co-operation from angling boat skippers and local professional fishermen. On either side of Stonehaven there are good rock fishing marks which should be approached with care especially during strong easterly winds.
Types of fish: Cod, haddock, coalfish, pollack, ling, catfish, plaice and other flatfish, ballan wrasse, cuckoo wrasse, whiting and Norway haddock from boats.
Boats: Boats are available from skipper: A . McKenzie, 24 Westfield Park, Stonehaven, Tel: (01569) 763411.
Bait: Mussels available if ordered from skippers of boats.
Season: All year
Further information from:
Information Centre, 66 Allardice Street, Stonehaven. Tel: (01569) 762806 Easter - October.

GREAT GLEN AND ISLE OF SKYE

Isle of Eigg
The Isle of Eigg lies 5m SW of Skye.
Types of fish: Pollack, conger, spurdog, skate, cod, mackerel.
Season: Summer - Autumn.

Isle of Skye

The many lochs and bays around the beautiful Isle of Skye provide ideal facilities for sea angling. There is a great variety of fish, most of which can be caught from the shore because of the deep water found close inshore off rocky shores and headlands. Local residents are very knowledgeable about fishing in their own area Loch-Snizort has now been found to hold a number of large common skate and anglers could well contact these during a session there.

Isle of Skye (Portree)

Portree, the capital of Skye, is situated half way up the east coast of the island. There is a very good harbour and good fishing marks in and around it. Ample free anchorage and berthing available for visiting craft. Slipping, refuelling and watering facilities are
easily accessible.
Types of fish: Cod, haddock, whiting, coalfish, pollack and mackerel.
Boats: Greshornish House Hotel, Edinbane, by Portree, Isle of Skye. Tel: (01470) 582266 , has one boat available.
Bait: Unlimited mussels and cockles available in tidal area of Portree Bay.
Season: May - September.

Isle of Skye (Camastianavaig by Portree)

To reach this sheltered bay which lies 4 miles south east of Portree, turn off the A850 to Braes. Although local tactics are the use of feathers, bottom fishing with trace or paternoster has yielded heavy bags with skate of 62.5lbs, cod 6 lbs whiting 3lbs, haddock

3lbs, spurdog 12lbs, gurnard 2lbs, pollacks 12lbs coalfish 14lbs , all from boats.
Types of fish: Shore - coalfish, pollack, wrasse and mackerel. Boat - cod, haddock and spurdog.
Tackle: Obtainable at Portree.
Bait: Lugworm at Broadford Bay and Balmeanac Bay. Cockles and mussels at Portree Loch.
Season: June - October

Isle of Skye (Uig)

Uig, a picturesque village amidst some of the finest scenery in the north west, has excellent fishing on its doorstep. Loch Snizort and small islands at its entrance, together with the Ascribe Islands opposite, are well worth fishing. Fishing can be arranged as far round the coast as Score Bay, known to some ring net fishermen as the "Golden Mile" .
Types of fish: Shore - coalfish, mackerel, pollack, conger and dogfish. Boat - coalfish, mackerel, pollack, conger, whiting, haddock, dogfish, flatfish, skate, cod and gurnard.
Boats: Available locally at Uig, Waternish and Kilmuir.
Season: May - September

Isle of Skye (Skeabost Bridge)

Skeabost Bridge is situated 5 miles from Portree at the south east end of Loch Snizort.
Types of fish: There is no shore fishing but many types of sea fish can be caught from boats.
Bait: Available locally.
Season: July - October.

Kyle of Lochalsh

The village of Kyle, on the mainland opposite Kyleakin on the Isle of Skye, there is a railhead and a car ferry link with Skye and the Hebrides.

Types of fish: Conger, coalfish, pollack and whiting from the harbour. Boat - pollack, cod, coalfish, mackerel and whiting.
Tackle: Available from John MacLennan & Co., Marine Stores, Kyle of Lachalsh IV40 8AE Tel; (01599) 534208.
Bait: Mussels from Fishery Pier and clams and cockles at spring tides.
Season: June - September.

NORTH SCOTLAND

Gairloch

Gairloch Bay is very popular with sea anglers. There is good fishing in this lovely sea loch, especially around Longa Island which lies near the entrance to the Loch.

Poolewe and Aultbea

Situated amidst magnificent scenery, the sheltered waters of Loch Ewe offer the sea angler opportunities of fine catches. Suitable accommodation is available in surrounding villages and local advice is always available.
Types of fish: Shore - pollack, coalfish, dab, codling. Boat - haddock, cod, codling, gurnard, skate, whiting, mackerel and flatfish.
Boats: Several boats available locally.
Bait: Mussels, lugworm, cockles, etc., from shore.
Season: April - October incl.

Little Loch Broom

Ten miles north east Aultbea/ Ullapool & The Summer Isles Loch Broom and the waters encircled by the Summer Isles offer excellent sea angling. The banks can be approached from Ullapool, which is an attractive holiday village

127

sited on a peninsula projecting into Loch Broom. The numerous banks and islands offer superb fishing and beautiful scenery in sheltered waters. Many attractions on shore via local shops; hotels and sporting facilities available throughout the season. Achiltibuie, a small village, also gives access to fishing grounds.

Types of fish: Shore - codling, coalfish, conger, pollack, mackerel, dabs, thornbacks, dogfish, flounders and plaice. Boat - as above plus haddock, whiting, wrasse, ling, megrim, gurnard, spurdog and turbot.

Season: June-October inclusive. Big skate best in autumn.

Lochinver

Lochinver is one of the major fishing pons in the north of Scotland. With a population of some 300 inhabitants it has a safe all-tides harbour with excellent shore services, including good moderately - priced accommodation and two fishing tackle shops. Excellent sea fishing within a short distance from the port specialising in jumbo haddock, cod, skate and conger. It is one of the few areas where large halibut are caught. Boats available. A large fleet of fishing vessels operates from the harbour and bait is readily available.

Types of fish: Cod, haddock, whiting, saithe, gurnard, ling, pollack, mackerel, wrasse, conger, skate. Coalfish, pollack, cod and mackerel from the shore.

Tackle: Tackle is available from Lochinver Fishselling Co., Culag Square, Lochinver. Tel: (01571) 844228.

Season: April - October

Drumbeg

Seven miles north of Lochinver

Caithness

With the prolific fishing grounds of the Pentland Firth, the north of Caithness has built up a reputation as being one of the premier sea angling areas in Scotland. It is now recognised that the chance of taking a halibut on rod and line is better in Pentland waters than anywhere else; more halibut have been taken here than in any other part of the British Isles. The presence of Porbeagle shark in these waters has been proved by the capture of many good heavy specimens, including the world record, with many more hooked and lost. Among the notable fish caught were European halibut records of 194 lbs. in 1974, 215 lbs in 1975, 224 lbs. in 1978 and 234 lbs in 1979. This fish represented a world record catch for the species. The Scottish shore record ling of 12 lbs 4 oz was caught in these waters. With countless numbers of rocky coves and sandy beaches there is much for the shore angler to discover along the whole of the north coast of Scotland. Accommodation is available to suit everyone, from first class hotels, private B & B to caravan and camping sites with full facilities. It is also possible to have a full sea angling package holiday with full board at a hotel and all boat charges included. The number of angling boats available increases each year, but it is still advisable to book boat places in advance.

Thurso and Scrabster

Thurso is the main town on the north side of Caithness and gives access through Scrabster to the waters of the Pentland Firth, where there are first class fishing grounds. Thurso Bay and the

Dunnet Head area are sheltered from prevailing winds and it is reasonably easy for anglers to get afloat to the marks. Scrabster 1.4 miles from Thurso, is the main harbour in northern Caithness. Most of the angling boats are based here. There is also some excellent rock fishing, while conger may be caught from the harbour walls.

Types of fish: Cod, ling, haddock, conger, pollack, coalfish, dogfish, spurdog, plaice, wrasse, mackerel, dab, whiting, rays, halibut and Porbeagle shark.

Tackle: Harper's Fishing Services, 57 High Street , Thurso KW14 8AZ. Tel: (01847) 893179.

Bait: Mussels, lugworm can be gathered at low water, mackerel and squid from fish shops and local fishermen. Most species take lures, feather and rubber eels, etc., and most fishing is done with this artificial bait.

Season: April - November.

Further information from: Caithness Tourist Board, Whitechapel Road, Wick. Tel: (01955) 602596. Jan-Dec.

Boat: Paul Gough - (01847) 895009.

Dunnet

Dunnet is situated 8 miles east of Thurso at the end of the famous Dunnet Sands, which are over 2.5 miles long. Few anglers fish this beach, as there is excellent boat fishing nearby. There is plenty of lugworm and the beach is well worth trying.

Types of fish: As for Thurso.

Boats and Tackle: As for Thurso.

Bait: Mussels from the rocks at low tide and lugworm all along Dunnet Sands.

Season: Shore - July and August. Boat - April - November

Keiss

Good shore fishing is to be had around Keiss, a small fishing village between John O'Groats and Wick. It might be difficult to get out in a boat. The shore fishing is from the rocks around Keiss, and from the beach at Sinclair's Bay to the south of the village. Here some very good plaice have been taken and also anglers have caught sea trout while spinning for mackerel.
Tackle: Tackle shops at Wick.
Bait: Mussels and lugworm can be obtained at low tide.

Sutherland and Easter Ross, Brora

Brora is a village situated on the A9, 12 miles south of Helmsdale. There is a small harbour and a few boats are available to sea anglers. There are rail links to Brora from the south and ample hotel accommodation and caravan facilities.
Types of fish: Cod, coalfish, cod, ling, haddock, rays and conger from boats.
Boats: Some owners are willing to take visitors at nominal costs.
Bait: Can be dug locally.
Season: July- September.

Grannies Heilan' Hame, Embo

This is a caravan holiday centre with extensive amenities 2 miles north of Dornoch.
Types of fish: Spinning for sea trout from the beach up to the mouth of Loch Fleet. Coalfish, mackerel and flatfish from the pier. The rocks provide good cod fishing. From boats, coalfish, mackerel, plaice, cod, haddock and whiting at times.
Bait: Lugworm can be dug at the ferry landing area and there are plenty of mussels and cockles near Loch Fleet.
Season: April - September.
Dornoch

Dornoch gives access to the fishing banks off the north coast of the Dornoch Firth. There is good shore fishing from the rocks at Embo, but to get afloat it is necessary to make arrangements in advance. Youngsters can enjoy good fishing from Embo Pier.
Types of fish: Sea trout from shore. Flat fish, haddock and cod from boats.
Boats: Boats are difficult to hire but there are one or two in Embo which is three miles from Dornoch.
Season: April - September.

Tain

Tain lies on the South side of the Dornoch Firth and gives access to excellent sea trout fishing, both shore and boat, in sheltered waters of the Firth.
Types of fish: Shore-wrasse, flatfish, pollack, mackerel. Boat - haddock, cod, skate, mackerel.
Boats: Available in Balintore, 6 miles from Tain and Portmahomack.
Bait: Available from the shore.

Balintore

The village of Balintore, near Tain has over the past 4 years increased in status and is now one of the recognised centres for big catches. Catches of up to 1,000lbs of cod and ling have been made (8 anglers) in a single morning's fishing.
Types of fish: Cod, ling, wrasse, pollack and mackerel.
Season: Mid-April to beginning of November.

Portmahomak

This fishing village is well situated in a small bay on the southern shore of the Dornoch Firth, 9 miles east of Tain and 17 miles from Invergordon to the south. There is a well protected harbour and a good, safe sandy beach.

Types of fish: Cod from the shore. Haddock and cod from boats.
Tackle: Available at Tain.
Season: Spring to Autumn.

North Kessock, Avoch and Fortrose

These villages lie along the north west side of the Moray Firth north of Inverness. This sheltered sea loch provides good fishing.

WESTERN ISLES

The Western Isles

The Western Isles form a north-south chain of islands off the west coast of Scotland. Separated from the mainland by the Minches, much of their rod and line fishing remains to be discovered, not only due to a lack of boats in the area, but also due to lack of communications between and within the islands. Car ferries run from Oban and Ullapool on the mainland and Uig on Skye. Regular air services to Barra, Stornoway, for Lewis and Harris and Benbecula for the Uists.

Isle of Harris (Tarbert)

The largest community on the southern part of the largest Hebridean islands. Tarbert stands on a very narrow neck of land where the Atlantic and the Minch are separated by only a few hundred yards of land. It is the terminal for the car ferry from Uig on Skye and Lochmaddy on North Uist.
Types of fish: Boat - mackerel, ling, coalfish, cod, rays, pollack and conger. Shore - plaice, haddock and flounder.
Boats: Check with Tourist Information Centre, Tarbert. Tel: (01859) 502011.
Bait: Mussels available on the shore, lugworm, cockles.

Season: May-October.
Further information from:
Tourist Centre, Tarbert.
Tel: (01859) 502011.

Isle of Lewis (Stornoway)

Stornoway, the only town in the Outer Hebrides, is easily accessible by air from Glasgow Airport (1 hour) and Inverness (25 mins); there is also a drive-on car ferry service from Ullapool (3.5 hours crossing). Another car ferry service connects Uig (Skye) to Tarbert (Harris), which is only an hour's drive from Stornoway. Stornoway is now recognised as a mecca for sea angling in Scotland. There is an enthusiastic sea angling club with club boats and licensed premises which overlook the harbour. Each August the club runs the Western Isles (Open) Sea Angling Championships. Many skate over the ton have been caught, the heaviest so far being 192 lbs. The Scottish blueshark record of 85.5 lbs. was off Stornoway in August 1972. Visiting anglers may become temporary members of the Stornoway Club (one minute from the town hall) and can make arrangements for fishing trips with club members in the club boats. Accommodation can be arranged through the Wester Isles Tourist Board, Administration and Information Centre, 26 Cromwell Street, Stornoway, Isle of Lewis. Tel: (01851) 703088.
Types of fish: Conger, cod, skate, rays, ling, pollack, whiting, dabs, bluemouth, flounder, dogfish, wrasse, haddock.
Bait: Mussels in harbour area; mackerel from local boats.
NORTHERN ISLES

Orkney

The waters around Orkney attract many sea anglers each year as big skate, halibut and ling are there for the taking. Ling of 36 lbs. skate of 214 lbs. taken by Jan Olsson of Sweden and the former British record halibut (161.5 lbs) taken by ex - Provost Knight of Stromness provide the bait which attracts anglers to these waters. The Old Man of Hoy, Scapa Flow and Marwick Head are well-known names to sea anglers. The Brough of Birsay, Costa Head and the Eday and Stronsay Firths are equally well known as marks for big halibut and skate. Fishing from Kirkwall or Stromness, there is easy access to Scapa Flow where wrecks of the German Fleet of the First World War provide homes for large ling and conger. In the fish rich sea surrounding Orkney the angler will find some excellent shore fishing, nearly all of which remains to be discovered. Furthermore skate of over 100 lbs. are still common while specimens of 200 lbs. have been recorded. More halibut have been caught in the waters to the south separating Orkney from the mainland than elsewhere in the U.K. Shark have also been sighted and hooked but none so far have beenlanded. Around the islands, in bays and firths, there is excellent sport for the specimen fish hunter and the Orcadians are eager to help sea anglers share the sport they enjoy. There is a regular car ferry service from Scrabster (Thurso) to Orkney and daily air services from Edinburgh, Glasgow and other points of the U.K.
Types of fish: Sea trout, plaice, pollack and coalfish, mackerel, wrasse from the shore. Skate, halibut, ling, cod, pollack, haddock; coalfish, plaice and dogfish from the boats.
Tackle: Available from Stromness and Kirkwall.
Bait: Available from most beaches and piers.

Season: June - October.

Shetland

Shetland offers the best skate fishing to be had in Europe; during the years 1970-74 more than 250 skate over 100 lbs. were caught. These included a European record of 226.5 lbs and 12 other skate over 190 lbs. During the same period, Shetland held nine British records, ten Scottish records and six European records, giving some indication that the general fishing is of no mean standard. Halibut and porbeagle of over 300 lbs. have been taken commercially in the Sumburgh area with porbeagle shark now being landed by anglers from this area. The Scottish record of many large porbeagle sharks of up to 450 lbs have been landed here and bigger fish have been taken by commercial boat. Shore fishing remains for the most part to be discovered.
Types of fish: Shore - coalfish, pollack, dogfish, mackerel, dabs, conger and cod. Boat - skate, halibut, ling, cod, tusk, haddock, whiting, coalfish, pollack, dogfish, porbeagle shark, Norway haddock, gurnard, mackerel, cuckoo and ballan wrasse.
Boats: Many boats available for hire throughout the islands. Boats can also be arranged through the Shetland Islands Tourism, Market Cross, Lerwick, Shetland.
Tackle: Available from J.A. Manson, 88 Commercial Street, Lerwick and Cee & Jays, 5 Commercial Road, Lerwick.
Bait: Fresh, frozen or salted fish bait available from fishmongers. Worm bait, crabs etc., from beaches.
Season: Limited to May to October by weather conditions.

SCOTTISH FEDERATION OF SEA ANGLERS OFFICIALS

Chairman
Mr. David Neil,
3 Roman Road,
Ayr KA7 3SZ.
Tel: (01292) 281945.

Vice Chairmen
Mr. Alastair Forsyth,
26 Trentham Court,
Westhill,
Inverness IV1 2DF.
Tel: (01463) 792412.

Mr. John Taylor,
1/1, 6 Tower Terrace,
Paisley,
Renfrewshire PA1 2JT.
Tel: 0141- 561 8554.

Hon. Treasurer
Mr. Robert Keltie,
76 Stewart Avenue,
Bo'ness,
West Lothian EH51 9NW.
Tel: (01506) 826274.

Fish Recorder
Mr. Paul King,
Harbour House,
Hopeman IV30 2RH.
Tel: (01309) 672161.

Coaching Co-Ordinator
Mr. Paul King,
Harbour House,
Hopeman, IV30 2RU.
Tel: (01309) 672161.

Public Relations Officer/Sponsorship
Mr. Brian Burn,
Flat 2, 16 Bellevue Road,
Ayr KA7 2SA.
Tel: (01292) 264735.

Office
Secretary Administrator
David Wilkie,
Secretary Administrator Office
Caledonia House,
South Gyle,
Edinburgh EH12 9DQ.
Tel/Fax: 0131-317 7192.
Weekdays except Wednesday 9am-1pm.

REGIONAL SECRETARIES

Central
Mr. Jim Beveridge,
72 Appin Crescent,
Kirkcaldy, KY2 6ES.
Tel: (01592) 269474.

West
Mr. I. B. McClymont,
41 Corrie Crescent,
Saltcoats KA21 6JL.
Tel: (01294) 461830.

North East
Mr. Jim Croal,
2 Strachan Avenue,
Westferry Park,
Dundee DD5 1RE.
Tel: (01382) 77422.

Eastern
Mr. Bill Murray,
189 Broomfield Crescent,
Edinburgh EH12 7NH.
Tel: Daytime 0131 - 334 4274.

Highlands & Islands
Mr. Willie Mackintosh,
"Schiehallion",
16 Glengarry Road,
Inverness IV3 8NJ.
Tel: (01463) 235850.

Western Isles
Mr. Angus Macdonald,
19 Clachan Biorach,
Tong,
Isle of Lewis HS2 0JD.
Tel: (01851) 703096.

131

FARLOW'S OF PALL MALL

5 Pall Mall
London SW1
Tel: +44 171 839 2423
Fax: +44 1285 643743

Farlow's established in 1840, is London's oldest fishing tackle shop and, fittingly, is situated at the corner of London's oldest arcade. The Royal Opera Arcade, on Pall Mall.

Farlow's three adjacent shops house London's largest selection of fishing tackle, shooting accessories and country clothing. They have been granted a Royal Warrant as suppliers of fishing tackle and waterproof clothing to H.R.H. The Prince of Wales.

The fishing shop, which specialises in trout and salmon fishing, also has departments covering course fishing, sea fishing, big game and salt water fly fishing. Amongst other leading manufacturers, Farlow's carries the whole range of House of Hardy rods, reels, clothing and accessories.

Farlow's country clothing shops contain ranges of clothing and footwear suitable for all aspects of country life. Fishermen, shooting people and those who simply enjoy country life are all catered for, with traditional tweed, wool and waxed cotton alongside modern fabrics. Farlow's also have London's largest selection of Barbour waxed clothing.

A separate shop, specialising in women's country clothing is just a few steps away from the main fishing tackle shop.

Farlow's is only two or three minutes walk from Piccadilly Circus and Trafalgar Square and their knowledgeable and friendly staff welcome customers from all walks of life and all parts of the world.

A beautifully illustrated colour magazine published twice a year, is available upon request. Free in the UK - overseas customers are asked to pay a nominal annual subscription to cover extra postage costs. Alternatively, visit our web site at http://www.farlows.co.uk.

Ardbrecknish
LOCH AWE

FREELANCE FISHING HOLIDAYS

British record wild brown trout 25lbs 5oz taken in Ardbrecknish boat Easter 1996..... *There are surely even bigger fish to catch!*

Unrivalled location for all anglers seeking wild brown trout, rainbow trout, char, pike and Autumn salmon. Early 17th century fortified tower house set amidst spectacular mountain glen and lochside scenery. Scottish Tourist Board 4 Crowns Highly Commended and Commended self - catering apartments and cottages. In house public bar and games room, with open log fires, serving excellent bar meals March to October.

Boat hire, fishing tackle, tuition and ghillie services are available at special rates for Ardbrecknish guests.

For non-anglers in the party our own tennis court, nearby golf courses, walking, mountain climbing, cycling and a great variety of birds, flora and fauna provide alternatives whilst waiting the day's catch.

Open all year from £175 to £840 per week for 2-12 persons, Spring and Autumn short breaks are particularly good value.

Call or write for details to:
**The Boden Family,
Ardbrecknish House,
South Lochaweside,
by Damally,
Argyll PA33 1BH.
Tel/Fax: (01866) 833223.
e-mail: ardbreck01 @aol.com**

SELF CATERING HOLIDAYS ON THE BERWICKSHIRE COAST

Secluded Holiday Cottages and Chalets centred on private Trout Loch in wooded country estate close to sea. Shops and sandy beach 2 miles. An ideal centre for anglers, naturalists and walkers or for touring the Borders, Edinburgh and Northumberland.

Write or phone for brochure

**Dr. and Mrs. E. J. Wise,
West Loch House,
Coldingham, Berwickshire.
Tel: (018907) 71270.**

Galloway for your 1999 Holiday

High-quality self-catering accommodation. About 200 houses throughout South West Scotland.

✳ **Peaceful Country Cottages** ✳ **Elegant Country Houses**
✳ **Convenient Town Houses** ✳ **Quiet Farm Houses**

RIVER FISHING FOR SALMON AND SEA TROUT, LOCH FISHING FOR WILD BROWN TROUT AND PIKE, SEA FISHNG FROM SHORE OR BOATS.

For free colour brochure, contact: G. M. THOMSON & CO., 27 King Street, Castle Douglas, Kirkcudbrightshire DG7 1AB. Tel: (01556) 504030 (24hr. answering service). Fax: (01556) 503277.

WHERE TO STAY

S.W. SCOTLAND

✓✓✓✓ THISTLE COMMENDATION ▶▶▶

Cock Inn Caravan Park

AUCHENMALG : NEWTON STEWART : WIGTOWNSHIRE : SCOTLAND

Peaceful, select Caravan Park adjacent to pleasant little beach and small country Inn. Panoramic view across Luce Bay. Bathing, sailing and sea angling etc. Also bungalow all year round.

GOLF • PONY TREKKING • FISHING

Modern toilet block, showers, freezing facilities, shaver points and all facilities, Shop on site   Sauna   Bar meals available at the Inn

FULLY SERVICED HOLIDAY CARAVANS FOR HIRE

TOURERS WELCOME E.H.U.

Please send for brochure or telephone **(01581) 500227**

THE ROMAN CAMP
COUNTRY HOUSE HOTEL

The Roman Camp sits on the north bank of the River Teith amongst 20 acres of mature and secluded gardens.

The house was built as a hunting lodge for the Dukes of Perth in 1625. We have 3/4 mile river running through our gardens, enabling guests to fish for wild brown trout and salmon on our private beat. The hotel can also arrange fishing on the many lochs and other private beats surrounding Callander.

The Roman Camp Country House Hotel, Callander FK17 8BG
Tel: (01877) 330003   Fax: (01877) 331533

Navidale House Hotel

Helmsdale,
Sutherland KW8 6JS
Tel: (01431) 821258
Fax: (01431) 821531

Comfortable Country House Hotel in a beautiful cliff top location, half a mile north of Helmsdale village. Salmon and sea trout fishing can be arranged on the Helmsdale river or wild brown trout on the numerous hill Lochs, with/without ghillie.

The Hotel has been recently refurbished to a high standard with most of the 15 rooms having dramatic sea views. Our Restaurant enjoys a reputation for fresh fish seafood and game. Two self catering Lodges within the Hotel grounds will be available in early Summer 1998. For full details and enquiries please contact the Hotel.

135

Hotels & Guest Houses

Name, addresses & telephone	Type of Accommodation	Type of fishing	Permits Available	Drying Facilities	Freezing Facilities	Prices	Special Features
ANGUS **Montrose** Mr and Mrs Dick, Lime Guest House, 15 King Street, Montrose DD10 8NL. Tel: (01674) 677236.	Guest House STB 3 Stars	River	Can be arranged	Yes	Yes	B. & B. from £20 p.p.	Lovely Georgian guest house set in the beautiful Angus Hills. En-suite bedrooms and traditional Scottish breakfast.
ARGYLL **Dalmally** Mr A.J. Burke, "Orchy Bank", Dalmally, Argyll PA33 1AS. Tel: (01838) 200370.	Guest House 2 Stars	Salmon Trout Pike	Yes	Yes	Yes	B. & B. from £18.00	Two miles from Loch Awe on bank of River Orchy.
AYRSHIRE **Barrhill** Miss Sylvain Broecking, The Glentachur Hotel, Barrhill, Ayrshire KA26 0PZ. Tel: (01465) 821223.	Hotel STB 3 Stars	Sea River & Loch	Yes	Yes	Yes	B. & B. from £22.50 B.B.E.M. from £34.50	Landscaped gardens. Deluxe accommodation. Excellent cuisine, beautiful countryside.
CAITHNESS **Dunnet** Mrs Anthea Skinner, Northern Sands Hotel, Dunnet, Caithness KW14 8XD. Tel: (01847) 851270.	Hotel 5 Double 2 twin 1 Family 1 Double - en-suite AA 2 Stars	Boat and Fly Lochs	Yes	Yes	Yes	B. & B. from £30.00 B.B.E.M. from £36.50	High quality food, service and accommodation at very reasonable prices.
DUMFRIES & GALLOWAY **Canonbie** Cross Keys Hotel, Canonbie Dumfries-shire DG14 0SY. Tel: (01387) 371205 Fax: (01387) 371878	Hotel	Sea Trout Brown Trout Salmon	Yes	Yes	Yes	B. & B. £24.00 p.p. (en-suite rooms - Special features)	Friendly, comfortable hotel. Good home cooked food. Famous Fishermans' rest.
Castle Douglas Mr McIntosh, Douglas Arms Hotel, King Street, Castle Douglas, Kirkcudbrightshire. Tel: (01556) 502231.	Hotel STB 3 Stars	Coarse Game Trout Pike	Yes	Yes	Yes	B. & B. from £32.50 p.p.p.n. B.B.E.M. £42.00 p.p	Cosy bars and restaurant. Secure undercover parking.

Hotels & Guest Houses

Name, addresses & telephone	Type of Accommodation	Type of fishing	Permits Available	Drying Facilities	Freezing Facilities	Prices	Special Features
INVERNESS-SHIRE **Invergarry** Mr Peter Thomas, Ardochy Lodge, Glengarry, Invergarry, Inverness-shire. Tel: (01809) 511232.	Hotel STB 3 Stars	Brown Trout Arctic Char	Yes	Yes	Yes	B.B.E.M. from £39.50	Family run hotel with boats available on Lochs Garry and Inchlaggan.
PERTHSHIRE **Birnam** Mr Bill Ormerwood, Merryburn Hotel, Birnam, Perthshire PH8 0DS. Tel: (01350) 727216.	Hotel STB 3 Crown Approved	Trout Salmon Course	From Hotel	Yes	Yes	B. & B. from £23.50 B.B.E.M. from £37.00	Packages arranged - single fishermen or parties. Wide range of choices.
Comrie Mr Edward Gibbons, The Royal Hotel, Melville Square, Comrie, Perthshire PH6 2DN. Tel: (01764) 679200.	Hotel STB 3 Stars	Salmon Grise Sea Trout Brown Trout	Yes	Yes	Yes	B. & B. from £65 p.p.	Aid of a local ghillie and delicious packed lunch with flasks of steaming soup provided. Hotel has rights to 2.5 miles of the River Earn. Shooting parties also catered for.
Kincraig Mrs L.E. Rainbow, Ossian Hotel, The Brae, Kincraig, Kingussie, Inverness-shire PH21 1QD. Tel: (01540) 651242 Fax: (01540) 651633.	Licenced Hotel 4 Crowns Commended	Trout Salmon on Loch & River	Bank/ boat permits	Yes	Yes	B. & B. from £20 -£28	Family run hotel. Beautiful lochside village. Good food and wine.
SUTHERLAND **Scourie** Mr P.J. Price, Scourie Hotel, Scourie, Sutherland IV27 4SX. Tel/Fax: (01971) 502396.	Hotel STB 3 Stars	Trout Salmon Sea Trout	Fishing inc. in hotel rates. Visitors permits available	Yes	Yes	B. & B. £22-£44 B.B.E.M. £32-£54	Long established fishing hotel. 25,000 acres of Hill Loch & River for Trout, Salmon & Sea Trout fishing.
SCOTTISH ISLANDS **Orkney** **Birsay** Mrs I. Clouston, Primrose Cottage, Birsay, Orkney KW17 2NB. Tel/Fax: (01856) 721384.	Guest House STB 3 Stars	Trout	Yes - Free to Residents	Yes	Yes	B. & B. £13-£18 B.B.E.M. + £8	Overlooking Marwick Bay. Good food and a friendly welcome.

Self Catering

Name, addresses & telephone	Type of Accommodation	Type of fishing	Permits Available	Drying Facilities	Freezing Facilities	Prices	Special Features
INVERNESS-SHIRE **Boat of Garten** Mr B. Gillies, Boat of Garten Caravan Park, Boat of Garten, Inverness-shire PH24 3BN. Tel: (01479) 831652.	Cabins Thistle 5 Ticks	River Loch	Yes	Yes	Yes	From £90-£375	River Spey, golf, tennis. Steam railway all within walking distance.
Struy Frank & Juliet Spencer-Nairn, Culligran Cottages, Glen Strathfarrar, Struy Nr Beauly IV4 7JX. Tel: (01463) 761285.	Holiday Cottages STB 2 Stars & 3 Stars	River	Yes	Yes	Yes	Prices on Application. Brochure available.	Salmon and trout fishing on the Rivers Farrar and Glass, tributaries of the Beauly. Guided tours of the deer farm. Bicycles for hire. All within a National Nature Reserve.
MORAYSHIRE **Grantown-on-Spey** Mrs A. Laing, Logie House, Forres, Morayshire IV36 0QN. Tel: (01309) 611278.	Shooting/ Lodge Cottage STB 3 stars	Brown Trout	Free	Yes	Yes	From £190-£1,500	Lodge sleeps 16. Cottage sleeps 4. Peaceful setting by Lochindorb. Bank fishing free. Boats for hire.
PERTHSHIRE **Bridge of Cally** Mrs J. Farmer, Persie Mains, Bridge of Cally, Blairgowrie, Perthshire PH10 7LQ. Tel: (01250) 886250.	Cottages STB 4 Crowns Highly Comm.	Salmon Trout	Yes	Yes	No	From £150 -£350	Quality accommodation on a Highland estate. Superb views and amenities.
Kincraig Mr David Kinnear, Dalraddy Holiday Park, by Aviemore. Alvie Estate Office, Kincraig, PH21 1NE. Tel: (01540) 651255. or Tel: (01479) 810330.	F'hse STB 4 stars	Salmon Sea Trout Pike Char Trout	Yes	Yes	Yes	From £300 - £500	Variation of lochs and river fishing.
Pitlochry Mr Stewart, Milton of Fonab Caravan Site, Bridge Road, Pitlochry PH16 5NA. Tel: (01796) 472882. Fax: (01796) 474363.	Static Caravans Thistle 4 Ticks	Trout Salmon	Yes	Yes	Yes	On Application	On banks of River Tummel. Couples and families only.

Self Catering

Name, addresses & telephone	Type of Accommodation	Type of fishing	Permits Available	Drying Facilities	Freezing Facilities	Prices	Special Features
SELKIRKSHIRE **Ashykirk** Mrs N. Hunter, Headshaw Farm, Ashkirk, Selkirkshire DG8 6SR. Tel: (01750) 32233.	Cottages STB 4 stars	Fly Fishing Loch rainbows & Browns	Lodge at loch	Facilities available in cottage	Freezer in cottage	£176 - £293	Secluded cottages on working farm with private 17 acre loch.
SUTHERLAND **Kinbrace** Mr M. Wigan, Borrobol, Kinbrace, Sutherland KW11 6UB. Tel: (01431) 831264.	Traditional House & Bungalow	Loch Trout Spate River Salmon and Sea trout	Yes inc. in price	Yes	Yes	From £226 inclusive of VAT	Managed wild trout. Boat provided. Roam 22,000 acre private estate.
WIGTOWNSHIRE **Newton Stewart** Mr Eric Hyslop, Borgan, Bargrennan, Newton Stewart, Wigtownshire DG8 6SR. Tel: (01671) 840247.	Cottages STB 3 stars	Salmon Trout Sea Trout	Yes	Yes	Yes	From £175 - £265	Exclusive salmon/sea trout fishing available. Central base for all fishing pursuits.

KEY TO MAPS

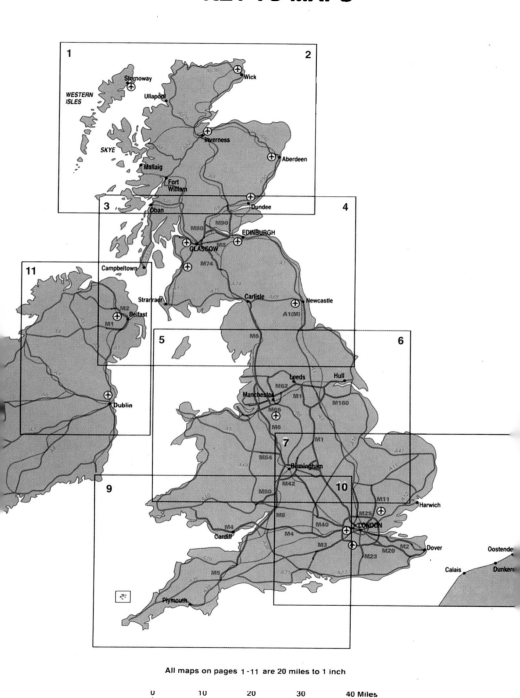

All maps on pages 1-11 are 20 miles to 1 inch

0   10   20   30   40 Miles

0   10   20   30   40   50   60 Kilometres

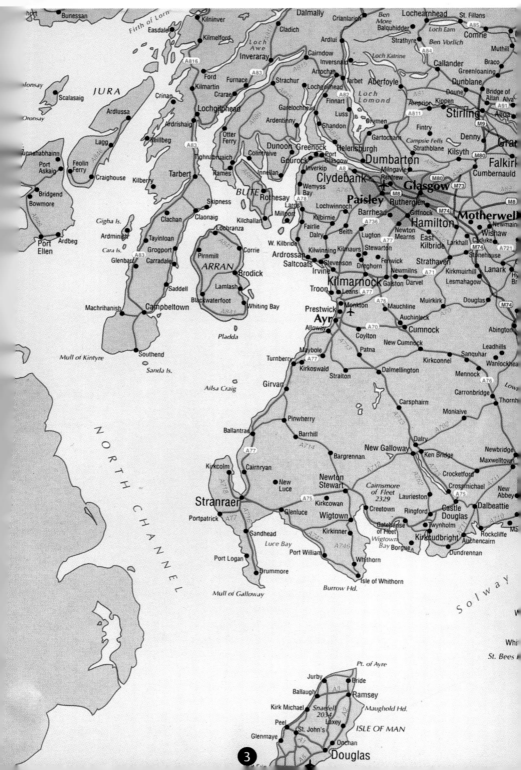

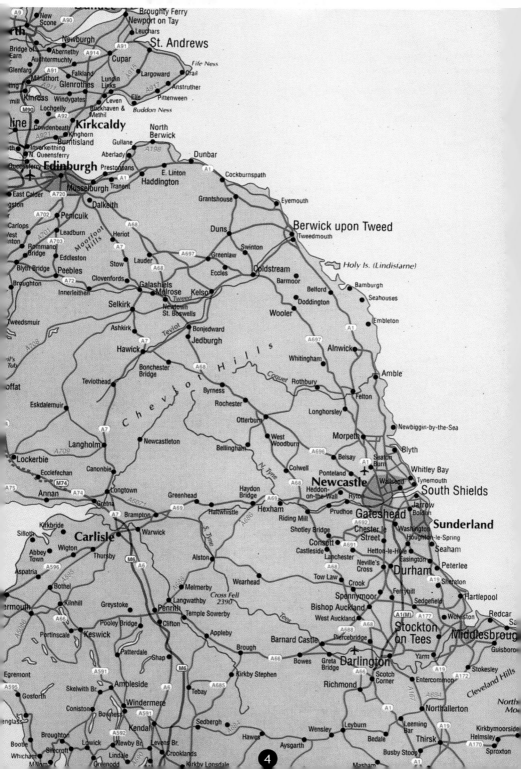

the-Sea
Cley
Sheringham
Cromer
Holt
A148
Roughton
Fakenham
North Walsham
Aylsham
A140
Sea Palling
Bawdeswell
Stalham
Attlebridge
A47
Horsham St. Faith
Rollesby
Caister-on-Sea
East
Dereham
Honingham
Acle
A47
Great
Yarmouth
Norwich
Blofield
Gorleston-on-Sea
Wymondham
A146
A11
A143
Attleborough
Long Stratton
Ellingham
Lowestoft
A140
Bungay
A146
Thetford
A143
Beccles
Kessingland
A1066
Diss
Halleston
Wrentham
Botesdale
Scole
Blythburgh
Ixworth
Peasenhall
Yoxford
ry St. Edmonds
Dennington
Saxmundham
A45
A140
Stowmarket
Wickham
Market
A12
Aldeburgh
Needham Market
A45
Claydon
Woodbridge
Ipswich
A12
Manningtree
Felixstowe
rl's Colne
Elmstead
Market
Harwich
s Tye
The Naze
Colchester
A133
Walton-on-
the-Naze
ham
Clacton-on-Sea
West Mersea
Blackwater
Foulness Pt.
Foulness Island
gh
Southend-on-Sea
l.
Shoeburyness
Sheerness
Isle of Sheppey
A249
Leysdown
Westgate
Margate
am
Herne Bay
Birchington
Broadstairs
Whitstable
A299
A253
Faversham
A28
Sarre
Ramsgate
ourne
A2
Sturry
A257
Sandwich
M2
Wingham
Deal
Canterbury
Bridge
A20
Barham
A2
Ashford
A28
dddenden
A760
A20
Dover
A2070
Sandgate
Folkestone
Tenderden
A259
Hythe
Dymchurch
haim
New Romney
Rye
Littlestone-on-Sea
Winchelsea
Lydd
Dungeness
tings
ds
59
Ooste
Middelkerke
Westende
Koksijde
De Panne
Dunkerque
N1
Calais
Gravelines
D916
N55
Cap Gris Nez
Guines
Ardres
N43
D928
A25
Marquise
Cassel
D933
Boulogne
8
St-Omer
© Bayfield Carto-Graphics Ltd
N42